YORKTOWN

YORKTOWN

The Strategy, People, and Events Surrounding the Final Battle in the American War of Independence

CONTRIBUTORS
Dr. Clarence Porter Jones, Sr.
J. Luther Kibler
W. T. Stauffer
Dr. L. S. Foster
Capt. Nelson C. Overton
Col. C. E. Lester
Prof. H. C. Krebs
W. B. Colonna
Prof. T. J. Stubbs, Jr.
Capt. George A. Mallison
Hon. John Weymouth
Col. C. E. Lester
Edwin K. Phillips

Coachwhip Publications
Landisville, Pennsylvania

Yorktown

ISBN 1-61646-101-2
ISBN-13 978-1-61646-101-0

Cover Image: *Capitulation de Cornwallis*, by Vernier & Torley (1837)

CoachwhipBooks.com

CONTENTS

INTRODUCTION

This book compiles papers published from 1930-1933 for the membership of the National Society, Sons of the American Revolution. These were part of a closer look at the people and circumstances surrounding the Siege of Yorktown, the last battle of the American Revolution, as Americans celebrated its sesquicentennial in 1931. The authors provide details on both strategy and personalities (the bravery and the treachery), providing significant insight into the formation of the United States of America.

THE GENERAL STRATEGY OF THE YORKTOWN CAMPAIGN

DR. CLARENCE PORTER JONES, SR.

As the Anniversary of Washington's Campaign at Yorktown is to be internationally celebrated in 1931, we think it would arouse interest to note the position of generals and armies at the beginning of the Dark Year of the Revolution in 1781.

Grasping the distances and meager methods of communication; the gigantic task to mobilize his army for the campaign; his generals scattered over this vast territory; these dark days spent with the generals and commands are as follows:

I. In January 1781 Benedict Arnold— "the lost pleiad"— was ravaging Virginia. Baron Steuben, Lafayette and State Militia under Nelson, Muhlenburg, Weedon and Clark (temporarily in Virginia from Kentucky.) Baron Steuben opposed Gen. Philips at Petersburg in March 1781.

II. Cornwallis in the Carolinas early in 1781.

III. Gates (at Charlotte, North Carolina) turned over command of Southern Army to Gen. Nathaniel Greene of Rhode Island early in 1781—army numbering 2,000. Under Greene were Morgan and "Light Horse Harry" Lee.

Morgan on January 17th, 1781, met Tarleton at Cowpens resulting in an American victory. Cornwallis in February 1781 began chasing Greene, following him to Dan River. Then he returned to North

Carolina, Greene following to resist uprising of Tories in North Carolina at Hillsborough. Cornwallis in April 1781 began march from Wilmington to Williamsburg. On May 20th he joined Philips at Petersburg.

IV. January 1st, 1781, in the North: Mutiny of the Pennsylvania Line put down by Anthony Wayne.

V. Washington in the Hudson River Valley in early 1781—at New Windsor above West Point. Washington on May 22nd, 1781, in conference with Rochambeau (with 4,000 men at Newport, Rhode Island) at Weathersfield, Connecticut. Gens. Knox, De Barras and Chastellux also present to plan for capture of New York.

VI. In March 1781 De Grasse sailed from Brest, France, for West Indies with twenty-five ships.

VII. Later advices from De Grasse led Washington to plan for Yorktown campaign.

L. C. Bell says: "On December 2nd, 1780, General Greene relieved General Gates of his command at Charlotte, North Carolina. Upon assuming the command he wrote Governor Jefferson: 'I find the troops in a most wretched condition, destitute of everything necessary for comfort or convenience, and may literally be said to be naked.'"

After burning his baggage, Cornwallis in the latter part of January 1781 marched forth to capture Greene. But Greene realized full well the insufficiency of his force to risk battle with Cornwallis. Instead, he conducted a masterly retreat. Upon being reinforced, General Greene recrossed the Dan and offered Cornwallis battle at Guilford Court House on March 15th, 1781. The battle was a stubborn and bloody affair.

The plight of Virginia at this state of the Revolution appears upon the verge of desperation. Leslie, who had commanded at Norfolk and Portsmouth, had joined Cornwallis. Sir Henry Clinton had placed Benedict Arnold (the traitor) in command, and Philips too came to Virginia and operated in conjunction with Arnold, Philips, however, being the superior in command.

"The British had the name; the Americans the good consequences of victory."

Fox said in the House of Commons: "Another such victory would ruin the British Army," and Pitt regarded it as the "precursor of ruin, to British supremacy in the south," and speaking of Cornwallis' situation on the eve of this battle, Schenck says: "It was a supreme moment in the life of Cornwallis and crisis in the Revolution. This victory won, there was no foe to obstruct his passage into the defenseless province of Virginia; North Carolina would be at the mercy of the Crown, and Georgia and South Carolina, already prostrate and subdued, could never rally for defense again.

"Should Greene be beaten, Cornwallis could take up his triumphant march to the sea to be welcomed by the English fleets that rode unchallenged in the harbors of Norfolk and New York.

"The prisoners of war at Charlottesville, Virginia, would be set free to plunder and pillage their captors. France, capricious and fickle, would forsake the waning fortune of the colonies, and making peace for herself, leave her allies to their fate. Washington would be crushed by the army of Clinton in his front and that of Cornwallis in his rear, or be driven into the frozen regions of the north for refuge. Congress would be scattered from its halls and carry dismay wherever they fled for safety."

Lafayette was ordered to Philadelphia, and then on April 6th, 1781, to join General Greene, but when Washington learned of the landing of Philips in Virginia with reinforcements for the British army, he countermanded the order and assigned Lafayette to command in Virginia under General Greene.

With the departure of Arnold from Virginia, and the arrival of reinforcements under Leslie, and the orders from General Greene to Lafayette to take command of all forces in Virginia and report direct to the Commander-in-Chief, Virginia became the theatre of the crucial and paramount military operations.

On the first of August 1781, Cornwallis proceeded by water to Yorktown, the main body of his army arriving on the fourth. On the sixth Tarleton sailed to Hampton, threw his horses into deep water, landed without loss, and joined Cornwallis on the seventh. General O'Hara's division remained at Portsmouth to destroy the works, and on the twenty-second of August 1781, the British Army was concentrated at Yorktown and Gloucester Point just across the river,

Count de Grasse had arrived in the Chesapeake Bay on August 30th, 1781. On September 17th, Washington with his aides called on the admiral to perfect plans of operations against Cornwallis.

General Nelson (then Governor) took the field at the head of the Virginia militia forces.

These are some of the outstanding factors incident to the preparation for the Yorktown Campaign.

GOVERNOR AND GENERAL NELSON AT YORKTOWN

J. Luther Kibler

That remarkable incident, usually related in the story of the bombardment of Yorktown, and which produced a halo of fame around the name of General Thomas Nelson, Jr., is a matter of common knowledge throughout the country. The story of his intense patriotism, as manifested on that momentous occasion when he offered five guineas to the gunner who would first hit his house with a cannon ball to drive out the British Earl—Charles Cornwallis—has been told to generations of American school children throughout the United States. And the financial sacrifices he made in the Revolutionary struggle for absolute independence will always be associated with his name wherever the story of Yorktown and Cornwallis is told. This much, at least, and perhaps a few other incidents in the history of his important public services as legislator and executive also, is about the sum total of public knowledge concerning this distinguished Virginia patriot, in particular as related in our school histories.

It is a matter of regret that after 150 years so little should be known generally of a man whose place in the galaxy of Virginia's honored war heroes and statesmen can be no lower than a star of the second magnitude—next to Patrick Henry, Thomas Jefferson, and George Washington—naming these in Revolutionary order. It is surprising to note that John Fiske, in his *American Revolution* does not even mention Nelson's name in connection with the Siege of Yorktown!

No biography of General Nelson, except brief sketches, has ever been published so far as I have been able to learn. The manuscript biography of Nelson, written by St. George Tucker, seems to have been lost—or if still in existence, is yet undiscovered. However, in view of the coming Sesquicentennial at Yorktown, the present is a most auspicious time for all thoughtful citizens to refresh their knowledge with new information—if it is to be found—about this true son of a famous family, at least by a review of the known public services of General Nelson when he reached the climax of his honorable career at Yorktown, which survey is sufficient for our present purpose.

Some day, when Virginia's historical treasures are once all uncovered and properly assembled for the erudite historian, a literary artist who can do historic justice to such a noble character will appear and limn the picture of the true Thomas Nelson, Jr., portraying the beauty of his character and revealing the glory of his patriotism to show him in all his majesty as a man, true-hearted and brave. For Nelson's nature and disposition responded to the demand: "Give us men"—men, who knowing the right dare defend it, whatever the hazard.

However, the subject of this paper: "General and Governor Thomas Nelson, Jr., with emphasis on the 'Yorktown Campaign'" calls for, first, a brief personal sketch of the general of Virginia's militia in 1779–1781, and then a review of his part in the preparations for the Siege of Yorktown.

General Thomas Nelson was the son of President William Nelson of the Governor's council, and the grandson of Thomas Nelson, the immigrant, sometimes called "Scotch Tom" Nelson because he came from Penrith, England, which once had been included in the territory of Scotland. Secretary Thomas Nelson was the brother of President William Nelson, and therefore General Nelson's uncle. The names of the three Nelsons—William and the two Thomases—and their titles—President, Secretary and General—have often been confused by writers in the public prints.

General Nelson as a man in active public life prior to the Revolution is not so familiar in the public mind as the staunch example of personal honor that he was, should make him. He entered the arena of politics when politics really meant the science of government, a school of practical experience in contending for the rights of English colonists which fitted him for executive duties when there came the testing time of Tarleton's raids and the Cornwallis campaign in Virginia's most trying period of the Revolution.

The character of General Thomas Nelson, Jr.,—Virginia's "War Governor"—and his unselfish devotion to the cause of American liberty can better be understood and appreciated when the staunch integrity of the elder Nelsons is kept in mind. Thomas Nelson, the younger, from earliest youth was under the watchful eyes and care of parents who were greatly concerned for his moral and religious welfare. It is the testimony of the written record that his father sent him, at the early age of fourteen, to England in the care of a friend there—who afterwards became the Bishop of London—in order to keep him from evil associations at home, earlier than he had intended his education in the mother country should begin.

No sooner than his education in England was completed, Nelson was elected to the House of Burgesses, serving from 1761 to 1774. He was also associated with his father in the mercantile business, that of importing goods for Baltimore and Philadelphia merchants. His grandfather has been called the founder of Yorktown, which is a matter of some significance.

The historian declares that William Nelson succeeded so well in his business, not alone by good judgment, but especially because of just and upright dealing in every transaction. In one case he refused to profit by a transaction which had resulted to his own advantage when he found that property then legally in his possession was morally due to another. And when we find a relation of the incident which credits his son, Thomas Nelson, Jr., as a member of the General Assembly when the proposal was made to sequester the English accounts of Virginia debtors for the benefit of the American cause, vigorously opposing such a measure, we can understand at once why he declared in most positive language that as an honest man he intended to pay his debts. When we see this example of honesty we recognize the wholesome influence of a training by forebears of inflexible integrity. In this particular case, Thomas Nelson's determined stand, as a man and as a legislator, for public honesty, despite the vicissitudes of war, saved Virginia from pursuing a questionable and dishonorable course in her economic affairs. Nor is this all that accounts for the true, moral manhood of General Nelson.

The Nelsons of Virginia were as religious as they were patriotic (a fine combination) and a fact not generally known. The church life of the Nelsons as it was reflected in their family life is a background on which, like an artist's canvas, is depicted the progress of the Nelson generations during the three-quarters of a century preceding the great issue of the Revolution at Yorktown in 1781. This rigid adherence to the line of conscientious conduct by the older Nelsons in recognizing and discharging their responsibility to their families, as well as to society in general, is illustrated by the custom practiced by the father of Thomas Nelson, Jr., and which example of the parent must have had a benign influence upon the future general and governor.

Bishop Meade tells the story: The York–Hampton Parish being of considerable length, it was impracticable for people living at the greater distances from their little Grace Church (larger in those days than now) where the Nelsons worshipped for several generations to return to their homes in time for their noonday meals. President William Nelson provided this meal Sunday after Sunday when all—rich and poor—enjoyed his bounty and hospitality. And this, it seems, Mr. Nelson considered the right thing to do, as a matter of course. Such generosity, combined with integrity of character and honesty of purpose was certain to produce a patriot of the highest order, a Thomas Nelson, Jr., whose like is nowhere else to be found in the annals of Virginia, whoever may emulate him by the more intelligence and intensity of his patriotism, for General Nelson's life example of liberality and devotion to his country has never been equaled, except by that of such men as Lafayette and Robert Morris.

Thus it becomes clear to every mind that it was no sudden impulse, no exigency of the moment that made General Nelson, in times of public need, rally to his country's call with all the wealth his father had bequeathed to him—about $40,000.00. It was part of the woof and warp of his character, woven through the experiences of a life enriched by the counsels of a righteous father and a God-fearing mother during that period of our State's history when men of iron will and unselfish singleness of purpose for the public good were needed—and actually produced, and actually making Virginia the Mother of Statesmen and of warriors for the right, too.

Those things are noted to show that General Thomas Nelson, Jr., was *not* an accident of the Revolution, but a real factor in it, which, because of his personal worth and popularity, he was able to help materially in bringing to a successful and triumphant conclusion.

Now as to General Nelson's direct connection with the Yorktown Campaign—with the Siege of Yorktown—two phases of the sane general event culminating in the surrender of the British forces under Lord Cornwallis. Cornwallis and his Waterloo at Yorktown are incomprehensible without the immediate antecedents of the closing scene of the struggle in that little Bethlehem of American Independence on the York River. Nelson is known as Virginia's "War Governor," ranking with Clinton and Trumbull of New York and Connecticut in that era of strife, and this in the epochal year when the State had three different governors: Jefferson, whom the British nearly captured; Nelson, who helped to capture the British; and Harrison who proclaimed the Treaty of Peace with the British.

In order to grasp the full significance of what Governor and General Nelson accomplished as Commander-in-Chief of the Virginia militia at Yorktown, we must see him first as Governor of Virginia—then as General Nelson in actual warfare, if the two offices can be seen as actually distinct in the same person in service at the Siege. And we must also keep in mind his personality and his temperamental qualifications for this task of being Governor when Virginia was almost overwhelmed by the enemy. Physical health is sometimes a vital factor in a critical hour (as witness Napoleon), and Nelson had on two or three occasions resigned positions of honor and trust because of ill health. More is the wonder then that he accomplished what he did as governor with the responsibilities also of a militia general. But, as he wrote to Washington, July 27th, "To have declin'd the appointment might have indicated timidity. I therefore accepted it with a determination to exert every power that I possess'd to give energy to Government and security to the Inhabitants of the State."

In thinking and speaking and writing about Yorktown in October, 1781, one is apt to visualize the struggle as purely local to Yorktown itself and the immediate vicinity. Certain it is that no one worked more industriously to make Yorktown the Waterloo of Cornwallis than Governor Nelson. Let us see him at work preparing for the actual siege.

With all the allied forces concentrated by Washington, Rochambeau, Lafayette and De Grasse as planned by the Commander-in-Chief of the combined armies, and awaiting the final movement of troops to capture the greatest prize of the six-year war, there was one thing most needful that remained to be done according to Napoleon's apt description of an army on the march. Before the troops concentrated on the peninsula to besiege the last citadel of Charles Earl Cornwallis could move from camp to storm a single outpost of the enemy, this army had to be fed! It had to be properly provisioned for the siege.

Now the question is seldom asked: Who fed the allied French and American soldiers—first at Williamsburg and afterwards at Yorktown? Who provisioned the fleet of Comte de Grasse watching on the York to keep Cornwallis *in* and Clinton *out*? The answer: *Virginia*. Virginia, already despoiled by the depredations of Benedict Arnold and Banastre Tarleton, was required by the logic of circumstances to serve as granary and storehouse for the exigencies of the campaign—to furnish provender for the horses and provisions for the men in camp and on the battlefield; and the troops, while at Williamsburg, were already desperately hungry for a while. How could the State relieve such a situation and collect necessary supplies after Cornwallis had added calamities inflicted by Tarleton and the arch-traitor of the war? The official correspondence of Governor Nelson gives the answer.

This record of General Thomas Nelson, Jr., as Governor of Virginia from June 12th, 1781, until after the Yorktown Surrender, tells most graphically the story which historians for 150 years have failed to condense into our common school text books! How many people, who know of Nelson's fame, have ever learned in what particular manner General Nelson proved his efficiency as Governor Nelson from June 19th (the day when he appeared in Staunton to assume his added responsibilities) so faithfully discharged during his short term, but especially while Washington, Rochambeau and Lafayette, at the former colonial capital, were setting the trap for Cornwallis and his army?

It is a fact to be deplored that so little is generally known at the present day about the energetic activities of Thomas Nelson, Jr., while in the gubernatorial chair at Richmond, at Williamsburg, and at Yorktown, moving his official headquarters from place to place as the campaign progressed and neared the crisis. Under such conditions *he made the Siege of Yorktown possible*; for all this time he was urging every proper official of the State Government and cooperating with every general commander of the mobilizing and united forces to secure the necessary supplies to support the military, both before and during the Siege of Yorktown.

Governor Nelson's official letters present him as a very busy executive, and picture to us, as it were, the stirring scenes around Williamsburg, because the whole issue of the Siege depended on the sufficiency of army and navy supplies. In fact, whether the Siege could be undertaken in time depended on Governor Nelson and his corps of assistants: County lieutenants, commissaries, quartermasters, private citizens in semi-official capacity, and the popular will to respond to his calls for immediate help. Washington's plan was to move promptly and quickly—to act before Clinton could come to succor Cornwallis. Had Governor Nelson been a laggard in office in this crisis—what then?

One can visualize every part of Virginia east of the Blue Ridge—every community in commotion, in hurried activity in its own particular way responding to Governor Nelson's urgent and repeated calls for wheat, corn, flour, meal, bacon, beef, salt, vegetables, vinegar, clothing, shoes, and every other article that an army in that day required, including rum, spirits and liquor as severally designated.

A multitude of items seems to have required the attention of the governor, and all were attended to with dispatch, for time was urgent—delay would be fatal. The imperfect postal system of that period was made to serve the needs of the military arm of the State as never before, for the army at Williamsburg was in distress for sustenance before Washington arrived on the 14th of September. Governor Nelson's letters, dated at Richmond from late June till September 12th, show how he sought during this time to employ every means available to provision and strengthen the allied arms. He kept the upper Tidewater region active to improve the roads for Washington's army coming through northern Virginia. He watched the public treasury; he levied an embargo on exportation of provisions; he rushed horses, wagons and forage of all kinds to the Peninsula; he inquired about ammunition; he secured boats, investigated the neglect of hides taken from slaughtered cattle, impressed (for future return) entrenching tools at Williamsburg, as he had previously done at Richmond, and more that cannot be mentioned here.

Until these things were provided, the war could not go on—the Yorktown Siege could not be undertaken. But Governor Nelson directed Virginia's governmental arm to build up the military for the final assault on British power in America. Let us hope that his intelligence and energies employed in this direction will no longer be lost sight of in studying the strategy of the Yorktown Campaign!

Picture, if you will, the scene that must have followed the receipt of this letter: "Wmsburg., Sepr. 26, 1781." (To Sir Peyton Skipwith) "Sir, Your's of the 24th was received only today. The difficulty I hope is removed before this time but if it should not, you are hereby authorized and empowered to impress boats, axes, knives, and all articles required for the slaughtering of the cattle collected at or near Hog Island, and transporting them across the river."

Food and extra implements of warfare were primary requirements; with these provided by Governor Nelson's ceaseless vigilance and exercise of his authority, the march to Yorktown was on, and the Siege began! But I would repeat that the first stage of that memorable campaign was wrought out by Virginia's General-Governor, Thomas Nelson, Jr., on the fields and in the mills and shops of Eastern Virginia. Without discounting the skill, genius, or prowess of a single commander or private in the ranks, it should not must not be overlooked that Governor Nelson's many-sided activities under the adverse conditions of limited resources, requiring him even to call upon the governors of Maryland and North Carolina for certain articles needed—these very activities made possible the Siege of Yorktown.

As the allied troops left Williamsburg we find the Governor's executive office moving also and he is in "Camp before York" September 30th, writing to Major Benjamin Day, Deputy-quartermaster general for the Virginia forces, politely requesting him to immediately establish a "Chain of Express from the Brick House to Camp." (The Brick House was in New Kent county.) In addition to his letters to various civil and military subordinates, Thomas Nelson had continuous correspondence with Lieut.-Governor David Jamison at Richmond, and with Lafayette, DeGrasse, the Continental Congress, Robert Morris, General Greene, and even with Cornwallis himself concerning the detention of prisoners. But while in "Camp before York" Nelson was still Governor of Virginia, as his thirty-three letters from the scene of final action show. His private secretary was Robert Andrews, a professor in William and Mary College. But in the popular mind, Nelson, the Governor at Yorktown, is all but eclipsed by Nelson, the General in the midst of the Siege.

On the battlefield he held command of the Virginia militia included in the three brigades of Weedon, Lawson and Stevens and Dabney's State regiment of 200—in all 3,200 men. These troops were stationed in the rear of Lafayette's Light Infantry between

Wormley's Creek and the Road to Hampton. Johnson, in his *Yorktown Campaign*, says that by the General Order of October 6th, "Lt. Col. Dabney's Regt. (Virginia) and one hundred and sixty men which his Excellency General Nelson was requested to have selected from the militia for the purpose of assisting the Artillery during operations in camp and guard duties," was subject to orders from General Knox.

Here, after his uncle, Secretary Thomas Nelson's house which had been Cornwallis' headquarters was made untenable by the allied artillery, General Nelson (not "Governor Nelson") sensed the British Lord's new headquarters to be in his own fine residence. Then, on October 10th, when asked by General Lafayette, "To what particular spot would your Excellency direct that we should point the cannon?" General Nelson replied: "To that house. It is mine—fire upon it, my dear Marquis, and never spare a particle of my property so long as it affords comfort or a shelter to the enemies of my country." Two cannon balls are still imbedded in the east wall of the "Nelson House," mute testimony to the lofty and conspicuous patriotism of Virginia's "War Governor."

Just one week later when Cornwallis raised the "white flag" the real strength—or rather weakness of the enemy was revealed, as Nelson had already, in his letter of July 27th to Washington, indicated by discounting the military prowess and successes of the British troops as Cornwallis led them down the Peninsula. A vein of hopefulness ran through many of Governor Nelson's letters throughout the campaign. And allied victory was assured on October 18th when Cornwallis, the constable of the Tower of London, was compelled to capitulate to the son of his own prisoner at the Moore House. The surrender of Cornwallis by proxy on the 19th of October was a decisive event in world history, which was made possible (let it be repeated) largely by Governor and General Thomas Nelson, Jr., whose just share of the honors of war attaching to "Yorktown" has never been fully accredited to him. Dr. Thatcher's diary for October 20th says: "To Governor Nelson of Virginia, Washington returned his grateful and sincere acknowledgments for the *essential* succors afforded by him and the militia under his command."

Hereafter our Yorktown hero is found living at his humble home "Offley" in Hanover County where his last letter as Governor was written on November 3rd, 1781; thereafter, until November 22nd, when he resigned the governorship on account of ill health, Robert Andrews was the medium between the retiring governor and the State officials at Richmond. While living in Hanover, despite the sacrifices he had made for the success of the American Revolution, he suffered the criticism of ingratitude and injustice. Lossing says: "Because Governor Nelson exercised his prerogative as chief magistrate of the State in impressing men into the military service on the occasion of the Siege of Yorktown, many influential men were offended and many mortal enemies appeared. But he outlived all the wounds of malice and posterity does honor to his name."

Today only the foundation walls of Secretary Thomas Nelson's house remain, though it stood in ruins fifteen years after the siege. This landmark has been saved from obliteration by the A. P. V A., while General Nelson's home is a Mecca for pilgrims, and the pride of Yorktown. Though his is one of the bronze figures in the Crawford Monument, no single monument stands today as a memorial to the bold and ardent patriot whose very name denotes Yorktown and Independence. But Nelson needs no new memorial to his honored name. One slight recognition of his services was given him while he lived—*Fort Nelson*, the second fort erected on the site of Louisville, Kentucky, in 1782. But like an ungrateful republic, Virginia has neglected the debt she should have repaid General Nelson, though State poverty may have been for years a valid reason for such "forgetfulness."

But if a grateful people in this generation would propose to erect another monument to the patriot-hero of Yorktown, I would say that an adequate memorial already stands there on sacred ground, conspicuous and the admiration of all visitors to this famous village of great shrines. Here is a Nelson "monument," built in advance of the day when service to his country placed the laurel wreath of victory on his fearless brow, and predestined his home to become in reality a national shrine. I refer to the "Nelson House" in Yorktown, of late called "York Hall." That stately mansion, now revered as a shrine of patriotism is a more significant memorial to keep bright in the public mind the record of Nelson's unselfish services than any monument of stone or product of sculptor's chisel that citizens of the Republic of States in this Twentieth Century could erect to glorify his name.

Could Thomas Nelson, Jr., but know today—and rejoice to know—that his former home, sacrificed to pay his obligations given to help bring the War for independence to a successful conclusion, is now devoted to purposes of charity. Grateful should all the "Sons of the American Revolution" be that such a monument invites all people to recall his noble character and essential services at the Sesquicentennial of Cornwallis' Surrender!

The stately Georgian architecture of the "Nelson House," combined with its historical associations, is an imposing and significant shrine. And with the name of Nelson associated with "York Hall," no other Nelson memorial at Yorktown could ever eclipse it in the powerful appeal it makes to American citizens as a landmark of liberty.

As if he needed no other monument, Time itself waited on the Future many years to mark his last resting place in the "city of the dead" around the church of his fathers. Here in the present century a modest granite slab has been placed over the spot where our hero is buried. His epitaph is testimony that his name can never perish. Chiseled in enduring stone, it reads:

> General Thomas Nelson, Jr., Patriot, Soldier, Christian Gentlemen, Born December 12, 1738; Died January 22, 1789. Mover of the Resolution of May 16, 1776, in the Virginia Convention Instructing Her Delegates in Congress to Move That Body to Declare the Colonies Free and Independent States; Signer of the Declaration of Independence; War Governor of Virginia; Commander of the Virginia Forces.
>
> He Gave All For Liberty.

GENERALS ARNOLD AND PHILLIPS (BRITISH) AT YORKTOWN

W. T. STAUFFER

The first British force led into Virginia in connection with the Yorktown Campaign was that of Benedict Arnold, the arch-traitor of the American Revolution.

Arnold was one of those dashing, reckless, at times foolhardy dispositions which are capable of the most brilliant exploits and which, strange to say, manage to escape danger at least with their lives. He was the great-grandson of Benedict Arnold, thrice colonial Governor of Rhode Island. He settled in New Haven, Connecticut, where he owned a drug store and engaged in the West India trade. Immediately after the battle of Lexington, in the face of the opposition of authority, he led the local militia to Cambridge. He suggested to Massachusetts an expedition against Crown Point and Ticonderoga, but was forestalled by Ethan Allen, under whom, however, he served. He led one of the expeditions against Canada; brilliantly engaged the British on Lake Champlain; took part in the New Jersey Campaign; raised the siege of Fort Stanwix; saved the second battle of Saratoga (after having been relieved of command); was placed in command of Philadelphia where he married Margaret Shippen, the daughter of a moderate Tory, and finally secured from Washington the command of West Point which controlled the Hudson River. Charges had been twice preferred against him, and he had twice been acquitted. His attempt to surrender West Point and with it perhaps Washington, who happened to be there at the time, the capture of André, and Arnold's escape are all well known to every American school child. Let me, however, call your attention to the fact that one of the men who captured André was an ancestor of our own compatriot, Mr. De Witt Crane. Let me also call your attention to the fact that Arnold's offense was not merely technical treason, but was the deepest treachery dyed with moral turpitude. He did not openly support the British cause like John Randolph, but for a year was in communication with Clinton and sought the command of West Point with a view to betraying it into the hands of the British.

Clinton sent Arnold to Portsmouth, Virginia, in December 1780 to replace the forces of Leslie who had been ordered from Portsmouth to Charleston, South Carolina. Arnold's forces were to carry on "desultory expeditions" and in a great measure to stop up the Chesapeake. He landed at Jamestown on January 3rd, plundered and burned Richmond on January 7th and then returned to Portsmouth. Washington sent Lafayette with a body of continentals to unite with Muhlenberg, Weedon and Nelson, who commanded militia in Virginia, and persuaded Rochambeau to despatch a small fleet and a few troops from Newport with the hope of capturing the traitor. But an English fleet intercepted the French and they were obliged to return to Newport. Lafayette marched his forces to the head of Chesapeake Bay and made his own way as far as Williamsburg, but, hearing of the withdrawal of the French fleet, he retired as far north as what is now Elkton, Maryland.

Meanwhile, Washington had learned that Clinton had sent General Phillips, an excellent officer who had surrendered with Burgoyne, to combine with Arnold's forces and to take command in the Chesapeake. This indicated a campaign of larger proportions in Virginia. Lafayette, accordingly, was ordered to return south and place himself under the command of General Greene. By forced march Lafayette reached Richmond on April 29th, 1781. Phillips appeared opposite the town next morning. Surprised at Lafayette's celerity, Phillips retired as far as Jamestown. On orders from Cornwallis Phillips returned as far as Petersburg on May 10th. Phillips died of fever on May 13th and Arnold succeeded him. Lafayette refused to have anything to do with the traitor even in the exchange of prisoners. Cornwallis arrived in Petersburg on May 20, took command, and ordered Arnold back to New York.

But this does not end Arnold's activities in connection with the Yorktown Campaign. When Clinton woke up to Washington's move he sent Arnold with 2,000 troops along the New England coast with the double object of capturing privateers in New London harbor and, by ravaging the coast, of drawing Washington back to its defense. The forces of Arnold sacked and burned New London, massacred the garrison of Fort Griswold, and returned to New York.

Arnold died in England in June 1801. As he felt the end approaching, he had his American uniform brought him to put on and asked that God might forgive him for ever having worn another.

MARQUIS DE LAFAYETTE, THE SOLDIER IN VIRGINIA

Dr. L. S. Foster

Let us see what manner of man he was who did so much for the American cause, and Virginia in particular, during the revolution. This distinguished character was born on the 6th of September 1757 in the province of Auvergne, France, a province celebrated for the valor and independence of its inhabitants from the earliest times. His ancestors ranked among the first people of the province and had ever been conspicuous for their independent spirit and chivalric contempt for danger.

In the year 1772 at the age of fifteen he was enrolled among the Mousquetaires, a core intended for the protection of the royal person, and composed of young men of the most illustrious extraction. The mildness and affability of Lafayette's manner soon attracted the universal esteem of his new comrades; and the influence of royalty, in a short time elevated him to the rank of a commissioned officer, a favor exclusively reserved for the most illustrious scions of nobility. The same spirit which guided his gallant father to a soldier's death on the disastrous plains of Minden, glowed with equal purity in the breast of Lafayette.

The star of political liberty was, at that time of his life, observed rising brightly in the West, and Lafayette was among the first who went from a distant land to worship it. He was a noble looking man. His forehead was fine, his eye clear hazel, and his mouth and chin delicately formed. The expression of his countenance was strongly indicative of a generous and gallant spirit. His mien was noble, his manner frank and amiable, his movements light and graceful.

His free principles were neither withered by the sunshine of royalty nor weakened by flattery and temptation.

Such my compatriots, was the man, so imbued with the principles of liberty and independence, that at his own expense he procured a ship and sailed with officers, men and army equipment to aid the cause of liberty. Arriving in America, he hastened to Congress then in session at Philadelphia and there offered his services to the struggling colonies battling for freedom. So desirous was he to cast his lot upon the side of liberty and independence, he was willing to enter the army as a volunteer without pay. Congress so impressed with the pleasing manner and soldierly bearing of the youth, lost no time in commissioning him a Major General without emolument in the army of the United States and referred him to the Commander-in-Chief for orders. Washington, with his scrutinizing eye and keen perception, soon discovered that he had in this young Frenchman, a soldier of worth of high ideals and strict integrity. So impressed was he with the Marquis, that he did not hesitate to entrust to him the most confidential and important orders. He felt for him a warm and sincere friendship, and paved the way for bestowing on him a command in the army equal to his rank. Under the care and tuition of the venerated man of the age whose adopted son he was, the principles of liberty which appeared to have been coexistent with his birth, were judiciously regulated and fostered. His conduct in the battle of Brandywine confirmed the already fixed opinion of him as a man and soldier, so much so, that when he lay wounded, Washington said to the surgeon in charge, "Take good care of him as if he were my son, for I love him the same."

When Generals Phillips, Simcoe and the traitor, Arnold were destroying property of every description in Virginia, Washington sent this trusted soldier with Wayne and Baron Steuben to her defense. As Lafayette entered Richmond the British array made its appearance in Manchester. The opportune arrival of Lafayette put an insuperable bar to the project of taking the Capital City in which a great proportion of the military stores of the State were collected. At Richmond the Marquis formed a junction with Baron

Steuben and found himself at the head of about one thousand regulars, two thousand militia, and sixty dragoons, while the British forces consisted of nearly four thousand veteran troops. Phillips moved his troops down the James River and the Marquis followed cautiously on the north side of the river as far as the Chickahominy. Under orders of Cornwallis, Phillips ascended the river and disembarked his army at Brandon on the south side of the river. Lafayette being advised of this move on the part of the enemy, hastened back to Richmond. Being persuaded that the purpose of this move was to join Cornwallis, who was now on his way to Virginia at Petersburg, Lafayette hastened to take possession of Petersburg before Phillips could reach that place. In this design, however, he was anticipated. The British general advanced with equal rapidity and being nearer to Petersburg reached it first. Taking possession of Petersburg on the ninth of May 1781, was the last exploit of General Phillips, the man who commanded the artillery on the field of Minden and from whose battery a shot had killed the father of Lafayette.

Now there comes to Virginia from the Carolinas, Lord Cornwallis with the intrepid, but cruel Tarleton to subdue this State and incidentally to capture the *Boy*, Lafayette. Without going into detail about Cornwallis' movements in this part of the State, we follow him as he pursued his march on the north side of the James to Williamsburg with Lafayette at his heels attacking his rear on every occasion that prudence would permit. In Williamsburg Cornwallis remained eight or nine days before crossing the James at Jamestown Island to proceed to Portsmouth where he expected to fortify himself and to send on the troops Sir Henry Clinton had demanded sent to New York, fearing he would be surrounded by Washington on land and the French ships by water. Cornwallis left Williamsburg on the forth of July 1781 for the Island. On the fifth, wheel carriages of every sort were transported across, and on the sixth the baggage and bathorses. Cornwallis intended to pass with the army on the seventh. Lafayette was aware of the intention of his adversary and was inclined to fall upon his rear when a major part of the army should have passed or was passing the river.

Lafayette put his army in motion on the afternoon of the fifth and discontinuing his former caution, rested his forces on the evening of the fifth within eight miles of the foe; a dangerous adventure was this. On the morning of the sixth Lafayette prepared to advance, believing that the hour was at hand for his meditated blow. He thought he had been accurately informed of the passage of the troops on the fourth and the continued crossing and recrossing of the boats ever since. At 11:00 A.M. he was advancing at the head of his troops prepared for battle and sanguine in the expectation that he would get up in time to fall upon the remains of the enemy on this side of the rivers He advanced as far as Green Spring, the former residence of Sir William Berkeley when governor of Virginia. At this place a report from Bushrod Washington and Ludwell Lee who had been sent to the river to observe the passage of the enemy, cast doubt on the passage of Cornwallis over the river. General Wayne, disquieted as he always was by losing a chance of battle, declared his conviction that the intelligence received applied only to a covering party, which would not fail to escape if our advance was longer delayed. Lafayette, indulging in his desire to finish his toilsome and cautious operations by a happy blow, accepted the decision of Wayne and began to make final arrangements for close pursuit. The British General, sage and experienced, presumed that the opportunity which his crossing James River would present, would be seized by Lafayette to follow him and so he took measures to encourage the adventurous spirit by holding his troops compact, covering as little ground as possible on his march and in his camp. He gave orders for his pickets to fall back with the appearance of alarm and confusion as soon as they should be seriously struck. Lafayette, by design probably, did not move from Green Spring until three in the afternoon, inasmuch as the remaining part of the afternoon gave sufficient daylight for the execution of his plan, especially if only a strong covering party of the enemy should be found on this side of the river. Should he stumble upon the entire army of Cornwallis, the quicker darkness approached the better it would be. Very soon after ordering an advance, he found himself almost completely surrounded by the enemy. By his consummate skill and the bravery of his officers and soldiers, he was enabled to make a hasty retreat, and fortunate for him and his army the enemy did not continue their advantage through the night. The failure of Cornwallis to pursue his enemy, made him lose the last opportunity to capture the Boy as he had promised to do.

Without going into further detail of this affair, suffice it to say, this concluded the summer campaign of Cornwallis in Virginia. For eight or nine weeks he had been engaged in the most active movements in Virginia at the head of an army completely fitted for the arduous scenes of war, conscious and proud of his own ability and ready to encounter every danger and difficulty to give success to his operations. The inferiority of Lafayette in number, in cavalry, in arms and equipment of every sort cannot be doubted. He had great difficulties to surmount, as well as to guard against his formidable foe pressing him on his retreat. Wayne, directing his most efficient aid, was far to his right and Baron Steuben with the Virginia levies was far to his left, The great body of inhabitants of the lower country flying from their homes with their wives, children and the most valuable of their personal property, sought safety in the mountains. The State authorities, executive and legislative were driven from the seat of government. In this period of gloom, disorder and peril, Lafayette was collected and undismayed. With zeal, courage and sagacity, he discharged his arduous duties, dispelling our despondency by his example and encouraging his troops to submit to their many privations with cheerfulness. He imparted the energy of his own mind to the country and impressed his high-toned spirit into his army. His efforts were finally crowned with success. No American should pass over the interesting occurrences of this period without reflecting that the defense of the great State of Virginia and with it all the States of the Union, was conducted with consummate fidelity and skill.

Before the twenty-third of August 1781, the whole British force under Cornwallis had concentrated in the position of Yorktown and Gloucester with a regular army of more than seven thousand. As soon as Lafayette received intelligence of the new position taken by Cornwallis, he crossed the Pamunkey and took position in New Kent. He had no intention of attacking the enemy because his force did not permit it, but he was disposed at least to harass them, to repress their excursions and to prevent their foraging in the country. On the 30th of August, Comte de Grasse arrived in the Chesapeake with twenty-eight sail of the line and several frigates. As soon as he anchored, his ship was boarded by one of Lafayette's officers announcing his situation and that of the enemy. In consequence of this information de Grasse immediately detached four ships of the line to block York River and employed some of his frigates in conveying the land forces, which amounted to 3,200 men under the command of the Marquis St. Simon, up James River to form a junction with Lafayette, then at Williamsburg. Lafayette was extremely gratified by being reinforced with so great a number of his own countrymen and by the increasing prospect of being able to render important services to a cause in which he had engaged with such noble and inextinguishable ardor. He had, however felt some disquietude relative to his position. He was apprehensive that Cornwallis, perceiving the circle that was traced around him, would profit by the superiority which he still possessed and, falling upon and overwhelming him, would escape into the Carolinas.

General Washington, attended by Rochambeau, reached Williamsburg, the headquarters of Lafayette on the 14th of September, and proceeding immediately to Hampton went on board of the *Ville de Paris*, where the plan of the siege was explained to de Grasse. The gallant Lafayette now had fresh opportunity to exert his personal influence in favor of the land in defense of whose liberty he had shed his blood. De Grasse was strongly inclined to leave a few frigates to block the James and York Rivers and to put to sea with his fleet in quest of the enemy. He informed Washington of his purpose. If the enemy had not left the harbor of New York, he proposed to block them up in that place. General Washington was exceedingly alarmed at this communication. Accordingly Lafayette was dispatched on board of the *Ville de Paris* with a letter, dissuading de Grasse from so dangerous a measure; and it is thought that without the interference and personal application of Lafayette, the French Admiral would have persevered in carrying into execution a design which might have given the enemy the opportunity to escape. When we consider that the surrender of Cornwallis sealed the destinies of the union, that his escape would have protracted the war and entirely changed the prosperous aspect of public affairs, and that a long period of bloodshed and desolation would have been renewed, we must regard this happy exercise of personal influence and persuasive talent, as one among the highest acts in his American career of glory.

The last division of the allied army landed in the vicinity of Williamsburg on the 25th of September and the whole force being now collected, moved on the 28th in four columns toward Yorktown and camped about two miles in front of the enemy. The next day the right wing, consisting of Americans, extended further to the right and occupied ground east of Beaver-dam Creek; while the left wing, consisting of the French, was stationed on the west side of the creek. In the course of the night Cornwallis withdrew his forces within his inner lines and the next day the abandoned ground was occupied by Washington, ready to open trenches whenever the ordinance and other requisite implements arrived at camp. The transportation of these implements of war was not completed before the 6th of October. On the night of the 6th the first parallel was commenced within six hundred yards of the British lines. Before the 10th several batteries and redoubts were completed, many of them mounted. They opened in succession, dismounted and silenced a number of the enemies' guns and demolished their works in many different places. When all of the batteries on the first parallel were complete, the fire on the 11th and 12th became so heavy it tore to pieces most of the enemies' batteries, dismounting their ordinance in every direction. The shells and red hot balls reached even the ships in the harbor, where the *Sharon* of 44 guns and three transports were entirely consumed by fire.

Washington now continued to urge his operations and on the 11th opened his second parallel within three hundred yards of the British lines. Two redoubts advanced three hundred yards in front of the enemies' works, flanked the second parallel and directed their fire with severe effect. It was necessary to possess these redoubts and Washington determined to silence them with the bayonet. To avail himself of the spirit of emulation existing between the two nations, the attack of the one was committed to the Americans led by Lafayette in person and the other to the French led by Baron de Viomenil. On the 14th of October, as soon as it was dark, the two detachments marched with equal firmness to the assault. The attack as extremely impetuous. On its success depended in a great measure that of the siege. Relying entirely on their bayonets, the Americans advanced with unloaded arms and rushed to the charge with so much ardor that they did not allow the sappers time to remove the abatis and palisades. Passing over them, they assaulted the works with irresistible impetuosity on all sides at once and entering them with such rapidity, that their loss was inconsiderable, and the enemy astonished at so much audacity, were instantly overpowered. The humanity of the conquerors was equal to their courage; they spared every man that ceased to resist. They were incapable of imitating examples of barbarity, as the recent horrid and barbarous outrage committed at Fort Griswold in Connecticut by a detachment under the command of the apostate Arnold. The taking of those two redoubts sealed the doom of Cornwallis, and without going further into the details of the surrender, let us my compatriots ever remember the debt of gratitude which we owe to the memory of Lafayette who ranked among the most active and intrepid of the general officers at the siege of Yorktown and promoted with unceasing perseverance the completion of the glorious scheme to which his efforts had been so long directed, and with the guiding hand of the mastermind, General Washington, and with the aid of the courageous Generals Laurons, Lincoln, Nelson, Wayne and others, made it possible for us to sing, "America the home of the free and land of the brave." And Yorktown, the spot which proved the terminating scene of the Revolution, will be revered by posterity, as long as liberty has an advocate, and reason and humanity have a friend.

LORD CORNWALLIS AT YORKTOWN

W. T. Stauffer

There were three major campaigns in the Revolutionary War. The first was an attempt to cut the colonies in two, and holding the line of Lake Champlain and the Hudson River to crush New England and then the remaining colonies from Pennsylvania south. The second was an effort to capture, first, Georgia and then conquer from the south northward. The third, an outcome of the second, was to conquer Virginia, and using it as a base to crush the remainder of the colonies. The first two were not ill-conceived as they were supported by the large Tory populations in New York, Georgia, South Carolina, and North Carolina. The third was unsuccessful largely because Virginia had so small a Tory population. In the Second and the third campaigns Earl Cornwallis was the ranking British general.

Cornwallis was six years younger than Washington. He was educated at Eton and at Cambridge, entered the army and saw service in Germany. As a member of Parliament, he opposed the ministerial action against the colonies. But when the Revolution broke out, he accompanied his regiment across the Atlantic. After the Revolution he was Governor-General of India, member of the Cabinet, Viceroy of Ireland, plenipotentiary to negotiate the treaty of Amiens, and again Governor-General of India. As to his generalship, we may quote General Greene in a letter to Lafayette after the battle of Green Springs: "Be a little careful and tread softly, for depend upon it, you have a modern Hannibal to deal with in the person of Lord Cornwallis." In the Revolution he had served at

Long Island, the capture of New York, Trenton, Brandywine, and Germantown.

He went south with the British General Clinton and was with him at the capture of Charleston. Clinton, returning to New York, left Cornwallis in command with the injunction to reduce Georgia and the Carolinas. Cornwallis pressed an energetic campaign, the very vigor of which was his final undoing. General Gates was made commander of the patriot forces in the south, contrary to the desires of Washington, and with powers which made Gates well-nigh independent of Washington. Gates, it will be remembered, had superseded Schuyler in command of the army opposing Burgoyne just as the latter had about won the campaign.

Through the strategy of Schuyler, the valor of Herkimer, the patriotism of both, and the dash of Arnold, Gates had gained a personally undeserved victory over Burgoyne. General Charles Lee seeing Gates on his way south, significantly remarked to him: "Beware your northern laurels do not turn to southern willows." Within four days after his arrival, Gates marched by a direct route through a sparsely settled country, the center of Toryism, to attack Cornwallis who had concentrated at Camden, South Carolina. Both Generals had selected the same night for a surprise attack. Their advance guards met each other in the woods. In the battle of the next day, the gallant DeKalb was killed, and the patriot army was utterly routed and scattered.

Half the white population of Georgia and the Carolinas was Tory, which the British made an effort to rally to their standards. Ferguson, a leader of the Tories, was attacked at Kings Mountain, utterly defeated and slain. Two months after Kings Mountain, General Greene took command of the Southern Army.

Nathaniel Greene was born in Rhode Island. He was reared a Quaker. At the beginning of the Revolution he joined the Kentish Guards for which fact he was expelled from the Friends. He joined Washington before Boston, and remained with him until transferred south. At the urgent request of Washington, Greene was made Quartermaster General, retaining, however, the right to command in the field. Cornwallis thus expressed his high regard:

"Greene is as dangerous as Washington; he is vigilant, enterprising, and full of resources. With but little hope of gaining an advantage over him, I never feel secure when encamped in his neighborhood." Washington sent the following message to the southern delegation in Congress: "I think I am giving you a general; but what can a general do without men, without arms, without clothing, without shoes, without provisions?" Greene found the southern army to consist of 2,000 half-starved, half-clothed men, many of them deserters from the British ranks, in a territory teeming with Tories. But no army of its size was ever richer in the personnel of its officers, including among others: Morgan, Marion, Thomas, Sumter, Clarke, Pickens, Kosciusko, Henry Lee, and William Washington. To force a division of Cornwallis' army, which would give greater opportunity for maneuvers, Greene divided his army into two parts. General Morgan in command of one part, by an unusual and superior strategy, administered a crushing defeat to Tarleton, Cornwallis' Lieutenant, at Cowpens. Tarleton fled to Cornwallis who began the pursuit of Morgan. Morgan crossed the Catawba just before Cornwallis appeared on the opposite bank. Night and heavy rains came on, and Cornwallis was delayed three days. Greene joined Morgan and conducted the retreat northward. They crossed the Yadkin. Again it rained and Cornwallis was compelled to march upstream to effect a crossing. Now came a race on parallel roads thirty miles a day for the fords of the Dan. Greene reached them first, and crossed the river which again became swollen. Cornwallis gave up the chase and returned to Carolina. Greene, having rested his men, again took the field and hazarded a. battle at Guilford Court House, in which Cornwallis defeated him. Tarleton called Guilford Court House "a pledge of ultimate defeat." Said Charles Fox in the British Parliament, "Another such victory will ruin the British Army."

Cornwallis had bought this victory so dearly that he retired to Wilmington, North Carolina. Greene, after making a feint on Wilmington, marched into South Carolina and fought and lost the battle of Hobkirk's Hill against General Rawdon; and fought a drawn battle against the British army under Stuart at Eutaw Springs. In the short space of nine months his lieutenant had won the battle of Cowpens; and he himself had fought and lost three major battles and had fought the drawn battle of Eutaw Springs. Yet by the remarkable strategy of dividing, eluding, and tiring his opponents by long marches, and in actual conflict forcing them to pay for a temporary advantage at a price which they could ill afford; in this short time, he rid North Carolina of the enemy and penned his forces in South Carolina up in the City of Charleston, thus winning one of the great campaigns of the Revolutionary War.

Refusing to follow Greene on his march into South Carolina, Cornwallis changed his plans moving northward into Virginia and forming a juncture with Arnold at Petersburg on May 20th, 1781. Cornwallis' scheme was to concentrate on Virginia from both north and south, and with the use of the British navy, to move up the large rivers and subdue the State. He relied much on the Tory element which he believed to be large, but which was, in fact, very insignificant. On May 24th Cornwallis moved forward and crossed the James at Westover, then through Bottoms Bridge and Hanovertown to Aylett's Warehouse on the Mattaponi. Lafayette also moved north, but on the inner line and encamped at the juncture of Goldmine Creek and the South Anna where he could look toward Wayne coming south with the Pennsylvania Line or toward Steuben, who had taken a position at the confluence of the Fluvanna and the James. Cornwallis then moved west and then northwest along the North Anna to prevent a juncture of Lafayette and Wayne, and with the expectation of destroying patriot supplies. Lafayette retreated rapidly until he reached Ely's Ford on the Rapidan, twenty miles above Fredericksburg. From the North Anna Cornwallis sent out two expeditions; one under Tarleton, who, but for Jack Jouett's strenuous ride, would have captured the Governor and the Assembly at Charlottesville; the other Simcoe, who compelled Steuben to retreat rapidly from Point of Fork.

On June 10th, Wayne, with the Pennsylvania Line, formed a juncture with Lafayette near Raccoon's Ford on the Rapidan. Lafayette now became less cautious, moved south from the Rapidan, and placed his reinforced army between Cornwallis who had occupied Point of Fork on June 7th, and the American stores at Charlottesville and Staunton. On June 15th Cornwallis broke camp, faced eastward, and by rapid marches reached Richmond on the 16th. Lafayette followed, hanging on the British rear. Leaving Richmond, Cornwallis marched coastward, Lafayette following at a safe distance. On June 25th, Cornwallis stood at Williamsburg, and Lafayette at New Kent with 1,500 Continentals and 3,000 militia.

Washington was now threatening New York and Clinton called on Cornwallis to send some of his troops north. Cornwallis obeyed and prepared to cross the James at Jamestown in order to retire to Portsmouth for embarkation. Being informed that Cornwallis was crossing the James, Lafayette broke camp on July 6th and moved toward Jamestown. The Continentals under Wayne halted at Green Springs. In the mistaken belief that the greater part of Cornwallis' army had crossed the James, the Americans were gradually drawn into a fight with the entire British army. Nothing but the caution of Lafayette, the decision and audacity of Wayne, and the lateness of the hour saved the American army at Greene Springs. Under cover of night Lafayette fell back to Chickahominy Church. On July 7th Cornwallis crossed the James at Cobham, and proceeded to Portsmouth with the intention of sending part of his army from there north to Clinton. But suddenly, early in August, he appeared at Yorktown with his whole force of 7,500 men, having come from Portsmouth by water. Clinton had ordered Cornwallis to fortify Yorktown also. Upon receiving from his engineers a report unfavorable to the fortification of Old Point, Cornwallis fortified Yorktown, with Gloucester Point beyond the York River. There was, afterward, considerable controversy between the two British Generals on this matter. Clinton contended that when Cornwallis received the report unfavorable to the fortification of Old Point, he should have returned to Portsmouth as the order to fortify Yorktown was merely incidental, and was predicated on the previous fortification of Old Point. Cornwallis contended that when he found Old Point unfavorable he carried out his orders in spirit by fortifying Yorktown and holding the Peninsula, which he considered the main object of Clinton's orders.

THE FRENCH ADMIRAL, COUNT DE GRASSE, AT YORKTOWN

Dr. Clarence Porter Jones, Sr.

Francois Joseph Paul Grasse, Count de Grasse, French Admiral, was born in Valettes Province, France in 1723. He died in Paris on the 11th of January, 1788. His first service as a sailor was with the Knights of Malta Navy, fighting against the Turks. In 1749 he entered the navy of France, received a Captain's commission in 1762, that of Rear-Admiral in 1778. He was then appointed to command a squadron sent to the West Indies. In 1781 he was made Admiral and was sent with a fleet to cooperate with the land forces of the American Colonies. He first assisted in the taking of Tobago in West Indies, then sailed to the mouth of the Chesapeake where he repulsed the attack of the British fleet under the command of Graves, prevented aid from reaching Cornwallis at Yorktown, and cut off his retreat; thus materially assisting the decisive American victory there. For these services he received the thanks of Congress. He then went to the West Indies where for a time he was successful against the British, capturing the island of St. Christopher; but on April 12th, 1782, was surprised by the British fleet under Rodney, and after a hard fight, was defeated and taken prisoner. He was accused of carelessness and even treachery, but was exonerated by an official investigation, and at the time of his death held the rank of Lieutenant-General of the naval forces of France.

From the diaries and the several biographies of Washington, the various accounts of the battles of the Revolution, of the Siege of Yorktown, Bell's Old Free State and other writings; with apologies to each of these authors, we deduce the following facts in brief:

De Grasse wrote Rochambeau under date of March 29th, 1781, advising that he (de Grasse) would sail for North America after reaching the West Indies, but that he would not be able to reach America until the 15th of July. A reply was sent de Grasse giving all advice possible concerning the strength, location, and apparent designs of the enemy. He advised him to enter the Chesapeake as there might be an opportunity of striking an important stroke there, and then to proceed immediately to New York and be ready to cooperate with the allied armies in an attack upon that city.

One is forced to the conclusion that Washington was deep in the conviction that New York must be attacked in the latter part of 1781 and was making his plans accordingly, but Rochambeau's answer to de Grasse's letter seems to have changed the plans of Washington, somewhat against the latter's will. On the 14th of August word came from de Grasse that he was sailing immediately for the Chesapeake direct with a view of undertaking operations there, rather than New York; that his stay must be brief as he was due to be back to the West Indies by the middle of October.

There was, accordingly, nothing also to do but to shape everything in readiness to carry out the plans as given by de Grasse. Washington immediately removed the French troops and detachments from the American Army to the Head of Elk (upper limit of the Chesapeake) to be transported to Virginia. Washington left Philadelphia for the Head of Elk on September 5th. At Chester, the same afternoon, he received dispatches from General Gist, at Baltimore, with the welcome news that de Grasse was at last in the Chesapeake. Overjoyed at the intelligence, he sent it at once to Congress and then pushed on to join the troops.

De Grasse sailed from Haiti on the 13th of August, reaching Hampton Roads on August 31st, and dropped in Lynhaven Bay. He had borrowed for allied land cooperation three thousand troops under the Marquis St. Simon which he had transported on his ships. He had a fleet of twenty-eight sail of the line and six frigates. His flagship, the *Ville de Paris* with one hundred and twenty guns was thought to be the mightiest craft afloat.

On the 5th of September, while a portion of his ships were transporting St. Simon's troops to Jamestown, Graves, the British

Admiral from New York, arrived in Hampton Roads with a fleet of nineteen ships of the line. Dr Grasse immediately went out to meet him, employing twenty-four of his ships of the line. He gave Graves such a warm reception as to persuade Graves to return to New York, leaving de Grasse master of the Chesapeake. Graves' losses were 336 killed or wounded, and three ships badly disabled. De Grasse's loss in men was somewhat greater, but his ships were intact after the battle was over.

In order to transport Washington and his army from the Head of Elk to Virginia, it was de Grasse's good offices here as he sent a part of his fleet, and by the 18th of September they were headed down the Chesapeake, and by the 26th, all troops were landed in the vicinity of Jamestown, Mulberry Island, and College Creek (Williamsburg).

On the 17th of October while the preliminary negotiations were underway looking to the surrender, Sir Henry Clinton left New York with seven thousand troops in transports with a convoy of twenty-five ships of the line, two fifty-gun ships and a frigate, resolving to break through de Grasse's blockade and relieve Cornwallis. He reached the Virginia Capes five days after the surrender. He returned to New York with a sad heart.

It is indeed surprising that in this enlightened nation there are so few persons who seem to appreciate Count de Grasse. This great man rendered the most distinguished service of cutting off Cornwallis' escape by water, and prevented reinforcements of troops or supplies. It seems to have been de Grasse who really forced the Yorktown campaign by his election to enter the Chesapeake instead of New York Bay. Had he elected the latter the tale might have been different. It is a fact that without de Grasse Yorktown could not have been won. Is it not that our people are not history conscious? Is it not a sad fact that our teachers of history lend their aid to the spectacular, as making a hero of Paul Revere, Molly Pitcher, Israel Putnam, all minor heroes who did something startling, and not mention de Grasse whose aid brought the Revolutionary War to a close years sooner (if it ever would have been won) than if he had not appeared on the scene of action?

GENERALS WASHINGTON AND ROCHAMBEAU AT YORKTOWN

W. T. STAUFFER

In the Saxon political firmament there are three stars of the first magnitude—Herman, Alfred the Great, and Washington. When Herman (Arminius) defeated the legions of Varus in the Teutoburg Forest he freed our forefathers from the tyranny of the Roman Empire and preserved to the world personal freedom, the great contribution of the Teutonic race to civilization. Alfred the Great united England under one rule, defended her against her enemies, and laid the foundation of Anglo-Saxon power and civilization. Washington not only freed his people from the tyranny of the British crown as commander of their armies during the Revolutionary War; but, as President of the Constitutional Convention and its pervading influence, laid the foundation of our government, and, as first President of the United States, welded the thirteen colonies into a single powerful nation. In short, the one dominant influence of the American Revolutionary period was the poise, the dignity, the personality of Washington.

But tonight we are concerned primarily with Washington as a general. His military ability has been much underrated. "That he had physical courage and could give orders calmly while bullets whizzed all about, one need not repeat. He was a strategist and a tactician too. Trenton and Yorktown do not cover his whole military record. With troops inferior in every single respect except natural valor, he outgeneraled Howe in 1776, and he almost never erred when acting upon his own good judgment instead of yielding to Congress or his subordinates. His movements on the Delaware even such a captain as Frederick the Great declared: 'the most brilliant achievement in the annals of military action.' Washington advised against the attempt to hold Fort Washington, which failed; against Gates for commander in the south, who failed; against the Canada expedition, which failed; and in favor of Greene for Gates' post, who succeeded. His army was, indeed, driven back in several battles, but was never broken up. At Monmouth his plan was perfect, and it seems that he must have captured Clinton but for the treachery of Charles Lee sent by wish of Congress to command the van. Indeed, of Washington's military career, 'take it all in all, its long duration, its slender means, its vast theatre, its glorious aims and results, there is no parallel in history.'"

The Count de Rochambeau was born at Vendome, France, on July 1st, 1725. He saw military service in Bohemia, in Bavaria, on the Rhine, and in Minorca. He was sent to America as lieutenant general with 6000 well-equipped troops, landing at Newport July 10, 1780. Here he remained a year owing to his reluctance to leave the French fleet which was blockaded in Narragansetts Bay. His part in the Yorktown campaign is told with Washington's. "Rochambeau displayed an admirable spirit, placing himself entirely under Washington's command and handling his troops as part of the American Army." After his return to France, Louis XVI made him governor of Picardy. During the French Revolution he commanded the Army of the North in 1790, but resigned in 1792. During the Reign of Terror he was arrested and narrowly escaped the guillotine. He was pensioned by Napoleon and died at Thoré on May 10th, 1807.

While Cornwallis was carrying on his southern campaign, Washington was encamped around West Point, New York, with headquarters at New Windsor. His army had been repeatedly reduced in order to send succor to the South, so that it now numbered only 3,500 men. Rochambeau by this time had only 4,000 effective men. On May 22nd, 1781, Washington and Rochambeau held a conference at Wethersfield, Connecticut. The only feasible plan of offensive warfare at that time in Washington's judgment was to make a demonstration on New York where Clinton's forces had been reduced to 10,500 men and where a combined French and American attack might place the city in their hands. Even if the attack failed, Clinton would recall to his defense a considerable portion of the British troops in the south, thus relieving Greene and Lafayette from pressure. Or, if the French gained the navel supremacy, a movement toward the south would be justified. Rochambeau returned to Newport. Washington remained a day longer end wrote urgent letters to the New England governors emphasizing the necessity of filling their Continental regiments, warning the militia to be ready to march on a week's notice, and calling for a liberal supply of provisions, powder, and wagons for transportation. He also wrote to the French minister, the Chevalier do la Luzerne, urging him to prevail upon the Count de Grasse with the French fleet to visit our coast in season to engage in an offensive operation. Returning to his headquarters, Washington devoted his entire attention to preparation for the campaign. Knox and Duportail, the chiefs of artillery and engineers, were ordered to put their departments into the best train for the "siege" of New York; the troops were set drilling; Continental detachments were ordered to be ready to join the main army; the Congress was appealed to for renewed exertions; Robert Morris was appointed Superintendent of Finance. But progress was slow. The French were six weeks coming to the Hudson.

By June 11th there was no doubt that Cornwallis had abandoned the Carolinas for the time being and had undertaken the conquest of Virginia. On June 13th word reached Washington through Rochambeau that de Grasse would appear on our coast with a powerful fleet in midsummer. Rochambeau sent a message in reply recommending that de Grasse "enter the Chesapeake on his way as there might be an opportunity of striking an important stroke there, and then to proceed immediately to New York and be ready to cooperate with the allied armies in an attack on that city." Rochambeau made a juncture with Washington the first week in July. On July 2nd Washington had made an unsuccessful attack on the enemy forts at the northern end of Manhattan Island, but failed. On August 14th word reached Rochambeau from de Grasse that on the 13th he would sail for the Chesapeake with a view to undertaking or facilitating operations in that quarter rather than in New York; and that he hoped the troops would be ready on his arrival as he must return to the West Indies by the middle of October. Washington was thus "obliged" to change his plans and make his attack on Cornwallis and not on Clinton.

"The march now undertaken from the Hudson to New York ranks among the famous episodes of the Revolution. No movement on so grand a scale had as yet been attempted. Brilliant in results, it was equally bold and scientific as a military venture. To break up a base of operations, leave the vicinity of a powerful enemy, and enter a new field more than four hundred miles distant in order to engage in a single enterprise, is no ordinary effort. For the men of that time it was a great effort." The force destined to move southward consisted of the French wing 4,000 strong and 2,000 men from the American Army, New York, New Jersey, and Rhode Island troops, and Hazen's old Canadian regiment. The remainder of the army consisting of Massachusetts, Connecticut, and New Hampshire regiments, less than 4,000 men were left under General Heath to guard West Point and the Highlands.

Breaking camp at Dobb's Ferry early in the morning of August 19th, the allied armies crossed the Hudson at King's Ferry. Washington with the Continentals took the route nearer the Hudson while the French moved south farther inland. Everything possible was done to make the movement appear as an attempt on Staten Island, the possession of which Clinton well understood would materially facilitate cooperation between the army and the expected French fleet. It was not until August 29th that the movements of the allied armies disclosed their objectives, which up to that time had been kept a profound secret at headquarters. From the 29th on, the march became an open movement. The two wings of the army united at Princeton and moved on to Trenton and then to Philadelphia, which the American army reached on September 2nd, and the French the next day. Washington and Rochambeau had arrived in Philadelphia on August 30th. The city was all astir, decorated and illuminated at night. The French paid the same honors to the Congress they would have paid to their king. They passed in review before the Congress, the French minister, and the commanding generals. The Continentals halted but part of a day and moved on through Chester and Wilmington to Head of Elk (Elkton, Md.) which they reached on September 6th. They were joined by the French on the 8th.

Washington left Philadelphia on the 5th. Not until he reached Chester did he receive the eagerly waited and welcome news that de Grasse was at last in the Chesapeake. It is said that this is the only time in his public life that Washington displayed boyish enthusiasm. He threw his hat in the air on receiving the news. Washington reached Head of Elk on the 6th and announced to the army the arrival of de Grasse with a favorable land and naval force. The soldiers were given month's pay in hard money which Robert Morris had borrowed from the Intendant of the French Army. Meanwhile Lafayette with his army and the Marquis St. Simon with 3,000 French troops which de Grasse had brought from the West Indies, took up a strong position across the Peninsula at Williamsburg, while Wayne with the Pennsylvania Line held the south bank of the James. At Head of Elk, the advance of each army embarked in light transports while the main body kept on to Baltimore and Annapolis and embarked in frigates sent up by de Grasse. By September 18th they were all off heading down Chesapeake Bay for landings near Williamsburg. The French landed at Jamestown Island and Burwell's Bay (Kingsmill Wharf) one mile below College Creek. The stores and artillery were unloaded at Trebell's (Grove Wharf) three miles below Kingsmill and six miles from Yorktown. On September 25th all the troops of Washington, Rochambeau, and Lafayette were concentrated in front of Williamsburg. Washington, not waiting for the embarkation of the troops at Head of Elk, pushed on with Rochambeau to Baltimore and riding sixty miles a day reached his home at Mount Vernon on September 6th, after an absence of six years. He remained three days and on September 14th arrived at Lafayette's headquarters at Williamsburg in advance of the army.

"The situation thus presented was the great surprise of the American Revolution. It appears as one of the few grand relieving features in an otherwise comparatively tedious war, for here we have a piece of strategy on Washington's part which involved for the first time extensive and critical operations, and whose details were carried out with singular precision and success. Clinton is quietly left in the lurch at New York; Washington boldly marches four hundred miles away, and suddenly falls upon his famous lieutenant at a point where assistance cannot reach him."

On September 27th Washington issued marching orders for the next morning. On the 28th the expectant troops moved forward on the Williamsburg–Yorktown Road. With the French in advance, they passed the Halfway House in single column. Then they took separate routes; the Americans filed to the right and halted at noon within two miles of the enemy's position in front of Yorktown. The militia marching farther to the right joined the Continentals at Munford's Bridge. The French held the line from Beaver Dam (Great Run) northwestward to the York, while the Americans held the line from Beaver Dam eastward to Wormley's Crook. General Weedon, with 1500 militia, the Duke de Lauzun's legion of 600 and 800 marines from the French fleet, all under M. de Choisy, hemmed in the British forces at Gloucester Point. As the object of this paper is simply to deliver Washington and Rochambeau with their forces Yorktown, the strategy will not be followed farther. The siege itself will be treated in a paper by Capt. Nelson Overton at the next meeting.

Having now concentrated the allied forces, let us see what manner of men were encamped before Yorktown. Of the officers we have heard much, but not so much of the men. The French sailors were experienced seamen who had worsted the British Admiral Graves beyond the Capes but three weeks before. The French soldiers were ill-equipped and were veterans of many a conflict and many a siege. As to the Americans: "It would be foolish to say that

Revolutionary soldiers never quailed. Militia too often gave way before the steady bayonette charge of British regulars, at times fleeing panic stricken. Troops whose term of service was out would go home at critical moments. Hardships and lack of pay in a few instances led to mutiny and desertion. But the marvel is that they fought so bravely, endured so much, and complained so little. The rank and file in this war, coming from farm, workbench, logging camp, or fisher's boat, had a superb physical basis for camp and field life. Used to the rifle from boyhood, they kept their powder dry and made every one of their scanty bullets tell. The Revolutionary soldier's splendid courage has glorified a score of battlefields; while Valley Forge with its days of hunger and nights of cold, its sickbeds on the damp ground and its bloody footprints in the snow, tells of his patient endurance. At Bunker Hill, an undisciplined body of farmers, unarmed, weary, hungry and thirsty, calmly awaited the charge of old British campaigners, and by a fire of dreadful precision drove them back. 'They may talk of their Mindens and their Fontenoys,' said the British General Howe, 'but there was no such fire there.' At Charleston, while the wooden fort shook with British broadsides, Moultrie and his South Carolina boys, half naked in the stifling heat, through twelve long hours, smoked their pipes and carefully pointed their guns." At Long Island, "By one of the most magnificent efforts of heroism and self-sacrifice in history, part of the Marylanders, at last reduced to five companies, held Cornwallis' entire host at bay till their comrades escaped; the survivors, after several desperate charges, being mostly bayonetted while making their last stand in a cornfield." "At Monmouth eight thousand British were in hot pursuit of the retreating Americans. Square in their front, Washington planted two Pennsylvania and Maryland regiments, saying: 'Gentlemen, I depend upon you to hold the ground until I can form the main army.' And hold it they did." Such were the men who beleaguered Cornwallis in Yorktown one hundred and fifty years ago.

THE SIEGE OF YORKTOWN

CAPT. NELSON C. OVERTON

When I first undertook to prepare a paper on the Siege of Yorktown I did not realize what a task was before me, but I soon came to the conclusion that to do it as it should be done, my problem was almost if not quite as difficult as was General Washington's in 1781. To attempt to set forth the composition of the armies and the many other details would place me in the position of the man in rural North Carolina of whom I have been told by my father's people. He had the reputation of being a tireless as well as a tiresome talker, and one evening he was holding forth in a country schoolhouse. After half an hour or so his hearers became a little restive and when another half-hour had past, they were very noticeably so. Pausing to catch his breath he said: "Usually where I talk there is a clock on the wall by which I may regulate my time, but I see none here, and I can't tell how long I have been talking." Whereupon a weary but indignant voice from some place in the hall shouted: "No, but gosh, but there is a calendar over there."

We have arrived at the gates of the city—all the participating troops have moved into their positions and we are ready to begin the Siege of Yorktown, that event of such vast importance to America and to the world.

"The whole army, officers and soldiers, will lay on their arms this night," ran Washington's brief order of September 28th, 1781, as the Americans took the right and the French the left of the allied line. Washington knew that the great moment had arrived. We cannot, of course, give Washington the sole credit for Yorktown, but his course of action from the time of the decision to march to the south stamps him as one of the real military geniuses of history. We may not even be positive that he contemplated trapping Cornwallis at Yorktown, or striking a. decisive blow there, but by taking every advantage that each day presented, he proved himself the real soldier and commander of soldiers. At the Weatherfield conference the plan was to move against New York City, as we have seen, but when word came that de Grasse would sail for the Chesapeake, Washington recognized that the situation was ripe for a change, and he did not hesitate to make it at once. To break up a base of operations, leave the vicinity of a powerful enemy and move a whole force more then four hundred miles distant, was tremendous effort, much more difficult then than it would be today. And such a move contained those two great essentials of military victory—boldness of purpose and surprise. I do not recall any parallel case in military history.

Now let us look at the position of the enemy so that we may move along with the events about to take place. "Nothing," said Cornwallis afterwards, "but the hope of relief would have induced mc to attempt its defense," speaking of Yorktown. The place might have served very well as a naval station—it was later so used by the United States, but as a position to be defended from a land attack, it had very little to recommend it. The British surrounded it with a line of fortifications as there were no natural eminences affording protection to its defenders. Two of the ten redoubts in the line covered the river road to Williamsburg; three were in the rear center of the town; and three were on the south, or British left, looking down the river. Two others known as Numbers 9 and 10 were also placed on the left, further advanced, as additional strength in that direction, for here was the natural point of attack of a besieging force. In addition to these redoubts which concealed in all about 65 guns, the British also constructed what Cornwallis called a "strong position out of town" consisting of one redoubt on each side of the main road to Williamsburg, and one on the road to Hampton. There were also fortifications at the head of the Creek to the left, Wormley's Creek, and a large work to the right near the river bank, close to the river road to Williamsburg, known as the Fusileers redoubt, garrisoned by the Royal Welch Fusileers and a small body of marines. Gloucester Point across the York River had also been fortified by a line of entrenchments which was to be defended by Tarleton and Simcoe, two able and experienced British officers.

I will not attempt to enumerate in detail the composition of the opposing forces. I assume that has been done by previous papers presented here. Suffice it is to say that the Allied Army was composed of the French Auxiliaries under Rochambeau and the American Continentals and the Virginia Militia, all under Washington as Commander-in-Chief. The Americans were divided into three divisions with Generals Lincoln, Lafayette and Steuben as division commanders. Lincoln, in addition, was given the temporary command of the whole American wing. Baron Steuben was the only member of the whole American force who had ever before been present at a siege, and it is probable that he had a great deal to do with every operation. In these divisions were troops of the line from the New England States, New York, Delaware, Pennsylvania, Maryland, New Jersey and Virginia; an artillery brigade under General Knox; a few sappers and miners and dragoons, and the Militia under General Thomas Nelson, all of whom were from Virginia.

Cornwallis, under his command, had the cream of the British veterans in America. There was, however, a serious lack of ranking officers. General O'Hara was his only Brigadier, and his list of field officers showed only two Colonels, twelve Lt. Colonels, and twelve majors in his entire force.

In numbers of all ranks there were about sixteen thousand besiegers and eight thousand besieged.

"There were the troops that lay on their arms on the night of September 28th just outside of Yorktown and whose exertions were to determine the control of this Continent."

On the 29th the allies further improved their position by moving closer to the enemy and reconnoitering the ground which they were to occupy. On the 30th a surprise awaited them, for it was discovered that during the night the enemy had abandoned their outer positions and had withdrawn within the immediate defenses of Yorktown. This move by Cornwallis provoked a great deal of speculation at the time by French and American officers, and later was a point of bitter controversy between Cornwallis and Clinton, his superior officer. Certainly, it seems, that if Cornwallis were awaiting and expecting relief (and he said that this was the only reason he attempted a defense of Yorktown) he should have used every means in his power to delay any decisive action by the Allies and to gain time which was the most vital element of his relief by Clinton. The position was a defensible one and should have been held as long as possible and its abandonment was held to be unmilitary by both French and American officers on the scene.

At any rate the Americans and French viewed the situation with satisfaction and occupied the abandoned defenses as their own on the same afternoon. "By this means," wrote Washington, "we are in possession of very advantageous grounds which command their line of works in a very near advance."

Now began a busy time of preparation by the besieging forces—reconnoitering, fortifying commanding knolls and ravines, making gabions, fascines and stakes, bringing up guns and placing batteries. Within a few days what had been Cornwallis' outer defenses became Washington's first fortified position extending from the ravine (Windmill Creek) above the town to the head of Wormley Creek below it. This was not done, however, without some difficulty, for the working parties were constantly under fire, and there were, of course, some casualties—in one instance four men of the Pennsylvania line were killed by a single shot.

Meanwhile about fifteen hundred militia under General Weedon of Virginia had been stationed on the Gloucester side of the river. These were later reinforced by six hundred French troops, the purpose being to prevent the foraging that had been taking place and also to shut the door of escape of the enemy at that point. On October 3rd a brisk encounter took place here which cost the British some loss of men and nearly resulted in the capture of the wily Tarleton. Afterwards the British retired within their defenses where they remained until the close of the siege.

By the evening of the 6th of October everything was in readiness for the final advance upon the town. This was to be made by parallels, which in our parlance is simply a trench affording protection to the besiegers and placing them in better striking distance of the enemies' works. Minute preparations were made for this important undertaking. Fatigue details and covering troops from each detachment were designated and the work was carried on with such precision and secrecy that Washington wrote "the enemy were, I believe, totally ignorant of our labor till the light of the morning discovered it to them." Not an American life was lost, but the French had twenty men and one officer killed and wounded, through the betrayal of their position by a deserter.

Industrious digging continued night and day until a sufficient number of batteries had been completed to begin the bombardment of Yorktown. The first shot came from the French battery on the left of the line. The American batteries opened on the town the same afternoon and according to the testimony of more than one office, Washington himself fired the first shot, which, there is reason to believe, was a fatal one, landing in a house where a party of British officers were having dinner. Secretary Nelson's house, situated on the outskirts of the town, had been Cornwallis' headquarters, but now had to be abandoned, so great was the firing upon it. On the 10th it is reported that General Lafayette was General Officer of the day and he invited General Nelson to be present at the opening of a new American battery. He asked General Nelson, where in the town the fire should be directed, and the patriotic General and Governor replied in the way familiar to us all, telling Lafayette to direct the fire upon his home because he knew that it was sheltering Cornwallis and his headquarters. By the 11th the fire from the enemy batteries had been nearly silenced and Cornwallis was writing to Clinton in New York that he could not hope to make a long resistance against such a powerful attack.

What may properly be regarded as the turning point of the siege came with the completion of the second parallel or trench which placed both wings of the allied array within storming distance of the British lines. This trench was opened on the 11th. To complete it, however, it had to be extended to the bank of the river and a serious obstacle stood in the way in the form of two British redoubts, numbers 9 and 10. As soon as the necessity of taking these positions was realized, it was, of course, decided to do it at once, and the storming of redoubts nine and ten became the most colorful incidents of the siege. Number ten was assigned to the pride of the Allied Army, Lafayette's Light Infantry. Number nine to the French Chasseurs and Grenadiers. With a friendly spirit of martial rivalry they were gallantly stormed and taken within a few moments of each other. The storming of these two strong positions took place on the evening of October 14th, and might well be made the subject of a much more detailed treatment, especially in the light of subsequent history which found French and American troops again going over the top to take the trenches of a common enemy, this time on the opposite side of the Atlantic.

On the part of the French a detachment of Grenadiers and Chasseurs, four hundred strong with Col. Wm. Dupont in immediate command, was detailed to take number nine and they did their work with bravery and enthusiasm with a loss of 18 killed and 77 wounded. As they approached the work they were challenged by a Hessian soldier, who of course, received no reply and the enemy opened fire The French were held up a few minutes by the abatis, or entanglements in front of the redoubt, but a passage was soon cleared. The redoubt was taken and its defenders made prisoners of war.

The American detachment, also four hundred strong was composed of Lafayette's Light Infantry troops as we have seen, all tried veterans, and were commanded by no other than Alexander Hamilton. These troops broke through the entanglements without waiting for a passage to be cleared for them, and succeeded in taking the redoubt within ten minutes after the movement started with only nine killed and 25 wounded. In both cases the British troops defending had behaved with their wanted courage, charging the invaders with the bayonet, but were overpowered.

The troops of America and France had exhibited extraordinary courage in the two exploits and Washington in his reports and orders gave to them his unstinted praise.

With those two works in their possession the allies had completed their second parallel. "My situation now became critical," wrote Cornwallis to Clinton. "The safety of the place is . . . so precarious that I cannot recommend that the fleet and army run any great risk in endeavoring to save us."

The end was near and Cornwallis realized it. No doubt he had realized from the first what the result of the siege would be.

After a gallant sortie on the night of the 15th, which was more to save his army from the disgrace of a passive surrender than for any other reason it is thought, and an unsuccessful attempt to effect his escape by crossing the York river on the night of the 16th, Cornwallis reported to his superior that, "We at that time could not fire a single gun. . . . I therefore proposed to capitulate."

The terms of the surrender were agreed to on the 19th of October and at two o'clock in the afternoon of that great day, the once proud soldiers of Great Britain marched out and lay down their arms.

As the news spread throughout the Colonies it was greeted with the wildest enthusiasm, but my mind returns to the scene enacted just a short way out of Yorktown and along the road to Hampton. The French with their Royal white standards flying in their brilliant uniforms formed one line and facing them stood Washington with his Continentals and Militia, some of whom had been with him at Trenton and at Valley Forge, ragged and lean. Between them marched a whole British Army in defeat with colors furled to the tune of an old English march.

The independence of the United States dates from that afternoon. It is true that peace had not yet arrived, but the people and statesmen of Britain as well as the people of America recognized the fact that the King's dominion in America had come to an end.

At Yorktown the American War of Independence moved out of the class of unsuccessful and undetermined rebellion and became a successful Revolution. It announced to the world that the Declaration of 1776 was not a groundless manifesto of unattainable rights but notice to the wide world that a people who willed to be free, could be free and independent. The Revolution and independence, of course, was not achieved at Yorktown alone—all the other struggles and events must be associated with it and be given their proper share of the credit, but it does represent the crowning achievement, the final victory. The resolution made at Bunker Hill was kept at Yorktown—here was the end of six long years of uncertainty, of hardship and sacrifice.

Before the eyes of Washington and his men and of all patriots of that day was the star of liberty, of freedom and of hope, as it must be before our eyes today. The obligation is upon such organizations as this to keep it there and to think and act and speak in terms of liberty. It is said that for 5000 years the literature of India in Asia contained not a single reference to the word Liberty or its equivalent, and today a handful of British soldiers hold in almost complete subjection three hundred million Asiatics. Liberty to be attained and retained must be constantly thought and written and spoken. And it must be fought for too—it is not usually granted through passive resistance.

This is the month of Washington's birthday anniversary, and may I pay a tribute, if a small one to him,—for to me Washington and Yorktown mean the same thing. Two years ago I talked to men in nearly all the places of any size in Virginia and whenever possible I spoke of Washington. Washington was the first as well as the greatest American, and possibly the greatest human that ever lived. When the other great minds of our Revolutionary period were thinking in terms of British Colonials and dreaming of Empires, Washington alone grasped the great idea of a Free Republic. That is one of the thoughts that Henry Cabot Lodge expresses about him, and that is praise indeed. When the enemy was at his very throat and he was in extreme personal danger, he actually sat down and wrote to the Continental Congress ideas and opinions that form the basis of constitutional government in America today. Through the dark years of the revolution the success of that struggle rested virtually on the shoulders of one man and that man was Washington, and his commanding figure and great mental force in the years following the Revolution more than any other one thing, or set of things, secured this country its place among the nations of the earth. Let us read again the story of Washington and we shall know the reasons for Yorktown.

WASHINGTON BEFORE THE AMERICAN REVOLUTION

J. LUTHER KIBLER

I. WASHINGTON'S BIRTH AT WAKEFIELD

George Washington, eldest son of Augustine Washington and his second spouse, Mary Ball of "Epping Forest," Lancaster County, was born February 11th, (O. S.) 1732. He was born at Pope's Creek, Westmoreland County—by some called Bridge's Creek, and later the plantation was named "Wakefield." The Washington Family Bible contains the following records:

"Augustine Washington and Mary Ball were married the sixth of March 1730/31, and George Washington, son to Augustine and Mary his wife, was born ye 11th Day of February 1731/32 about 10 in the morning and was baptized the 5th of April following. Mr. Beverly Whiting and Captain Christopher Brooks, godfathers, and Mrs. Mildred Gregory godmother." (Mrs. Gregory was George's aunt).

At "Wakefield" also were born his sister Elizabeth, known to posterity as "Betty," and his brother Samuel. Washington has two half-brothers: Lawrence and Augustine, who were educated in England, Lawrence later becoming a seaman and sailed with Admiral Vernon to South America.

In 1735 when George was only three years old, the family moved to "Epsewasson," later called "Mount Vernon." This place George's father had bought from his sister. It was also known as "Hunting Creek." Here his brothers John Augustine and Charles were born in 1736 and 1738 respectively. The home at "Epsewasson" or "Hunting Creek" in that lonesome neighborhood with few and distant neighbors, burned when George was only seven. The father was away from home at the time; the mother and the slaves, however, saved most of the furniture, fighting the fire with water from the Potomac. But now, what about a new home for the family? A move was imperative. Too little is generally known about Washington from his seventh year until the death of his father.

II. Washington's Boyhood Home at "Ferry Farm"

The fire at "Hunting Creek" gave the Washington family the reason for moving to "Ferry Farm." Note the circumstances so little known: An advertisement in the *Virginia Gazette* in April 1738, gave Augustine Washington the golden opportunity that seems to have been intended for him. Lands belonging to the estate of William Strother, "gentleman," deceased, of the Fredericksburg region, were advertised to be "sold for cash on the 25th day of October next by way of auction." One tract, said the advertisement, "contains 100 acres lying about two miles below the falls of the Rappahannock close on the riverside, with a handsome dwelling house and a ferry belonging to it, being the place where Mr. Strother lived." Another tract of 160 acres also was advertised. Washington's father bought both. On November 2nd, 1738, Strother's executors conveyed by deed recorded in King George county, "The mansion house wherein the said William Strother lately lived and those several parcels of land adjoining thereunto and containing by estimation 260 acres."

This is the genesis of the Washington "Ferry Farm," as such named from the ferry mentioned in the old *Virginia Gazette* advertisement of April 14th to April 21st, 1738. Soon after the family of Augustine Washington moved from the Epsewasson region on the Potomac to this Strother farm near Fredericksburg. Here the Washington family remained. *As a family,* the Washingtons never moved again. The father resided here until his death in 1742. Mrs. Washington, the mother, lived here for 37 years—until 1775.

From this Ferry Farm, George with his sister (Betty) and his brothers went to school in Falmouth. Falmouth has restored recently the old field school there which Washington is said to have attended. The story is related of "getting even" with a certain schoolmate, who, in a snowball battle struck little George on the eye with a rock concealed in a snowball. The boy's name was William Bustle, and young George afterwards made him "hustle." This occurred once while George played "soldier."

At Falmouth George's teacher was the sexton of Falmouth Church, named Grove, but who was called "Hobby." Peter, the family servant, accompanied Master Washington to school on horseback, so the story goes. Following his school days with "Hobby," George's brother Augustine took him to "Wakefield," near which place he studied surveying and other practical subjects. Here at "Oak Grove" school he took a course that laid the foundation of his later success in the early experiences he had while he surveyed for Lord Fairfax. His mentor had considerable influence on the young mind of Washington. In school he was fond of mathematics, and several years later he is said to have attended a more advanced school in Fredericksburg with Rev. James Marye as his instructor.

One writer says that this rector of St. George's Church, as George's teacher, required him to memorize a hundred "Rules of Civility and Decent Behavior in Company and Conversation," which rules were also made the subject-matter for copy-book lessons in writing. What is the origin of these "Rules of Conduct" forever associated with Washington's youth? It appears that as a young man Washington was a serious-minded person. It is believed by some people that he composed these rules himself. He did not. Two books of ancient printing are in existence containing these rules in modified form, one in English which one literary critic claims was the source of Washington's knowledge of them and of the inspiration they gave him. Another delver into the literary past has found them originally in French—the product of some priestly mind in a monastery. But whatever their origin, Washington has immortalized them with his own name.

As all the world knows, Parson Mason L. Weems seems to have been acquainted with Washington's early days spent on the Ferry Farm, or "Cherry Farm" as it has also been called. (Pine Grove is another modern name for it.) It was here that the scene of the Hatchet and Cherry Tree story is laid. Whether the youthful and truthful George, at the age of about nine years, ever actually hacked that cherry tree matters little. Weems' story has had its salutary moral effect for generations past, and will have in long years to come. The story of the colt, his mother's pet animal, that burst a blood vessel and killed itself (one writer says "broke its neck") when George attempted to break the unconquerable creature, was also a Ferry Farm incident about which George again "told the truth." Here also he performed the feat of measuring his strength by the width of the Rappahannock river and a Spanish silver dollar, or was it just a plain smooth stone from the river bank? I imagine that silver dollars were quite scarce then, as American dollars some times are today. The cabbage seed also "came up" here to spell George's name, by chance, so the boy believed until his father explained this garden wonder to his son.

On April 10th, 1742, Augustine Washington, father of our subject, and who was one of the leading "gentlemen" of his community, was elected one of the trustees of the Town of Fredericksburg, On April 12th, just two days later, he died. So early was Washington deprived of his father by death—at the age of only 12 years. Provision had been made in his father's will for each of his children. To George and his mother was given the home place, and also two lots in town to George himself. A fuller statement would be to this effect: The estate at "Epsewasson" where the family had lost its second home by fire, fell to Lawrence, the oldest son, by the law of primogeniture with the provision in Augustine Washington's bequest that George should succeed his half-brother Lawrence in possession of the place. John Augustine Washington, George's second oldest full brother received the old homestead at "Wakefield"—the plantation now a national cynosure and to be made a national memorial in 1932.

Mrs. Washington, the widow, held Ferry Farm until George became of age, but observing the spirit of his father's last words: "Be good to your mother," the embryo "Father of his Country" allowed his mother to keep the "Cherry Tree Farm" until the end of her life. It was in 1746 that Washington essayed to live a life at sea. He was now 14 and his trunk was packed, but he was prevailed upon by his mother, who could not spare her boy, to remain at home. Evidently this was one important turning point in Washington's career. He continued to live on the old Strother "Ferry Farm" until 1754 when he acquired Mount Vernon, where he dwelt for a time with his brother Lawrence. But he had been much away from home from Ferry Farm after he began his work as a surveyor.

III. Washington, the Surveyor

In 1848 Washington did his first work as surveyor for Lord Fairfax in marking the western boundary of his lands in the "Northern Neck." In this surveying expedition young Washington became educated in woodcraft of the frontier along the Shenandoah and the South Branch Valleys. In 1749, at the age of 17, he received his commission as public survey or for Fairfax County, from the College of William and Mary. (I pause here to say that Washington was never a student at this famous seat of learning. He only passed his "test" here for "surveyor," having gotten his education in mathematics elsewhere as already noticed. But when he died in 1799 at the age of 68, he was Chancellor of William and Mary.)

Here now, we see Washington in his middle teens, becoming dependent upon himself upon his own efforts to earn a livelihood, for the Washington family was not wealthy, only respectably well off. At this time his services brought him a doubloon a day ($15.00) from his friend, the Lord of the Northern Neck domain. Some of his experiences while on this exploring expedition (for Lord Fairfax had not yet known the limits westward of his territory) are worthy of note here because thus early did Washington get a knowledge of frontier life which fitted him for a more romantic field of operations a few years later. But I must refer all who might be interested to Washington's Diary, which he began to write when he began surveying for Thomas Lord Fairfax.

This period of his life began in March 1748. One morning in the month of Mars, Washington and his companions left "Belvoir" (the old Fairfax home at the time but now long since disappeared) the property of George's half-brother Lawrence, who had married a daughter of Hon. William Fairfax, whose son, George William Fairfax, Washington's friend and neighbor was also here on this March morning, ready for the adventure into the wilderness.

Lawrence Washington, educated in England, was able to add something to George's store of general knowledge; and here opportunity opened the door for the young would-be surveyor, for this profession, or occupation offered employment in laying out lands for new settlers continually seeking new homes. Many "squatters" had occupied at random land belonging to the Baron Fairfax whose domain was a small empire, including 22 counties at present in northwest Virginia and northeast West Virginia.

George Washington Fairfax, commissioned by the colonial Assembly at Williamsburg, was at the head of the surveying party; George Washington was his assistant. One can easily understand how and why young Washington came to be chosen for this work even if he needed official appointment. A portion of the road this party traveled from Alexandria (then the village of Belle Haven) was a portion of the same trail Washington afterwards followed three times on fateful trips to the Ohio Valley.

At Lacey's Ordinary (a portion still standing) at Aldie in Loudoun County, was the end of the party's first day's journey—forty miles to the head of Bull Run. This old tavern was forty by sixty feet with fire places eight feet wide. Here were guests in other days who are known to fame: Boone, Nellie Custis, the King of France and his brother Louis Philip, so the chroniclers tell us. Washington seldom slept in a bed during the whole month the party was gone. Having left "Belvoir" on the 11th of March, Fairfax and Washington were back home on April 1st, 1748. The next year Washington received his Surveyor's Commission from the College of William and Mary and afterwards his surveys bore official certification.

On November 4th of the same year (1752) Washington became a Mason at Fredericksburg. The old Lodge was not the present building in that historic town. On the 6th, two days after he was made a Mason, he was chosen adjutant-general of the Virginia militia at a salary of 150 English pounds a year. It was in this same year an eventful one for a man of only 20 years, that George Washington became full owner of Mount Vernon by the terms of his father's will, as already mentioned. (This was also the year in which Washington lost a birthday by the changing of the calendar from the Old Style to New Style, for January, February and 25 days of March were dropped from the calendar on December 31st, and the year 1753 began on January 1st instead of running 1752 until the 25th of March when the new year would have begun on March 25th, 1752/53.)

But the next year, 1753, was to mean much to both Washington and to Virginia. On October 31st, anniversary of the burning of the last State House at Jamestown (October 20th, O.S.) Washington started from Williamsburg on his journey to carry a protesting message from Governor Dinwiddie to St. Pierre at Ft. Venango, above the site of the present Pittsburgh. He returned January 16th, 1754. His journal, covering many pages, was published by the governor. (See Marshall's *Life of Washington.*)

IV. Washington's Early Military Career

Soon after Robert Dinwiddie became Governor of Virginia the colony was divided into four military districts, and George Washington was appointed for the northern division. He had previously when only 19 years of age been made adjutant-general, ranking as major for training the militia in defense of the frontier against the Indians, but under Dinwiddie his duties were enlarged.

In 1753 the encroachments of the French upon the northern, or Ohio River frontiers, became alarming to the Ohio Company of which the Washingtons, the Lees, and Governor Dinwiddie were members. Their grant of thousands of acres on the Ohio were in danger of falling under French control. Consequently, we have the story of Washington's journey to the Ohio Country at the age of 21. No one was better fitted for this memorable journey—physically, intellectually, and by knowledge of the country gained in his surveying of certain frontier regions for Lord Fairfax.

As already stated, young Washington left the Virginia capital on October 31st and by November 16th he was at Wills Creek—now Cumberland, Maryland. His guide was Christopher Gist; his French interpreter was Jacob Van Braam, whom he secured at Fredericksburg. Reaching Fort Venango in northwestern Pennsylvania, he delivered Governor Dinwiddie's message. Marshall says: "He returned with infinite fatigue and much danger from hostile Indians." On January 16th, 1754, we find Washington back in Williamsburg with the reply of Monsieur Gardeur de St. Pierre, declining to vacate the territory claimed by Virginia.

Virginia's rebuttal to St. Pierre's letter to Dinwiddie was a regiment of 300 men "in command of a Mr. Fry," as Marshall puts it, "with Major Washington as lieutenant-colonel." "Mr. Fry" was Joshua Fry, professor of mathematics at William and Mary College, and who had, on July 30th, 1732, laid one of the first bricks in the foundation of the "President's House," under restoration this year by Mr. Rockefeller. ("Viewmont," Fry's old home, the oldest in Albemarle county, is still standing.) Colonel Fry died at Patterson's Creek while his command was marching to join Washington who had led an advance contingent of troops into the disputed territory. The command of Fry's regiment now devolved upon Washington. His progress was halted by the approaching French.

Arriving at Great Meadows, Washington built Fort Necessity. Villier, the French Commander, attacked the Virginians on July 3rd, 1754. On July 4th—significant date for a surrender—Washington capitulated with the honors of war conceded to him. In this campaign 58 men were lost, besides those among the troops furnished by South Carolina and New York.

The following winter orders from England placed all officers of royal troops sent over to America in superior command over those of the provincial troops. This led Washington to resign his commission rather than submit to such humiliation. When General Edward Braddock came early in 1755, he invited young Washington (at the Carlyle House in Alexandria) to become one of his aides-de-camp. It should be remembered, however, that Braddock landed first at Hampton, and went to Williamsburg to confer with Governor Dinwiddie; he then proceeded to Alexandria.

Washington accepted Braddock's invitation, but he was only partially recovered from illness when Braddock entered battle on the Monongahela. In "Braddock's Defeat"—the popular name for the battle—Washington had two horses killed under him and four balls were shot through his coat. Dr. James Craik said: "I expected every moment to see him fall." Providence has been credited for his preservation here— "the angels of the Lord encamping round about him." Reference is here made to the comment of Rev. Samuel Davie on this point. When Braddock was buried Washington read the Episcopal burial service over his grave. (Braddock required his soldiers to attend religious services conducted by the army chaplain in camp.)

In letters written by Washington afterwards, we learn that he was disappointed and disgusted with the regular English troops in this engagement—the Battle of the Monongahela. Virginians fought bravely; only thirty men remained out of three Virginia companies!

The Virginia Assembly now planned for a regiment of sixteen companies, placing Washington at the head of the recruiting service. After recruiting men for this regiment, Washington set out for Williamsburg, but at Fredericksburg he was entreated to return to Winchester to protect the people in the Valley, who were in a state of panic almost, on account of Indian attacks. This was in 1755. In the Spring of 1756 Indians again alarmed the frontier settlements. It was during this period of suffering—alarm, suspense, attacks, and helplessness that Washington uttered that famous declaration: "The supplicating tears of the women, and moving petitions of the men melt within me such deadly sorrow that I solemnly declare, if I know my own mind, I could offer myself a willing sacrifice to the butchering enemy, provided that would contribute to the peoples' ease." (Washington must have been familiar with the 12th chapter of Romans.)

Washington next urged upon the Virginia government at Williamsburg an increase of the military forces and recommended a fort to be built at Winchester since the mountains beyond the Valley had now become the Indian Frontier. He also visited the line of frontier forts, and found everything everywhere unsatisfactory, and frequently advised with Dinwiddie, the governor. The fort was built and named "Fort Loudoun" after the English general placed in command of all the provincial troops in America. The French and Indian War was now in progress, the "Seven Years War" as it was called in Europe, which ended in 1763.

Washington's correspondence with Dinwiddie was not very complimentary to the Governor because Dinwiddie's hesitant policy was not satisfactory to Washington. But nowhere is there just reflection of the military activities of the now already famous young Virginia colonel, who plead for a more resolute prosecution of the war in men and supplies. John Marshall writes that the Lieutenant-Governor (Dinwiddie) "seems to have been a weak, obstinate and rude man without just conceptions of the situation or real interests of the colony." Washington, on one occasion, had asked Dinwiddie for absence from the service to settle some accounts, etc., but the governor denied him the privilege "in abrupt and discourteous terms" we are told.

Dinwiddie vacated the Governor's Palace in Williamsburg in January 1758, and John Blair, Sr., President of the Governor's Council, acted as Governor, and a campaign against Fort DuQuesne, the French Fort at the forks of the Ohio, was decided on. John Campbell, known as Lord Loudoun, had arrived in America as Governor-General of all the English colonies in America. In the winter of 1757 Washington visited him in Philadelphia. John Blair was Acting Governor until June 1758, when Francis Fauquier became Lieutenant-Governor under Lord Loudoun.

While recruiting men in Winchester for the Fort DuQuesne expedition, Washington found it necessary to make a hurried trip to Williamsburg to procure supplies and money for the soldiers being enlisted. This visit to the Capital was made in May 1758 while John Blair was still acting as governor. It was while on this trip—a journey made be it remembered *in a hurry*, that Washington met the wealthy widow, Mrs. Martha Custis, at M. Chamberlayne's "Poplar Grove" plantation residence on the Pamunkey river. Bishop, his faithful body servant (with him since "Braddock's Defeat") accompanied him on this doubly historic journey. In the ensuing campaign Washington and Forbes captured Ft. DuQuesne, the Virginia colonel himself replacing the French flag with the British flag. Returning from this campaign Washington resigned his commission the last week in December 1758, about a month after he and General Forbes had made Ft. DuQuesne "Fort Pitt." General Forbes died soon after returning to Philadelphia and Washington married the widow of Daniel Parke Custis in New Kent County on January 6th, 1759.

A summary view of Washington's military career thus far has its significance here. Jared Sparks, President of Harvard College, writes of the influence the frontier war of 1753 to 1758 had on the future life of the military hero of Virginia as follows: "The events of this war proved to him and to the world his mental resources, courage, fortitude and power over the will and actions of others. They were in fact a school of practical knowledge and discipline, qualifying him for the great work in which he was to be engaged a future day. The duties of his station at the head of the Virginia troops, and the difficulties he had to contend with during an active warfare of five years, bore a strong resemblance to those that devolved on him as Commander-in-Chief of the American armies in the Revolution. They differed in magnitude and in the ends to be attained, but it will be seen that they were analogous in many striking particulars, and that the former were an essential preparation for the latter."

Washington's struggles with the colonial government at Williamsburg was almost as trying as his military campaign, paralleling to a great extent his after experiences with the Continental Congress. But the popular mind has little knowledge of these discouragements. The story of his patient efforts is almost thrilling, though involved and complicated it seems without orderly treatment. Therefore his activities during the French and Indian War deserve fuller consideration than is possible in this sketchy paper.

V. Washington as a Burgess

While yet at Fort Cumberland on the expedition to Ft. DuQuesne, Washington had been elected to the House of Burgesses from Frederick County. A side light on this election according to the "custom of the times" is not out of place here. In 1757 George Washington as a "prohibitionist" (let us say) received only 40 votes for a seat in the House of Burgesses. He complained to the Governor (Dinwiddie) about so many tippling houses in Winchester as a "great grievance." But when, on July 24th, 1758, Washington was chosen to the House of Burgesses, he was at Wills Creek—now Cumberland—and his friends managed his campaign in their own way. The vote was as follows: For Washington 310; for Thomas Bryan Martin 240; for Hugh West 199; and for Thomas Swearington 45. Gabriel Jones, the "swearing lawyer from Augusta County," and Colonel James Wood, founder of Winchester, were Washington's "seconds" in this election. The expenses for mint julep, etc., were 39 pounds and six shillings.

Now while in Williamsburg as a member of the House of Burgesses, he was also on his honeymoon, residing at the old Custis "Six-Chimney House" until the end of May when he and Mrs. Washington moved to Mount Vernon. In the Old Capitol he was complimented in the highest terms for his services in the late campaign which ended five years of close attention to military affairs. On this occasion occurred the well-known incident of his utter inability to prove himself any kind of an orator, when Speaker John Robinson of the House of Burgesses, extricated him from his trepidation and confusion in this dilemma by saying: "Sit down, Mr. Washington, your modesty equals your valor; and that surpasses the power of any language that I possess." For seven years he represented Frederick county, and then for eight more years he represented Fairfax county in the House of Burgesses.

It was ten years later in 1769 that Washington introduced the resolutions prepared by his neighbor, George Mason, providing for the Non-Importation Association pledged against the use of British goods in the House of Burgesses in session at the Raleigh Tavern, following the proroguing of the Assembly by Lord Botetourt.

The Old Capitol Marker bears a bronze tablet with the names of the 149 members who signed this "Association" paper, Washington's name among them. Mason was not a member of the House then. If only his name were there, too!

VI. Washington as Commander-in-Chief

The year of the First Continental Congress came at the end of Washington's services at the Old Capitol in Williamsburg as a burgess (whenever the Assembly was in session), and having been elected to both the First and the Second Continental Congresses, he was present at Philadelphia in 1775 when John Adams announced his intention to propose the famous military leader for Commander-in-Chief of the continental troops assembled around Boston. Hearing his name mentioned in this connection, Washington quietly left the convention hall. John Hancock, President of Congress, was seen to color in his face when he was passed by for Washington, for Hancock had military ambitions of his own it appears from history.

Washington was chosen head of the Revolutionary forces June 15th, the same day the New England army was adopted by Congress as its own. He was nominated not as "General," but as "Commander-in-Chief" of the Continental Army by Thomas Johnson of Maryland. We now soon see Washington bidding a last farewell to his mother, and before long he is under the famous *elm* at Cambridge—July 2nd, 1776, the date of his arrival there. His headquarters in Cambridge was the "Craigie House," afterwards the home of Henry W. Longfellow; of Jared Sparks, President of Harvard College and a historian who wrote an interesting biography of Washington; and of Edward Everett, the orator and statesman. (We recall "Bell and Everett" for President in 1860.)

On July 3rd, the day before the Declaration of Independence was adopted, George Washington, the American from Virginia, drew his sword on Cambridge Common for the defense of the rights of Englishmen; and this sword, eventually, gave America her independence at Yorktown.

WASHINGTON FROM CAMBRIDGE TO VALLEY FORGE

COL. C. E. LESTER

Guedella says in his *Treatise on Truth*: "Of all the gods which man has ever made—the most singular are those which he made out of other men. Frequently the venerated person's career has a national significance and the deification of such a political or military figure has produced a queer sort of sub-religion which, fascinating as folklore strangely complicates the task of the historian. Patriotism is one of the greatest enemies of Truth. The shy lady seems to retire into the cool depths of her well when she hears a brass band coming or detects the deeper note of memorial orators tuning up. She is nowhere harder to discern than in those careers which have been overlaid by this odd craving for mythology."

Having somewhat similar thoughts in mind when routed with Washington through the two most hectic years of his career, limited by time and therefore to but a few highlights in his most strenuous public life, I have confined myself so far as possible to *known facts*, discussing briefly events and actions with which he was directly connected: the operations of the Army directly under his command and control; the operations in the Northern Department adjacent to Canada; some personal views and observations concerning Washington as an individual, and things which directly concern his leadership.

Some of the events and actions were concurrent, while some things had to be given precedence in assembly. So if it be observed that something that happened in 1777 is spoken of prior to something occurring in 1776, it has no significance and does not affect history.

Washington was a delegate from Virginia to the Second Continental Congress in March 1775, and as such was a member of the Committee for fortifying New York and various other military committees. It may be said here that it appears that Washington, like John Adams, thought Independence not so much desirable as inevitable. In a letter to Capt. McKenzie in 1774 he wrote: "It is not the wish (referring to Massachusetts in particular, and all the Colonies in general) to set up for independence, but you may rely on the fact that none will submit to the loss of rights and privileges without which life, liberty and prosperity are rendered insecure."

The beginning of the war was in Massachusetts and the New England troops began to mobilize almost without direction in the vicinity of Boston. Virginia was a strong colony and New England needed not only her support, but also that of the other Southern Colonies as well in the forthcoming struggle.

The Virginia Colonel in Congress, who had achieved some popularity in Braddock's campaign, seemed to be one of the outstanding figures for a military leader. Though lacking greatly in technical knowledge, he was in many ways probably as well qualified as any other known aspirant for the position. In addition to that, as a person of prominence in Virginia it was doubtless a master-stroke of political strategy on the part of John Adams when he moved for the selection of Washington as the Commander-in-Chief of the Colonial Army. Gen. Charles Lee was a formidable contender for the position as well as others, including John Hancock, a friend of Adams who had very high hopes of landing it. Adams, however, had the canny political view of the situation and wrote: "The appointment will have a great effect in cementing the union of the Colonies." Yet later, as Chairman of the Board of War, he unceasingly hampered Washington and his Army.

In the manner of the modest gentleman that he was, Washington accepted the post and declared with the utmost sincerity that he felt himself unequal to the command with which he was honored, and wished to serve without a salary and be reimbursed only for his expenses. We may feel assured that his record of expense was a most accurate one. His well-known peculiarity of putting on record all monetary transactions, no matter how small, no doubt was most methodically put into use here. On July 3rd he took command of the whole Colonial Army and the local troops assembled at Cambridge for action against the British troops in Boston.

The Fall and Winter following were doubtless trying ones for Washington. To make an effective army out of raw and undisciplined troops was no small job. Organization, discipline, and training were necessary. Propaganda was essential. The populace had to be educated to see conditions as they were. The impending struggle cannot be said to have been altogether popular. Whigs and Tories were indiscriminately mixed in every community with the Tories perhaps somewhat predominant amongst the well-to-do and influential people. There was a powerful opposition toward forcing the issue. Many were inclined to offer a passive resistance to the movement simply by non-support. There were personal and party differences in Congress. There was the usual number of vocal patriots who stood on the side lines and vociferously condemned such movements as were made and equally loud in their denunciations of inactivity. There was the never-ending jealousies in the Army over rank and promotions. Col. Reed (Washington's Aide de Camp) brought to Washington's attention in several letters the dissatisfaction which his appointment and actions had caused in places. Washington wrote him in reply: "I will endeavor at a reformation and can assure you that I wish to walk in a line that will give the most general satisfaction." Ammunition and military stores were hard to obtain and desperate measures were often taken to secure them. Taken as a whole, the winter was a hard one for Washington and had he not been a big man in mind as well as physique he might well have broken under it. As has been said however, if he was not a great man when he went to Cambridge, he was a general and a statesman in its fullest sense when he drove the British from Boston in 1776. Congress and the Provincial Congresses had to be dealt with, and the all-important matter of Commissary supplies was a never-ending source of trouble.

Shortly after Washington's appointment Congress appointed Ward, Charles Lee, Schuyler and Putnam as Major Generals and

Cates as Adjutant General with Brigadiers rank. Lee and Schuyler had accompanied Washington on his trip from Philadelphia to Cambridge and a stop was made at New York. The Tory Governor, Tryon, arrived about the same time as Washington and the sentiment seemed to be about equally divided between him and Washington.

The situation in the north was difficult, and Schuyler was placed in command of the Northern Department. Canada was unfriendly. Practically all the influential people along the border were Royalists and the Indians were ready and willing to fight the Colonists.

The colonialists' enterprise to annex the province of Canada was somewhat disastrous, though at the time it promised to be a fruitful one. They started too late in the Fall with lack of proper preparation. This with the unfortunate delays of Arnold and short-time enlistments defeated what appeared to be an auspicious movement. John Marshall voiced an opinion somewhat prevalent and which has the approval of some writers when he stated that efforts would have been more judiciously employed in securing Lakes Champlain and George and the fortified towns on them. General Carleton conducted a most energetic campaign against Arnold, and defeated him on Lake Champlain. Active operations ceased when cold weather set in, with Schuyler holding Ticonderoga and Carleton back in Canada in winter quarters.

In Boston, Howe had succeeded Gage and had strengthened his defenses. Washington held him to Boston and the adjacent shores until February when he obtained sufficient supplies and some additional troops, and decided to drive Howe out.

By a brilliant night maneuver Washington secured a position that menaced all Boston and Howe was compelled to evacuate. He sailed with his troops for Halifax with several hundred Tories, and there prepared for a movement on New York, British strategy being to force the line of the Hudson and Lakes George and Champlain and separate New England from the rest of the Colonies. Washington wasted no time after the evacuation of Boston, but as fast as possible moved his troops to the defense of New York. Early in August, Washington had a force at New York of about 27,000 men with about three-fourths of them effectives.

As Commander of the defending forces Washington certainly experienced all the handicaps that Providence could provide. Himself most ill-informed as to the technical knowledge of a soldier, without regular army training, educated only as an Indian fighter, Washington faced difficulties many times greater than at Boston. It was here he began to show his natural genius for leadership and the essential element of command to utilize fully scant resources. Raw levies of troops, shortage of food, forage, arms, ammunition and clothing was his daily menu. A Coast line from Maine to Charleston to defend with no fleet, a small force thinly dispersed to guard strategic points and keep lines of communication caused him much concern. Taking from less than twenty thousand effectives scattered about on Long Island, York Island, Governors Island, Paulus Hook, New Rochelle, and East and West Chester the necessary details for camp duty, quartermaster details, medical corps, wagon trains and other non-combatant work, he had left probably less than 15,000 men to meet the assault of Howe's troops. These troops, which began to arrive early in June, were estimated at somewhere about 24,000.

To add to Washington's difficulties, his views heretofore expressed in regard to Tories were now verified by Governor Tryon's conspiracy, which included the Mayor and other officials of New York City and had even penetrated Washington's Life Guards.

With trained men, experienced officers, superior equipment and supported by a large fleet, there was no great glory in it for Howe when he defeated Washington at Long Island.

The American forces under Putnam and Sullivan took a severe drubbing from Howe's troops with considerable losses.

Howe had apparently over-estimated the strength of his adversaries and failed to make the most of his opportunities and Washington successfully withdrew his troops, crossed the East River and escaped the trap. The advisability of defending Long Island had been debated at considerable length and with some fervor. Had General Greene not been ill and had General Sullivan's subordinates been more diligent in protecting Jamaica Pass, the story might have been different. In any event the abandonment of

Long Island without a fight would have made it just that much easier for Howe to take New York. The army's deficiency in cavalry assisted them to defeat. The importance of patrol and reconnaissance cannot be over-estimated. The element of surprise is of inestimable value. A troop of cavalry on patrol might well have changed the whole aspect of the situation at this battle.

Washington was greatly discouraged. The militia was in some cases mutinous. Deserting in large numbers, they refused to obey orders and had an entire lack of subordination. This caused Washington to write Congress concerning his lack of confidence in his men and to reiterate his former statement that no dependence could be placed upon men of short-term enlistment. It was a sorry jest of the time that Washington never could be sure that his men would fight and the British never sure that they would run.

Unfortunately, then as well as many times since in the history of our country, Congress could not see the necessity for trained men. Many persons apparently think and have thought that all that is necessary to make a soldier is to give a man a gun and perhaps a uniform and a band to march to. However, it takes many weeks of weary and intensive training and severe discipline to instill into the average recruit's mind even a cursory view of what it is all about. Thoroughly trained and competent instructors in the science of war are necessary to impart instructions to raw troops. Washington had few of these. His officers in large numbers were of the most mediocre calibre. The criticisms of officers then, during the World War, and intervening times were pregnant with justice as well as injustice. The just accusations were that they were too often incompetent. Incompetence on the part of an officer is, in general, not a direct reflection on the officer, but rather a reflection on the appointing power. A reasonable amount of vigilance would prevent the appointment of an incompetent, and should he get by that—his first action should prove his calibre. Probably a large percentage of Washington's officers lacked nothing in courage, determination and intelligence; they simply lacked the one prime essential of training and the great lesson of experience. To fight battles successfully requires teamwork in the highest degree.

In the ranks of the Army it is necessary to subjugate individualism to collective action. Washington was a pathetic figure then rather than a heroic one. The fate of a nation lay in his hands and he was surrounded by dissatisfied incompetents.

I should, perhaps, qualify that statement. He had quite a number of high-ranking officers who had seen considerable service and were men of training and intelligence; however the derelictions of several of these officers in whom he had the utmost confidence detracts considerably from their accomplishments

Officers of the line and non-commissioned officers are the backbone of any army; herein lay the greatest weakness in Washington's personnel. No army is better than its non-commissioned officers and as a whole they were a poor lot. Short-term enlistments ruin any army, for about the time that men begin to get some idea of what they are there for, it's time for their enlistment to expire.

Without Washington's personal efforts it is doubtful if his army could have escaped Long Island. It was from this time that Washington began to use resourcefulness in lieu of resources and which caused John Fiske to say of him: "In Washington were combined the highest qualities of a general-dogged tenacity of purpose, endless fertility of resource, sleepless vigilance and unfailing courage, with a rare geographical instinct. He always knew where the strongest position was and how to get there." All these qualities and more he displayed in the year following. Lord Howe, as a result of the battle of Long Island, deemed it an opportune time to suggest compromising differences, but Congress held firmly and insistently for Independence of the Colonies.

The untenability of Washington's position in New York became increasingly evident. In a letter to Congress he writes: "On every side there is a choice of difficulties." His keen knowledge of his Army's weakness convinced him as to the necessity for "avoidance of any general action" to side step, if you please, engagements where the chances were against him or even equal. The Army was on the verge of dissolution due to expirations of enlistments, dissention amongst his officers and men, and many other internal difficulties. Added to this was the facing of troops superior in numbers, discipline, leadership and necessities. Congress had not given him the support he had a right to expect, and he put before them at length his views which were, in general, that the contest would be a drawn out one, and that the Army should be placed on a firm basis by proper pay and inducements so as to attract men of character and principle, and equal the inducements that the British were able to offer.

The movements of the British forced the conclusions that his line of communications would be cut and his army bottled up in New York unless a move be quickly made. The withdrawal of stores was started and after two Councils of War the evacuation was begun and the movement of stores expedited. On September 15th Howe sent some ships up the Hudson that quickly stopped the movement of stores. A division under Clinton landed at Kipp's Bay and the militia entrenched there became panic-stricken and fled the place. Two brigades sent to sustain them were of the same calibre and Washington had the humiliation of attempting to rally without success.

All troops were withdrawn from New York and positions were taken up on the heights to the north with serious loss of baggage, provisions and stores. Howe now had New York and Washington had a strong position which Howe was not inclined to attempt to force. From early in October until November 1st there were frequent skirmishes and local engagements with varying fortunes on both sides.

Howe was prudent; he was 3,000 miles from his base, and like Washington, could not afford ill-timed or inauspicious enterprises. There was constant maneuvering for position with Howe as the aggressor and Washington on the defense attempting to checkmate the moves of Howe and as a whole doing it well.

Howe, finding Washington's position too strong to force, changed his plans and decided to take Forts Washington and Lee. Washington knowing the precariousness of these positions wrote General Greene concerning their untenability and advised the evacuation of Fort Washington. His reliance in General Greene, giving him discretionary powers, was here misplaced, although

General Greene, who commanded Fort Washington, had heretofore given Washington his unqualified and efficient support. He was later to prove one of the Revolution's ablest Generals. Greene stated later in extenuation of the loss of the Fort that "there were men enough to have defended themselves against all the Army had they not been stricken with a panic." In the meantime Howe returned down the North River. Washington in a letter to Congress concerning this move states: "I cannot believe that Howe, presuming him to be going to New York, intends to close the campaign and do nothing more. I think it almost certain that he will move part of the troops into the Jerseys and as soon as I know that the move is real and not a feint I shall move a part of my force to counteract his designs." The loss of Fort Washington was a severe blow to the Colonists, they losing about 2500 men, and quantities of artillery and arms.

Washington wrote a letter to his brother Augustine to the effect that the post was held contrary to his wishes and opposition after having been determined upon by a full Congress of general officers and a Resolution of Congress.

Col. Tilghman, Washington's aide de camp, wrote Robert Livingston: "We were in a fair way of finishing the campaign with credit to ourselves and I think, the disgrace of Mr. Howe had the General followed his own opinion."

The vainglorious General Lee wrote to Washington: "O, General, why would you be overpersuaded by men of inferior judgment."

These criticisms here seem to be not ill-timed or inappropriate. Washington, with all his outstanding characteristics, was a modest gentleman willing to accept the opinions and advices of others whom he deemed loyal and worthy supporters, and defer his judgment to that of his general officers and Congress. Congress by no stretch of imagination could be even slightly familiar with local conditions, particularly as there was but little military talent in the body. Washington's deference to Congress was maintained even after that body later had given him dictorial powers.

It is a military principle that upon the commander rests the responsibility of decision. It is also another principle that orders be concise, direct and positive. An order should never be given that is possible to misconstrue or misinterpret. Military commanders in instructions should never suggest; they should direct. It is quite possible that had Washington been more dictatorial as his station demanded, this fiasco could have been prevented as later he might have effectively squelched the disloyal aspirations of Gates and Lee.

Washington had hardly been able to conceive that Howe would abandon his movement up the Hudson until Howe moved into the Jerseys. It was a fortunate circumstance for the Colonies that Lord George Germain, the British Colonial Secretary, failed to give Howe orders to continue up the Hudson and form a junction with Burgoyne who was headed south in that expectation. What the results might have been had Howe moved north instead of south is a matter of conjecture. The fact remains that as things went Burgoyne was decisively defeated at Saratoga.

Washington moved to a position between the Hackensack and the Passaic Rivers, and as Howe advanced he retired fighting rear guard actions to Trenton where he at once moved his supplies across the Delaware. In the meantime Gates had been ordered to take part of the Northern Army and join Washington. Gates through his clique in Congress had superseded Schuyler and received the credit for defeating Burgoyne which rightfully belonged to Schuyler and Arnold. The Battle of Bennington and the defeat of St. Leger practically sealed the fate of Burgoyne. Credit for the greater share of the preparatory events leading up to the Saratoga defeat belongs to Schuyler and incidentally to Lord Germain, and a lion's share of Saratoga itself belongs to Arnold. Gates in his high-handed manner practically ignored Arnold's bravery and generalship and also deliberately failed to report the battle officially to Washington.

Washington had also ordered Lee to join him with his troops shortly after the surrender of Ft. Washington. Lee in his disloyal and treasonable attitude toward Washington delayed his movement until he was captured by Howe—some have said by design. Huddleston, Librarian of the British War Office and author of *Gentleman Johnny Burgoyne*, calls Lee a traitor to the American cause and refers specifically to what was called Mr. Lee's plan exposed in 1860 by Mr. G. H. Moore. This was a plan for the capture of Philadelphia by the British, a plan which it is claimed was devised and submitted to Howe while Lee was his prisoner and which Howe to some extent followed. Washington having been reinforced by some Pennsylvania militia returned to Trenton. Here he saw the futility of fighting and moved his Army across the Delaware.

Putnam was sent to Philadelphia to put the city in a state of defense. Still expecting Lee and his troops and the seven regiments under Gates, Washington had hopes of dealing Howe a good blow. The retreat through the Jerseys by our Fabius Maximus had been a masterly one. The tactics of Fabius against Hannibal had not been through any lack of valor, but rather the prudent action of a wise and far seeing Commander. It is but a sound principle of command to avoid battle when such action promises defeat, a stalemate or even a lack of decisive advantage. Action without any benefits accruing is but a waste of resources. Washington's ability was most evident when he was in difficulties and he outgeneraled Howe at every move.

The eminent Historian, John Richard Green, said of him: "It was only as the fight went on that the Colonists discovered his clean judgment, his calmness in defeat, the patience with which he waited, the quickness and hardness with which he struck and the serene sense of duty that never swerved through resentment or jealousy."

On December 20th Sullivan arrived with what was left of Lee's troops and Gates put in an appearance the same day. Washington felt it necessary to attempt some action. Howe had returned to New York and had left his troops cantoned through the Jerseys. Washington felt that as soon as the Delaware was frozen over Howe would attempt to take Philadelphia, and he therefore determined to attack the British posts on the Delaware. The plan called for three distinct phases of the operation; however only the one directly commanded by Washington succeeded and his success at Trenton doubtless saved his army from an early defeat. Gates was asked to command one phase of the operations, but he feigned illness and requested leave. He had other irons in the fire, and like Lee, had thought his star in the ascendant and doubtless pictured himself soon the Commander-in-Chief.

The crossing of the Delaware, the capture of the Hessians, and the invasion of Jersey caused Howe to hasten Cornwallis back, who drew in his forces and assembled them about Princeton. Washington began to see his command in trouble unless decisive steps were taken. An attack by the British was imminent. Washington thought his command was too weak to risk it, yet he could not very well retreat across the Delaware without suffering the loss of the Jersey militia, and the decidedly helpful change in sentiment that his coup at Trenton had given him. He decided to risk an engagement on the Assumpink River and there he held Cornwallis for a day. Cornwallis was sure that he had Washington trapped. A brilliant scheme of a night march on the British rear and stores was put into effect, and Washington defeated Cornwallis' Reserve at Princeton the next morning, caused Cornwallis to reverse his movement, captured a number of British prisoners, escaped the trap set for him and by a continuous harassing of the British troops, forced Cornwallis to withdraw to New Brunswick and Amboy.

Washington had again proven himself an able and resourceful leader. With a force inferior in numbers and discipline he had practically freed the Jerseys and saved his little army from destruction. Charles Botta, the Italian historian, in his *History of the American Revolution* said: "Achievements so astonishing gained for the American Commander a very great reputation and were wondered at by all nations." During this winter Washington made brave attempts to secure a powerful army for the Spring Campaign, but met with indifferent success. Necessarily the Army in the North must maintain considerable strength; the New York Highlands must still be held, and smaller enterprises elsewhere that entered into the general scheme served as a severe drain on Washington's Army while recruitment was at a very low ebb.

Howe wanted Philadelphia and expected to march through the Jerseys, subdue the colony across the Delaware and take the city. To do this he must get Washington out of his fortified camp at

Middlebrook and defeat him as he could ill-afford to take a chance on crossing the Delaware and leaving an undefeated army in his rear. But Washington now chose to fight on ground of his own choice or not at all, and refused to be let into any general engagement. Howe finally perceiving that Washington could not be drawn from his strong position withdrew his army to Brunswick, for what appeared embarkation to the Delaware or Chesapeake or possibly up the Hudson. Washington immediately disposed his troops to expedite a movement in either direction depending upon events of the near future. As it developed, Howe put to sea for Philadelphia and Washington overland for the same place. They met later on the Brandywine, Howe seeking the engagement, and Washington not disposed to avoid it. Washington was defeated here although the battle was not a decisive one, Washington was outnumbered, outdisciplined and armed with small prospects of victory. He retreated to Chester, to Philadelphia, and another engagement took place later on the Lancaster Road. Suffice it to say, the British took Philadelphia, although as John Marshall reported: "With an inferior force he employed the British army nearly thirty days to advance sixty miles, fought one general action and was defeated, offered battle again within five days, pulled himself out of trouble and, still maintained a respectable opposition."

Washington kept up his attempts on the British communications with their fleet. The Battle of Germantown was fought and local engagements of every character harassed the British for several weeks. During this time the several forts on the Delaware were evacuated and the British cleared the way for free communications with their fleet. There was some clamor that Washington should attack the city, but fortunately superior judgment prevailed and such a move was not attempted. Early in December Howe sallied out with his full force to attack Washington. There were several local engagements while maneuvering for position. Howe finally took up a position on Washington's front, but Washington was disinclined to be drawn from his works, and Howe, apparently convinced of the improbability of defeating him, withdrew again into Philadelphia.

Cold became intense and Washington withdrew his forces into winter quarters at Valley Forge. It may be stated here that after the defeat at Brandywine, Washington foresaw the advisability of securing what supplies he could before it was too late, and this resulted in the withdrawal of practically all public property before the city fell. Valley Forge had been selected because of its strength and it was so situated strategically as to cover the surrounding country and cut off supplies from the country to Philadelphia.

The suffering here of the troops for want of food and clothing is a matter too well known as to require comment. The Army Commissary Department from the beginning had been somewhat of a failure. Lack of experienced men coupled with the complications of assembly and distribution of supplies left the troops many times insufficiently supplied. The folly of Congress in reserving the right to the appointment and control of the Commissary General was only too apparent, and to make a bad matter worse, they appointed four deputy generals who were not accountable to, nor removable by the department head, but only to and by Congress, thus withholding from the Commander of the Armies the control that should have been his exclusively. In a lengthy letter on this and other subjects Washington wrote: "Unless some great capital change suddenly takes place the army must inevitably be reduced to one of three things—to starve—dissolve—or disperse in order to obtain subsistence."

May I add here that there was an abortive attempt to place Pershing in the same position in 1918, but he immediately took the bull by the horns so to speak, and handled the matter to his own satisfaction. He placed a man at the head of the Service of Supply who would have been hard to beat and still retained control. This was the so-called Goethals incident, and comes to public view in Frederick Palmer's *When Mr. Baker Made War.*

On July 16th, 1918, Secretary of War Baker wrote Pershing as follows: "The President and I have had several conferences about your situation in France, both of us desiring in every possible way to relieve you of unnecessary burdens, but of course to leave you with all the authority necessary to secure best results from your forces, and to supply all the support and assistance we possibly can. As the American troops in France become more and more numerous and the battle initiative passes to you the purely military part of your task will necessarily take more and more of your time and both the President and I want to feel that the planning and executing of the military undertakings has your personal consideration and that your mind be free for that so far as possible.

"The American people think of you as their Fighting General and I want them to have that idea more and more brought to them, For these reasons, it seems to me that if some plan could be devised by which you would be relieved from any necessity of giving attention to the Service of Supply, it would help.

"One plan that suggested itself was to send General Goethals over to take charge of the Service of Supply, establishing a direct relationship between him and Washington and allow you to rely upon him just as you would rely upon the Supply Departments of the War Department if your military operations were in America instead of in France.

"Such a plan would place General Goethals in a coordinate rather than subordinate relation to you, but, of course, it would transfer all of the supply responsibilities from you to him and you could then forget all about docks, railroads, etc,"

Baker asked Pershing to think the matter over and tell him just what he thought about it.

It didn't take Pershing but a very few minutes to express his opinion and also to end the matter as far as he was concerned.

In a cable marked RUSH RUSH RUSH RUSH he wrote: "I very much appreciate your desire to relieve me of every burden that might interfere with the direction of military operations. However, there seems to be an exaggerated view concerning the personal attention required in handling the details of administration of this command, The whole must remain absolutely under one head. Any division of responsibility or co-ordinate control would be fatal. The man who fights the armies must control their supply through subordinates responsible to him alone. The responsibility is then fixed and the possibility of conflicting authority avoided. This military principle is vital and cannot be violated without inviting failure. When it becomes necessary for me to be constantly at the front I shall retain control through the General Staff. General Kernan (who then had command of the SOS under Pershing) has worked very hard but has not all the necessary qualifications for success. I have already selected General Harbord to relieve Kernan." (Signed—Pershing)

Phillip Guedella says in his *Fathers of the Revolution*, "It has been the depressing destiny of many military commanders to conduct operations on behalf of legislative bodies. With an acute sense of their imperfections and a lively resentment of their control they victoriously extend their boundaries in a mood which must always recall the uncertain relations of General Washington to Congress. It was the misfortunes of the American dictator which must engage the sympathies of every soldier to have his Senate in constant session."

To add to the many vexing problems confronting him Washington had the humiliation of learning that public adversaries and secret foes under the mask of friendship were attempting to destroy his influence and ruin his character. Sparks thinks that the antagonism of Gates and Mifflin dates from Cambridge when Gates was Adjutant General and Mifflin was Quartermaster General. They both asked for commands there, but were refused by Washington in the interest of the service.

The battle of Saratoga having given Gates a reputation somewhat different from what he would have gained had all the facts and conditions surrounding the affair been known, he developed a decided following. Huddleston says that Burgoyne's defeat was entirely due to Arnold and that Gates spent the greater part of the action in his quarters in a hot discussion with Sir Francis Clark, who taken prisoner after being wounded, lay upon Gates' bed.

A number of members of Congress, Generals Gates, Mifflin and Conway entered into a combination against Washington with the object of having Gates displace him. Conway was another disgruntled officer with nothing but his own interests in view. The disgraceful behavior of Gates and Conway in their correspondence concerning Washington gained them nothing, but the unkind regard of level headed people.

Washington wrote in a private letter to Mr. Laurens, President of Congress: "I am not unapprised that a malignant faction has been for some time forming to my prejudice. My enemies take an ungenerous advantage of me. They know the delicacy of my situation and the motives of policy that deprive me of the defense that I might otherwise make against their insidious attacks. They know that I cannot combat their insinuations without disclosing secrets of the utmost importance to conceal. But why should I expect to be free from censure, the unfailing lot of an elevated station?"

Many volumes have been written of him by many eminent authorities from whom I have gleaned this brief summary of some of the events, actions and characteristics that concern him during this period. I leave you with him at Valley Forge, serene in the knowledge of the loyalty of a large share of the supporters of the Revolution, the respect of his adversaries and continental Europe, and the wholesome self-satisfaction of knowing himself to be what history has proven him—an able leader—an unselfish spirited gentleman with the healthy, generous, self sacrificing interest of his country always uppermost in his thoughts and actions. I think John Fiske expresses most aptly Washington's value to the Colonies in the frequently quoted sentence: "Other men were important—he was indispensable."

WASHINGTON FROM VALLEY FORGE TO THE TREATY OF PARIS

Capt. Nelson C. Overton

This paper on the life of "George Washington from Valley Forge to the Treaty of Peace" must of necessity be sketchy and incomplete, for it deals with the character who was virtually himself the Revolution during more than half the period of that conflict.

Valley Forge was the supreme test of fortitude of the American Army and of George Washington. "To see men," said Washington, "without clothes to cover their nakedness, without blankets to lie on, without shoes by which their marches may be traced by the blood from their feet, and almost as often without provisions as with them, marching through the frost and snow, and at Christmas taking up their winter quarters within a day's march of the enemy, without a house or hut to cover them till they could be built and submitting to it without a murmur, is proof of patience and obedience, which, in my opinion, can scarcely be paralleled."

Characteristically, Washington says nothing of his own patience and obedience—obedience to his own will and sense of duty of which there *is* no parallel. He had marched into winter quarters at Valley Forge, an army without training, without discipline, without organization and without equipment, and in June 1778 he marched from Valley Forge a highly disciplined, well drilled army. He had attained one of the greatest hopes of his life—an army that was at least equal to the enemy in a pitched battle.

While the army and Washington were at Valley Forge, two of the great contributing causes of the success of the American Revolution took place—one was the French Alliance and the other, the arrival at Washington's headquarters of Baron von Steuben. With the former of these all Americans are familiar, but there is a rather surprising lack of familiarity with the latter; and while I know that the members of this organization are not without knowledge of von Steuben's relationship to the life and success of Washington, I do not think it will be out of place to point to it here.

Steuben had been in the Army of Frederick the Great of Prussia, and a member of that Monarch's personal staff. He came to America fired by ideals of liberty, and offered his services in its cause. He found an unorganized camp at Valley Forge filled with little but misery and hardships, turned it into a great training camp, and taught officers and soldiers something that they had never known before—precision in the technique of war, the disciplined use of the bayonet and the mastery of the charge.

The Americans to this time had followed the English custom of delegating to a corps of non-commissioned officers the drilling and instruction of troops; the officers' duty consisting merely of being present and at the proper time leading their men into action. This custom still prevails in the British Army, which has in its company sergeant majors, a superb class of men, unexcelled anywhere in their intelligence and knowledge of their work. Washington had not been able, due to constantly changing personnel, to build up such a corps of instructors, and neither he nor his officers were able to give the necessary instruction to the soldiers. Washington at once saw the value of von Steuben to the American cause and made him Inspector General of the Army. Soon everything in the camp began to change. A better spirit prevailed, there was something to do, something which the men at once realized would be of immense value to them when the weather opened up and the spring campaign began. Steuben appointed inspectors for each division and brigade and thoroughly drilled them in his methods. These inspectors were sent out to their contingents and in a short time his doctrines were adopted throughout the army.

Washington now had an army he felt he could depend upon, and disregarding the advice of his council of officers, was determined to fight. He attacked the British at Monmouth Courthouse on June 29th, and it was here that we see the first fruits of von Steuben's work. With defeat eminent through the treachery or cowardice of Charles Lee, whose troops were in full retreat, Washington came up with the main body and ordered Steuben to rally the fleeing men. Steuben shouted to them a few words of command, and "they wheeled into line with as much precision as on ordinary parade." After a general engagement in which there was considerable loss on each side, the British withdrew from the field, and an impending defeat became a victory for Washington's Army.

I like to think of Washington at Monmouth. In his exchange with Lee we see something of the fire of the man and find that he is, at least, somewhat akin to us all. He has been set apart on such an elevated level, far above other men, so highly praised by historian and biographer, that to the ordinary mind he has been almost "put outside the range of human sympathy." As someone has said, "he has been regarded as a great forbidding figure, almost hidden from view by a misty haze, devoid of heart and feeling toward men and free from human failing." Fortunately, in the last few years, the Parson Weems picture of Washington is being dispelled, and we see him in a fairer light. It was at Monmouth that Lafayette said of him, "I have never seen so superb a man." Lodge says, "A part of this myth-like character is caused by a genuine love for the man and a real gratitude given by men to the hero and the founder of a race or nation." A hero worship which is not at all out of place and which has had and always will have an important part in the building of a nation.

Another fact which has helped to create this impression of Washington is the fact that he rarely spoke of himself. I quote from the same author: "He did as great work as has fallen to the lot of man; he wrote volumes of correspondence; he talked to innumerable men and women and of himself he said nothing. A brief sentence here and there is all that we can find. The rest is silence. In all that he wrote, all that was done or said important to the business in hand was set down and nothing was overlooked, but that is all. The work was done and we know it was done, but the man is silent as to all else. Here indeed is a man of action and of real silence, a character to be wondered at in these or any other times."

During the remainder of the summer and the following winter Washington was in New York and Philadelphia watching the British, and preparing for the campaign of 1779. This was the period following the announcement of the French Alliance, and was an anxious time for Washington. To others the Alliance brought great confidence, but the very confidence felt by them filled Washington with apprehension and solicitude. A baneful feeling of security was abroad, which it seemed to him was paralyzing the energies of the country. Many of those patriots whose names were beacons at the Declaration of Independence had withdrawn from activity in the Revolution and were engaged in private pursuits or those of the individual states. Washington in his letters and utterances deprecated this growing sectional feeling and urged that never was there greater need for exertion among the patriotic sons of America than now. He was in constant communication with the Congress, with individual members of that body and with other personages about the country, advising, exhorting, and urging.

From this time to the arrival of de Grasse in the Chesapeake was perhaps the most trying period of the Revolution for Washington. The winter at Morristown was even more severe than that at Valley Forge, and the army was subjected to more suffering, but Washington now commanded a disciplined army, and history has little to say of the suffering at Morristown. Washington was constantly with his troops. "To share the common lot," he said, "and participate in the inconveniences which the army from the peculiarity of our circumstances, are obliged to undergo, has been with me a fundamental idea." During this period also Arnold's treason was disclosed, and this was a severe blow to Washington, who reposed great confidence in the ability and patriotism of Arnold. In this incident, which is one of the saddest pages of our history, Washington acted with the calmness and firmness which characterized nearly all of his actions. Then followed the surrender of Charleston in the south by General Lincoln, and the defeat of General Gates at Camden, which was the worse defeat ever suffered by an American Army.

But there was also a bright side to the picture for Lafayette returned from France with news of the success of his mission there. We see Washington and Rochambeau at the Weatherfield Conference. We see Clinton preparing to defend New York, and being completely surprised by Washington, who with Rochambeau turned to the south to join forces with de Grasse to surprise Cornwallis at Jamestown.

In this operation with the French, Washington has exhibited to us another extraordinary quality of his ability. "History teaches that every allied army should have a commander, subject to the orders of a commander-in-chief, who, himself, should not be an army commander. But Washington commanded his own army, and at the same time secured the most loyal support and obedience from Rochambeau, who commanded the French Army, and loyal cooperation from two admirals commanding French fleets. Nothing is more difficult in war than to command allied forces in joint operations. Washington did it so well that we often overlook the fact that he furnished the most successful instance in history during the exercise of such a command."

On his way southward to Jamestown and victory, Washington stopped by Mount Vernon, the first time he had been to his home since 1775. Six years away from home and family. This fact is to me significant as well as remarkable. Remarkable because he absented himself from a family to whom he was extremely devoted and from one of the finest homes in America surrounded by broad acres in the cultivation of which he was intensely interested; significant because it speaks volumes to us of his devotion to the principles of free government, and his determination to implant them and secure them forever to his country.

Hurrying to Williamsburg, Washington and Rochambeau joined forces with the divisions of Generals Lafayette, Lincoln, and Steuben, and the Virginia Militia under General Nelson, and the siege of Yorktown began.

Following the reduction of Yorktown, Washington's idea was a combined operation in the south, and he addressed a communication to Count de Grasse on this subject, but the Count in reply stated that the orders of his Court made it impossible for him to take part in the operation. Leaving Rochambeau in Williamsburg, Washington proceeded to Newberg on the Hudson where he established his headquarters.

During the darkest years of the Revolution Washington's steady mind had been exercised in raising and holding the enthusiasm of the public when sinking into despondency, but he now had an opposite task to perform—that of guarding the people against overconfidence inspired by the recent triumph. "No nation," said he, "ever suffered in treaty by preparing, even in the moment of negotiation, most vigorously for the field."

Great discontent now became apparent in the army among both officers and men. There was not sufficient money to feed the troops from day to day, and the pay of the officers was far in arrears. In connection with this trouble Washington received an extraordinary letter from one of his veteran officers, in which letter the officer attributed the present ills, including the army's, to the Republican form of government and advised a form of government similar to that of England and suggested Washington as the head of such a government. And again, Washington, raising above the level of men of meaner ambition, and looking as he had always done far into the future, made this reply to the letter: "If I am not deceived in the knowledge of myself, you could not have found a person to whom your schemes are more disagreeable. Let me conjure you, if you have any regard for your Country, concern for yourself or posterity, or respect for me, to banish these thoughts from your mind, and never communicate as from yourself or any one else a sentiment of the like nature." If any one anywhere can improve on the phraseology of this reply, the lofty ideals contained in it, or the completeness of the answer it makes, I, for one, would be interested in hearing the improvement.

At length arrived the wished for news of peace. A general treaty had been signed at Paris on the 20th of January, 1784, and Washington directed himself to the task of settling accounts, taking leave of his army and turning back his authority to the people. He addressed a letter to the governors of the Colonies in which he set out in clear and concise manner the very fundamentals of American institutions even as we know them today. "Liberty," he wrote, "is the basis; and whoever would dare to sap the foundations or overturn the structure, under whatever specious pretext he may attempt it, will merit the bitterest execration and severest punishment which can be inflicted by his injured country." It might be well to carve that sentence deeply in some place where it could be seen plainly and understood well, for by a thorough search, there may be found some men who would say that a knowledge and understanding of it would do no harm today.

On December 23rd, 1783, with ceremony and formality he returned his commission to the Congress, sitting at that time at Annapolis. "The scene is at last closed," said he in a letter to Governor Clinton, "I feel myself eased of a load of public care. I hope to spend the remainder of my days in cultivating the affections of good men and in the practice of domestic virtues."

This hope was not to be realized, for the young republic was not yet ready to relinquish the grip of his steady hand. "The character of Washington," said Irving, "may want some poetical elements which dazzle and delight the multitude, but it possessed fewer inequalities and a rarer union of virtues than perhaps ever fell to the lot of one man."

From his greatest biographer I gather these thoughts, which I present to you in closing this paper: Washington, considered from every viewpoint, was the first American as well as the greatest, and perhaps the greatest mortal who ever lived. While the other great minds of our Revolutionary Period, even our own Jefferson and Henry, were thinking as British colonials in revolt, Washington alone grasped the Great National Idea of the Free Republic.

He lead an ill-equipped army to victory against superior numbers and brought ordered, free government out of the crumbling federation of British Colonies. With the enemy at his very throat, trapped and in extreme personal danger many times, he wrote ideas and advice to the Continental Congress, which ideas in a few years formed the basis of constitutional government in America.

Through the darkest years of the Revolution the success of that struggle rested virtually on the shoulders of one man, and that man was Washington, and later during his administration as President, his great personality and commanding figure, more than any other thing or number of things, possibly secured this Country in its place among the great nations of the earth.

WASHINGTON FROM THE TREATY OF PARIS TO HIS FIRST ADMINISTRATION

Prof. H. C. Krebs

On the twenty-fifth day of November, 1783, the American troops took possession of the City of New York. One week later the last of the British troops left New York harbor under the command of Sir Guy Carleton. On the fourth day of December Washington bade farewell to his officers at Fraunce's Tavern, and proceeded via Philadelphia to Annapolis to yield up his commission to the Continental Congress. On the twenty-third day of December he met the Congress, and read to them his message of abdication. His short address was masterly in diction, felicity, and simplicity. Jefferson, who was present, afterwards wrote, "the address was worthy of him." It was the irony of fate that the President of the Congress at that time was General Mifflin, who in the dark days of Valley Forge had conspired with the rest of the Conway Cabal to deprive Washington of his commission. General Mifflin, with as good grace as he could muster, replied in terms of high praise to Washington's remarks. Indeed, his speech was most fitting—it had been prepared for him by Thomas Jefferson.

Two days later Washington spent Christmas at his home, which, except for a few hours in 1781, he had not set eyes on for more than eight years.

Washington's highest ambition now was to rehabilitate his estate, and to devote himself to its simple interests. "My manner of living is plain," he wrote, "and I do not mean to be put out of it. A glass of wine and a bit of mutton are always ready, and such as will be content to partake of them are always welcome. Those who expect more will be disappointed." To Lafayette he wrote: "I have not only retired from public employments, but I am retiring within myself, and shall be able to view the solitary walk and tread the paths of private life with heartfelt satisfaction. Envious of none, I am determined to be pleased with all; and this, my dear friend, being the order of my march, I will move gently down the stream of life until I sleep with my fathers."

At this time Washington was not yet fifty-two years of age, and he sincerely thought his public life was at an end. He did not dream that in a few years he would again be called to be helmsman of the ship of state when it was about to founder upon the rocks.

During the war Washington had learned by bitter experience that the government was totally inadequate to the task of controlling the country. His main troubles as commander of the armies had been due to the impotence of the Continental Congress, and this not only because the personnel of the Congress was then of a low order, but because the Articles of Confederation were in themselves fatally defective. While still at the head of the army, that is to say on June 8th, 1783, Washington had sent a circular letter to the governors of the several states, which he meant to be his legacy to the American people. In it he insisted that four things were essential to the very existence of the United States as an independent power. First, there must be an indissoluble union of all the states under a central government that had power to enforce its decrees. Secondly, the national debt must be paid to the uttermost farthing. Thirdly, there must be a uniform organization of the militia in the several states. Fourthly, local interests must in some cases be sacrificed to the common weal. None of these four essentials could be performed by the government then in existence. Washington's letter, because of the high regard in which he was held, exerted a powerful influence on the public mind, and prepared the way for a great reform.

For many years Washington had been deeply interested in the development of the territory west of the Allegheny mountains. In early life he had done surveying in this region, and had bought for himself over thirty thousand acres of land. In 1770 he had begun to advocate easy channels of conveyance between the east and the west. After the close of the war he urged on many occasions the closer union of the eastern and western regions, without which he greatly feared that in time to come they would break asunder; and during the three years 1784-7 he devoted his time largely to the establishment of a line of communication that afterwards became the Chesapeake and Ohio Canal and the Baltimore and Ohio Railroad.

To carry out this project a commission of the states of Virginia and Maryland met at Washington's residence, Mount Vernon, early in 1785. At Washington's suggestion it was agreed that the commission should formulate a uniform system of duties and other commercial regulations, a uniform currency, and recommend the same to their respective legislatures. Pennsylvania was invited to become a party to the commercial compact, as the head waters of the Potomac and the Ohio were involved.

Shortly afterward Madison proposed in the Virginia Legislature that a meeting of commissioners from all the states should be held to discuss pending commercial questions, but this motion was laid on the table. The Mount Vernon compact was, however, agreed upon by Maryland and Virginia, and Maryland suggested that Delaware and Pennsylvania should be consulted as the project contemplated a canal between the Delaware River and Chesapeake Bay. It might be feasible at the same time to consult these two states also on the subject of uniform duties. Indeed, would it not be a good plan for commissioners to be invited from all the thirteen states for this discussion? Virginia at once passed Madison's resolution, and Commissioners from all the states were invited to attend a meeting at Annapolis on the first Monday in September, 1786. The invitations to this meeting were sent out by the Governor of Virginia.

Interest in any movement to secure any kind of uniformity between the states was at so low an ebb that four states took no action whatever in the matter. Four other states appointed commissioners, but they were not represented at the convention because these commissioners failed to attend. Thus only Virginia, Delaware, Pennsylvania, New Jersey, and New York were represented at the meeting. One of the commissioners from New York was Alexander Hamilton.

The New Jersey delegates had been instructed to bring up not only a uniform system of commercial regulations, but other important matters that might be necessary to the common interest and permanent harmony of the several states. This expression, "other important matters," was hailed with delight by all the delegates as opening the way for a broader consideration of pressing national questions. Hamilton now took a step further. He urged that commissioners be appointed from all the states to meet in Philadelphia on the second Monday in May 1787, "to devise such further provisions as shall appear to them necessary to render the constitution of the federal government adequate to the exigencies of the Union, and to report to Congress such an act as when agreed to by them and confirmed by the legislatures of every state, would effectually provide for the same." This report was brought before Congress in October, but Congress refused to sanction it.

However, during that very winter, 1786-7, the difficulties of the country seemed to reach a climax. The paper money craze agitated many states. There were insurrections and riots in Vermont, New Hampshire, and Massachusetts. There was a fierce dispute with Spain regarding boundary lines, and the navigation of the lower Mississippi, with threats of secession by the western states if their rights were not maintained, and threats of secession by the New England states if they were. An amendment was proposed to the Articles of Confederation to enable the Congress to raise funds that were absolutely necessary to the government; but New York defeated it. Thus Congress, having no means whatever of raising revenue, was compelled to accept the recommendation of the Annapolis convention and to give its sanction to the proposed meeting at Philadelphia.

Virginia did not wait upon the action of Congress, but through the influence of Madison appointed delegates, the chief of whom was George Washington. This appointment was most happy; for when the other colonies learned that Virginia considered the proposed convention so important that she selected as one of her representatives the foremost citizen in the country, they also chose as delegates the ablest men at their command.

Washington had long viewed the state of the country with anxiety and had frequently expressed his views in letters and in conversation, In 1783 he wrote: "For my own part, although I am returned to and am now mingled with the class of private citizens, and like them must suffer all the evils of a tyranny or of too great an extension of federal powers, I have no fears arising from this source in my mind, but I have many and powerful ones indeed, which predict the worst consequences from a half starved, limping government, that appears to be moving always on crutches, and tottering at every step."

Later Washington was confirmed in his views when he learned that New York sought to make an independent treaty with the Indians at the time that Congress was negotiating to the same end. He was alarmed at the local jealousies that existed, the hostile tariffs that were enacted at home and abroad, retaliatory legislation between the states that practically ruined trade and commerce, In 1785 he wrote: "I confess to you candidly that I foresee no evil greater than disunion; than those unreasonable jealousies which are continually poisoning our minds and filling them with imaginary evils to the prevention of real ones." The next year he expressed himself as follows: "There is more wickedness than ignorance in the conduct of the States, or, in other words, in the conduct of those who have too much influence in the government of them, and until the curtain is withdrawn and the private views and selfish principles upon which these men act are exposed to public notice, I have little hope of amendment without another convulsion."

Again he wrote: "Thirteen sovereignties pulling against each other, and all tugging at the federal head, will soon bring ruin on the whole, whereas a liberal and energetic constitution well guarded and closely watched to prevent encroachments, might restore us to that degree of respectability and consequences to which we had a fair claim and the brightest prospect of attaining."

Now that Washington had been appointed one of the delegates to attend the Constitutional Convention at Philadelphia, he had grave doubts whether he should accept. He was President of the Order of Cincinnati; and being anxious to be relieved of that office he had informed them that he could not attend their annual meeting in Philadelphia in May. Now to attend the Constitutional Convention at the same time and place seemed inconsistent, and might give offence to his old comrades. He feared his reputation might suffer if the convention came to naught. Was the public mind ready to insure success? Was the country ripe for so radical a proposition as a new constitution? And would not every attempt to alter the old constitution exhibit its defects more clearly, and thus hasten its collapse? Would not every State strenuously oppose any decrease in its powers, and would not every office holder be against any proposition to abolish his office? But Madison, Governor Randolph, Knox, Hamilton, and other close friends urged him strongly to accept from a sense of public duty. His absence would be construed as a defection from republicanism. To these considerations he yielded, and notified Governor Randolph that he would attend the convention.

The convention was called by the Continental Congress to assemble on the second Monday in May, which was the fourteenth day of the month; but it was not until eleven days later, that is on the twenty-fifth day of May, that delegates from seven States had arrived. Of course, the convention could not organize until a majority of the thirteen States were represented. The dilatoriness of this assembly may be explained partly by the uncertainties of travel in those days, partly by the indifference of some of the delegates, but more especially because in the meetings of the Continental Congress it had come to be a waste of time to be on hand during the opening days of the session.

The first duty of the convention was to elect a presiding officer. Benjamin Franklin was at this time President of Pennsylvania despite his eighty-one years. He and the people of his State were the hosts of the convention. It might have occurred to some that it would be complimentary to Franklin as host, and a recognition of his long patriotic services, to make him presiding officer of the convention. But the ascendancy of Washington was so great that no one seems to have thought of anyone but him for the honor. Indeed, Franklin himself intended to nominate Washington for the position; but the state of the weather and of his health forbade his attendance at the first session. Robert Morris, at whose home Washington was a guest, presented his name in behalf of the Pennsylvania delegation. John Rutledge of South Carolina seconded the nomination. Although there were no other nominees, the convention took a formal ballot. Every vote was for Washington. Morris and Rutledge conducted him to the President's seat. Washington expressed emphatically his appreciation of the honor conferred upon him, and asked the indulgence of the members for the involuntary errors he was sure to make owing to his want of better qualifications for the office.

George Wythe, Chairman of the Committee on Rules, reported three days later on the methods of business procedure. One of the rules would be welcomed by every presiding officer today: "Every member, rising to speak, shall address the president; and whilst he shall be speaking, none shall pass between them, or hold discourse with another, or read a book, pamphlet, or paper, printed or manuscript. And if two members rising to speak at the same time, the president shall name him who shall be first heard."

This convention met in one of the hottest cities of the country, in the hottest part of a hot summer. The debates often partook of the nature of the temperature. Disagreements were diametrical. Delegates from small states were at loggerheads with delegates from large states. Their views seemed to be irreconcilable. Many times more than one delegate rose at the same time to speak; yet there is no record whatever of any protest when Washington made his recognition, nor was a single appeal made from the decision of the chair during the entire Convention. Nothing could more clearly demonstrate the high respect in which Washington was held by the delegates, and the calm equity of his rulings.

Only once did Washington enter into the discussions of the convention, and that was at the very end of deliberations. When the engrossed constitution had been read, and Franklin and others urged upon all the delegates to sign it as the best instrument of government to be arrived at by this convention, Delegate Gorham of Massachusetts moved that, if not too late, the basis of representation in Congress should be reduced from forty thousand to thirty thousand. After a short debate, Washington, when rising to put the question, expressed the hope that the change might be made, as giving the people a larger proportion of representatives, thus assuring them added security in their rights and interests. When the vote was taken, the change was made unanimously.

The influence of Washington in this convention should not be underestimated even though, as presiding officer, he felt it his duty to refrain from participation in the debates. Much of the thought of this convention was determined when not in session. Groups would gather informally to discuss pending questions. Private conversation between individuals was constantly occurring. In such cases Washington sometimes expressed his views; and on all difficult questions his opinion, as far as he had formed one, was usually known. There is one recorded instance as follows: "It happened one morning in the convention hall before a quorum had arrived, that some of those present advocated half measures as more likely to meet the approval of the people than any thoroughgoing reform. Washington interrupted the discussion with an expression of opinion that established his position beyond all question: 'It is too probable that no plan we propose will be adopted. Perhaps another dreadful conflict is to be sustained. If to please the people we offer what we ourselves disapprove, how can we afterwards defend our work? Let us raise a standard to which the wise and the honest can repair. The event is in the hand of God.'" Washington may not have been an orator; but these five short sentences constitute a great speech.

It is also to be noted that, as a member of the delegation from Virginia, Washington frequently cast his vote; and it is interesting that his vote was always in favor of the position taken by James Madison. This persistent endorsement of Madison by Washington added greatly to the power which Madison wielded in the debates.

The most difficult question before the Convention was the reconciliation of the rights and interests of the larger states with those of the smaller. Three weeks were devoted to this discussion with little result but the intensification of hard feelings.

Luther Martin of Maryland was especially bitter in his denunciation of the plan to elect members of the House of Representatives in proportion to the number of people in each State. "This proposition on the table," said he, "is a system of slavery for ten states, as Virginia, Massachusetts, and Pennsylvania have forty-two ninetieths of the votes, they can do as they please without a miraculous union of the other ten. They will have nothing to do but gain over one of the ten to make them complete masters of the rest. They can then appoint an executive, and judiciary, and legislature for them as they please."

Mr. Madison strongly contended that if each State had the same number of votes in the House, a combination of several small states would determine the destinies of the country, and that the interests of the large majority of the people of the country could not rightly be controlled by a small minority.

Mr. Wilson of Pennsylvania pointed out that the equality of vote by states was exactly the plan found obnoxious in England, whereby Old Sarum, with no inhabitants, had as many representatives in Parliament as the city of London.

These few arguments indicate the trend of thought of the two hostile camps—the small states and the large states. No agreement being in sight, Benjamin Franklin brought forth a most interesting proposition, namely, that after four or five weeks of groping in the dark getting nowhere, it was very strange that no one had thought of appealing to God, the Father of lights, to illuminate their understandings. During the Revolutionary War, said Franklin, daily prayers were uttered in that very room for divine protection, and God had manifested himself unmistakably in response to these prayers. He therefore moved that every morning, on opening the convention for business, prayers imploring the assistance of Divine providence be offered by one or more of the clergy of the city.

It was objected to by Hamilton and others that to introduce prayers at such a late day would give the impression to the public that the convention was torn with dissension and animadversions. Franklin afterwards said that all except three or four of the delegates considered prayers unnecessary. Hamilton remarked that he did not think foreign aid helpful. Mr. Williamson said the convention had no funds to pay the clergy for officiating. The convention silently postponed the matter by adjourning without any vote on Franklin's motion, and the subject was never again brought up.

It was at the end of the three weeks of futile discussion of proportional representation that the convention was on the point of dissolution. No agreement or other satisfactory solution was in sight. The small states men were firm, and the large states men immovable. Gouverneur Morris afterwards said that the "fate of America was suspended by a hair." "Might as well go home," said some of the delegates, and they began putting on their coats. It was at this point that Washington rose in his place and addressed the delegates. He reminded them that the convention had been called together with the utmost difficulty; that if this body were now to disintegrate, it was most unlikely that any other convention would ever be called; that this would mean the ruin of the country; and that all the hardships of the Revolution would have been in vain. He besought the delegates to resume their seats, and continue their deliberations. These solemn words had their effect; the delegates removed their coats, and with a chastened spirit took up again the vexed question before them. The matter of representation in the lower house was then abandoned for the time being, and that of the upper house was taken up. Here it was soon proposed and carried that all states should have equal representation in the Senate. This concession on the part of the larger states paved the way for a similar concession on the part of the smaller states relating to the composition of the lower house, and the greatest of all the compromises in the convention was speedily reached.

It is to Washington that the credit belongs of having prevented the dissolution of the convention at this point. No other man could have kept the delegates in session. It may truly be said that here again Washington saved the country.

The proceedings of the convention were secret; but it is probable that some rumors of dissension among the delegates became current. It was, of course, desirable that the public should not be stirred up to demonstrations of feeling. Therefore in several of the newspapers of Philadelphia an inspired item appeared a few days after the great compromise as follows: "So great is the unanimity, we hear that prevails in the convention upon all great federal subjects, that it has been proposed to call the room in which they assemble Unanimity Hall."

The silent influence of Washington was powerfully in play when the delegates took up the question of the Presidency of the United States. Everyone felt that the inevitable person for the first Presidency would be Washington, and that, of course, he would conduct the office in every respect above reproach. Therefore the debates on this question were really swayed by the thought that the successors of Washington might not be of his exalted character, and that it would be necessary to safeguard the country in the future against the failings of ordinary human nature from which Washington seemed to be exempt.

On Saturday, September 15th, the real work of the convention was brought to a close. When Washington put the question as to agreement on the constitution as amended, all the states voted aye. Three of the delegates, however, declared they could not sign the document as at that time constituted. Edmund Randolph of Virginia, made a plea for a second convention to act upon amendments that might be suggested by individual state conventions. George Mason, also of Virginia, took the same position as Randolph. Elbridge Gerry of Massachusetts refused to sign for other reasons.

Of course, no one in the convention was entirely satisfied with all parts of the document. But it was the best that could be constructed by that body. Benjamin Franklin made a strong speech urging the delegates to give up some of their personal views and join in promoting the adoption of the constitution in the interests of the whole. He said that after a long life he had found that views he had at one time taken had later been found wrong; and while he did not approve of some things now before them, he was not sure that he might not find his position wrong in time to come. He illustrated by the story of a certain French lady who, in a dispute with her sister said, "I don't know how it happens, sister, but I meet with nobody but myself that is always in the right."

On Monday, September 17th, the members met to sign the document. Washington, as presiding officer, took the pen in hand to sign first. Before writing his name he said: "Should the states reject this excellent Constitution, the probability is that the opportunity will never be offered to cancel another in peace; the next will be drawn in blood."

All the delegates then signed except Randolph, Mason and Gerry. Several other delegates would not have signed had they been present; but they had gone home in disgust some days before. Among them was Luther Martin of Maryland.

After the signing the delegates adjourned to the City Tavern, dined together, and took cordial leave of each other. Washington started for Mount Vernon the next morning, September 18th, and arrived there four days later.

Washington was now exceedingly anxious that the Constitution should be adopted by the States. He was much concerned that a number of his compatriots of revolutionary days viewed the adoption of the constitution with hesitation, and in some instances with outspoken opposition. He wrote in December: "My decided opinion is that there is no alternative between the adoption of it and anarchy; I am not a blind admirer of the Constitution to which I have assisted to give birth; but I am fully persuaded that it is the best to be obtained at this day, and that it or disunion is before us."

Cheering news began to come in during December. Delaware, the first to act, adopted the Constitution December 7th. Pennsylvania followed five days later. Six days afterward New Jersey came in. Georgia, the first southern state to act, adopted the Constitution January 2nd. On May 23rd South Carolina acted, making eight states up to that time. Only one more was needed to establish the Constitution over the nine states. Washington was very anxious that Virginia should be the ninth state. Alexander Hamilton was moving heaven and earth to bring New York in for the ninth. While these two states were engaged in strenuous debate, New Hampshire slipped in on June 21st. Virginia was the tenth state June 26th, while New York followed a month later.

Before any of the states had adopted the Constitution, Washington had already been singled out as the man to be the first President. There was no opposition to him in any quarter. He was averse to going into public life again, but the call to duty was insistent. He wrote to a friend: "The first wish of my soul is to spend the evening of my days as a private citizen on my farm; and if circumstances will not allow me this last boon of temporal happiness, and

I should once more be led into the walks of public life, it is my fixed determination to enter there not only unfettered by promises, but even unchargeable to creating or feeding the expectancy of any man living for my assistance to office."

The electoral vote was taken on April 6th. All the electors voted for Washington. There were sixty-nine votes, New York not being represented, and North Carolina and Rhode Island not yet having ratified the Constitution. How Washington felt about his elevation to the Presidency is well expressed in a letter to General Knox: "In confidence I tell you (with the world it would obtain little credit) that my movements to the chair of government will be accompanied by feelings not unlike those of a culprit who is going to the place of execution. I am sensible that I am embarking the voice of the people and the good name of my own on this voyage, but what returns will be made for them heaven alone can foretell. Integrity and firmness are all I can promise."

Washington's journey from Mount Vernon to New York for his inauguration was a triumphal procession. Crowds greeted him everywhere. The date set for the ceremonies was April 30th. On the balcony of Federal Hall, on Wall Street, on the site of the present Federal Treasury Building, Chancellor Livingston administered the oath. When it had been repeated, Washington said, "I swear, so help me, God." Then the Chancellor turned to the crown assembled on the street below, and swinging his arm cried, "Long live George Washington, President of the United States!" It was a great day for America.

WASHINGTON DURING HIS FIRST ADMINISTRATION

W. B. Colonna

Washington did not want to be President. He got very little pleasure out of being President and he added very little glory to his fame by being President.

Having won the Revolution and concluded a peace with England, he resigned his commission on December 4, 1783, and retired to Mt. Vernon with the announced determination of spending the balance of his days there, living the life of a country gentleman.

Five years later he yielded to the importunities of his friends and consented to accept the presidency of the newly established Republic.

The constitution having been adopted by nine of the thirteen states, an election was called and when the electors met to select a President, Washington was the unanimous choice. This was no surprise to him, as he had previously agreed to accept the office, and in anticipation of election, he had pursued a course of study of the history of previous republics.

When, on April 30, 1789, he took the oath of office as "The President of the United States" an entirely new and different period in his life was begun. The erstwhile retired army officer, living in comfort on his farm, was now to assume the role of Chief Executive of the greatest experiment in republican government of which history has any record.

He came to the office not as a politician, for he had nothing selfish to seek; not as a statesman, for he was not qualified for this either by education or training, but rather as a strong parent seeking to harmonize the petty disagreements of his children and to organize them into a homogeneous body strong enough to take and hold its place in the family of nations.

Fortunately the country was not yet divided into two contending and rival parties, but he was to see and to be plagued with the beginnings of this contest, which has lasted to the present day.

He found a form of government existing, and without discarding that further than was necessary, he proceeded to avail himself of the services of the members of that government, supplementing and strengthening it in order to make it conform to the new constitution. With what success he was able to harmonize discordant elements and establish the structure of our government is attested by the fact that it has lasted 143 years, and, with the guidance of Providence, we trust it will last forever.

The inaugural ceremonies were in New York, of course, the then seat of government. They were accomplished with a good deal of pomp. Those nearest to the government were so close to the history and conventions of royalty in England and Europe that it was impossible to have the first President assume his office without, in some measure, imitating the customs of the Old Country.

Even here became an issue that often arose to annoy the President. Questions of ceremony and governmental etiquette constantly arose, and, although they meant very little to Washington, personally, they frequently caused him much annoyance in his efforts to respect the opinions of others. His retort, when criticised for his awkwardness in making courtly gestures upon a certain occasion, is informing, as well as amusing:

"That I have not been able to make bows to the taste of poor Col. B— (who, by the by, I believe never saw one of them), is to be regretted, especially, too, as upon those occasions, they were indiscriminately bestowed, and the best I was master of. Would it not have been better to throw the veil of charity over them, ascribing their stiffness to the effects of age, or to the unskillfulness of my teacher, rather than to pride and the dignity of office, which God knows, has no charm for me, for I can truly say I would rather be at Mt. Vernon with a friend or two about me than to be attended by the seat of government by the officers of state and the representatives of power of every nation of Europe."

Congress was in session at the time of the inauguration and many weighty matters demanded consideration. The question of taxation was among the most important. The status of the vast western lands required immediate attention,—the Government, under the Articles of Confederation, had been able to do very little for the pioneers in this great unknown and they were restive; this territory presented a temptation to the Spaniards to exploit the Indians and particularly was tempting to the British who were still holding certain positions there on the excuse that the United States had not fulfilled its obligation under the Treaty of Peace. This Treaty provided that claims due British subjects should be paid, but there was great delay in paying them because the Federal Government had no money with which to pay and the individual states were slow in following the recommendation of the Federal Government that they be paid. The greatest problem, however, was that of establishing the public credit.

The paper money issued by the Continental Congress had small value. The currency issued by the several states and lesser governmental sub-divisions was almost worthless and the script issued to the soldiers and officers of the Revolution in lieu of their pay had become a snare and a delusion. The national debt, together with the debts of the several states, incurred during the Revolution, amounted to $79,000,000.00.

Washington turned promptly to Hamilton with these financial troubles, but he had to be very patient. The machinery of government authorized by the Constitution was not provided for in detail until September 1789.

As soon as Congress passed the necessary legislation, Washington proceeded to select the members of his cabinet. Edmund Randolph of Virginia was chosen as Attorney General; Alexander Hamilton of New York as Secretary of the Treasury; General Knox as Secretary of War, and Jefferson, who was to be the Secretary of

State, was still in France representing the interests of the Colonies united under the Articles of Confederation. By the selection of Hamilton, Washington chose perhaps the ablest and best man for the office, but one who was to have more difficulty in the conduct of his department than any other member of the official family. To him fell the duty of devising means of raising revenue so much needed and establishing the credit of the New Republic. Hamilton was definitely committed to the assumption by the Federal Government of the combined national and state debts contracted during the Revolution.

A tariff on imports offered the most available source and thus our tariff policy, which was begun for revenue only, and later developed to foster infant industries, and now seems to threaten the life or death of our foreign commerce, had its beginning. Hamilton also proposed the establishment of a national bank and levying an excise tax on foreign liquors.

During this year, Mrs. Washington and her family, who had remained at Mr. Vernon, came to New York to make their home with the President. Washington is said to have insisted on the observance of the homely virtues in his domestic life there, and to have been very punctilious in the observance of the Sabbath. During this year, also, he suffered a very severe illness, so at one time his life was almost despaired of.

One of the serious responsibilities of the new President was to select a Chief Justice of the Supreme Court and his associate justices. The history of these selections as given by Warren in his *History of the Supreme Court* is interesting, even to one who is not a lawyer. Suffice it to say, however, that he chose the following:

John Jay of New York, Chief Justice
John Rutledge of South Carolina
James Wilson of Pennsylvania
William Cushing of Massachusetts
James Iredell of North Carolina
John Blair of Virginia

In October of this year Washington made a tour through the New England states and had some interesting experiences with reception committees and those seeking to maintain their own dignity, while at the same time, doing him proper deference as President.

Washington's love for LaFayette had not ended with the return of the Marquis to France. Col. John Trumball, the famous painter of Washington portraits, came home from France bringing Washington affectionate messages from LaFayette, who had visions of leading a sort of revolution in France. It will be recalled that later LaFayette sent Washington the key to the Bastille.

In January, 1790, the Second Congress met. Many weighty matters were still pending and demanding attention. The national defense was unprovided for. Our diplomatic intercourse with other nations needed to be established. The naturalization of foreigners required attention. The establishment of a post office and the ever present issue of national credit and finance were all urgent.

The question which created the widest difference of opinion was the assumption by the Federal Government of the state debts as urged by Hamilton. Jefferson, who had now returned and accepted the duties of Secretary of State, was never disposed to agree to anything that Hamilton proposed and his attitude was hostile to the assumption. The story of how Hamilton secured his influence in favor of assumption in exchange for his (Hamilton's) influence in locating the national capital on the north bank of the Potomac, is a familiar passage. Jefferson always thought that Hamilton outwitted him and he never forgave Hamilton.

Many of the States, notably Virginia, objected to the assumption by the Federal Government of its debts. This seems somewhat anomalous, but the reason assigned was that the Federal Government would become so great as to jeopardize the rights of the individual states. We know, however, that the policy of assumption was finally agreed upon and its wisdom is not now questioned.

By this time the revolution in France was assuming an alarming proportion. LaFayette continued his correspondence with

Washington, but Washington's replies indicate an anxiety for the personal safety of his friend and for the ultimate outcome of the revolution.

The seat of Government had now been moved to Philadelphia, where it was to remain for ten years, while the capital on the north bank of the Potomac was being built. The next Congress was to meet in Philadelphia. Hamilton again presented his plan to lay a tax on foreign liquors, and this was done with the approval of Washington. Washington's argument favoring this tax is facetious and ingenious. He said he favored the tax because no person had to pay it unless he chose to. At this session of Congress the national bank was authorized under Hamilton's recommendations. Here again he locked horns with Jefferson. Before Washington would approve the national bank act, he took counsel with a number of those whose opinions he considered most highly and finally gave his approval. The bank turned out to be a great success.

This but served to widen the breach between Hamilton and Jefferson. The latter's chief criticism of Hamilton was that he was an admirer of the English Constitution—at heart a monarchist—and that his policies tended to convert the Federal Government into a powerful centralized state at the expense of its component parts. Thus began the two schools of political thought which waged such a hot and uncompromising warfare during Washington's First Administration that he grew weary and almost disgusted to the point of wishing to be relieved of the burdens of the presidency.

After the adjournment of the Third Congress in March, 1791, Washington took a long trip through the Southern States. He was away about four months and visited Fredericksburg, Richmond, Charleston, Columbia and many other places. In the fall of the year 1791, he spent some time at Mt. Vernon.

In October Congress met again. Washington's address to Congress commented upon the general prosperity of the country and the success with which the public finances had been managed. The only trouble which the Government was experiencing was with the Indians. General St. Clair had been put in command of the forces operating against the Indians and was on constant duty. Alas, General St, Clair was destined to suffer a disastrous defeat at the hands of the Indians.

At rare intervals Washington is said to have had outbursts of temper, which did little credit to his dignity. His display of temper upon an occasion when he thought Alexander Hamilton had kept him waiting, is an instance in point. When Washington heard of St. Clair's defeat, it is said that the news reached him while he was entertaining at dinner and he restrained himself until the meal was over. Thereafter, he flew into an uncontrollable rage. His temper was probably accentuated by the fact that before St. Clair undertook the expedition against the Indians he was specifically warned against a surprise and it was in a surprise attack that his forces met such a disastrous defeat. Later Washington regretted the incident and made the *amende honorable.*

At this session of Congress a law apportioning representation in Congress was vetoed by Washington. Later it was amended to conform to his views and passed with his approbation.

Toward the end of the first administration, the issues between Hamilton and Jefferson became acute. Two newspapers were established, one to champion Hamilton theories of government and one to champion the Jefferson theories of government.

Jefferson was exceedingly critical of Hamilton and, while Hamilton may have exhibited a greater degree of dignity and self-control in dealing with the issues between him and Jefferson, his course was by no means conciliatory. Washington was forced, on more occasions than one, to assume the role of peacemaker. He considered that the services of both these men were needed by the country and he feared the result of disrupting his cabinet. Almost at the cost of sacrificing some of his dignity, he pleaded with these irreconcilables and succeeded in keeping both in his cabinet.

As the end of his four-year term was approaching, Washington declared his purpose not to accept a second term. At once, both Hamilton and Jefferson turned the full force of their persuasive arguments upon him to induce him to reconsider. They agreed that the country was at a crisis and Hamilton even suggested that unless Washington was willing to make the sacrifice and see the country through the emergency, it might have been better if he had not accepted the presidency in the first instance.

These efforts were successful and so we leave our hero at the end of his first administration reluctantly agreeing to accept his second term.

In this paper I have followed the historical account given by Washington Irving in his life of Washington.

I have been unable to discover any evidences of either a great politician or a great statesman in Washington during this first administration, but he furnished the steadying influence so essential to a successful beginning of the new form of government. He seems to have initiated very little in the way of governmental policy, further than to proceed in a conservative, orderly way to attend to our own affairs without intermeddling with the affairs of foreign nations or seeking their influence in domestic affairs. There was nothing radical or spectacular about him and he presided with dignity and decorum, seeking at all times to avoid unnecessary dissention.

The greatness of George Washington as President during his first administration consisted largely in his personality.

WASHINGTON DURING HIS SECOND ADMINISTRATION

PROF. H. C. KREBS

The Presidential Election of 1792 was conducted with a simplicity that is very refreshing in these days of political complexity. There were no primaries, no conventions, and no platforms. No one person was nominated for either the presidency or the vice-presidency. There were no national nor state campaign committees, and no campaign funds. The whole machinery of election consisted of the appointment of electors in the several states, who were to meet on the first Wednesday in December and cast their ballots for any qualified persons whom they might fancy. Each ballot was to contain the names of two persons; but there must be no mark or other sign to indicate which was the preference for president and which for vice-president. Thus each elector technically voted for two persons for president, and not at all for a vice-president. Practically, of course, the person having the second highest number of votes for the presidency would be vice-president.

Another interesting item in the situation was that no one gave any thought in regard to the presidency. Washington was sure of a unanimous vote. But there was a contest for second place. Since Washington's name would be on every ballot, the other name must, in accordance with the constitutional provision, come from a State other than Virginia.

Friends of George Clinton, Governor of New York, urged his election on the basis of his democracy, but it was recalled against him that four years before he had bitterly opposed the adoption of the constitution. John Adams, of Massachusetts, had his enemies, but his proponents contended that the first administration had done so well that no change should be contemplated.

There were one hundred and thirty-two electors. When the ballots were counted, one hundred and thirty-two were for George Washington, seventy-seven for John Adams, fifty for George Clinton, four for Thomas Jefferson, and one for Aaron Burr. Clinton had all the votes of New York, Virginia, North Carolina, and Georgia. The four votes for Jefferson came from Kentucky, and were obviously illegal, as Jefferson was from the same State as Washington. Adams carried all the other states.

Washington's second administration began at a time of popular excitement. News had reached America of a great victory by the French Republican troops over the allies. The people of the United States had a lively recollection of the cooperation of France during the American Revolution. They also had deep sympathy for a people who had followed our example in ridding themselves of royalty. Hence the news of this victory was received with unprecedented rejoicing and hilarity. Meetings, parades, feasts, flag-raisings and banner-wavings enthused every city in the country. The amount of punch consumed was almost incredible. Even poets broke forth, and one delivered himself thus:

> "Brunswick's old Duke, with ninety thousand men
> Marched into France, and then run out again!"

People went wild over republicanism. They demanded a liberty cap in every house, and a French cockade on every hat. Such titles as Sir, Mr., Dr., and Rev. were diabolical terms that must be heard no more. Men must be called Citizen, and women Citess.

News now arrived that the French King had been beheaded, and that France and England were at war. This put a new aspect on the situation. For America to assist France would be construed as a declaration of war against England. This would mean millions added to our debt, the destruction of our trade, ruin of business, and a probable military invasion.

But our Treaty of Alliance with France in 1778 bound two us to guarantee to France forever all her possessions in America, the opening of our ports to French privateers and prizes, and a denial of these privileges to all other nations. Clearly we must observe this treaty and offend England, or preserve neutrality and thus fail our ally.

Washington hastened to Philadelphia, and discussed with his cabinet all the points involved. It was agreed that this country was in no condition to go to war with England. Self-preservation being the first law of nations as well as of nature, no course other than neutrality was open to us. It was strongly argued that a treaty made with the French monarchy in 1778 was not strictly binding after the overthrow of said monarchy. At any rate, Washington issued a proclamation calling on all good citizens to take no part in aiding or abetting either of the belligerents, and threatening full punishment on all who failed to observe neutrality.

On the very day that Washington issued this proclamation, news reached Philadelphia that the new French minister, Citizen Genet, had landed at Charleston, South Carolina, on April 8th, and had proceeded to do acts so high handed as to be almost beyond credence. Before he had been recognized by the Federal Government, and before he had received the official records of his predecessor, he issued orders constituting every French consul in the United States a court for the trial and condemnation of any British ships that might be brought in as prizes. He bought two ships, equipped them as privateers, manned them with American sailors, and sent them out to capture British merchantmen. Prizes were soon sent in—four to Charleston, one to New York, and one to Philadelphia.

Citizen Genet made an overland trip from Charleston to Philadelphia. He was received with great enthusiasm by the populace in every town, many of whom were so blinded by their sympathies for republican France that they began to look on Washington as a recipient of monarchical honors during the Federalist celebrations on his birthday, and could hardly contain their wrath.

Genet was received by the republicans of Philadelphia with ovations and addresses that turned his head. On May 18, he was recognized by President Washington as Minister from the French Republic. Genet was enraged because Washington's speech on that occasion was chillingly polite and dignified.

Genet now asked for a new treaty with the United States, and for prepayment of part of the loan due France from the United States. Jefferson courteously informed him that no treaty could be made without the consent of the Senate. Hamilton wrote him that the Federal Treasury was empty; but that even if it were filled to overflowing his request could not be granted because it would be aiding France against a nation at peace with the United States.

Complaints from the British government began to come in, and were laid before Genet, whose reply to Washington tried to justify his acts by quoting the provisions of the treaty between France and the United States. Washington was unmoved by this argument, and at once took steps to nullify the various orders and acts of Genet.

However, for many months, riots occurred between French and English sympathizers. French sailors on shore were mobbed by adherents of the British, and British sailors by republicans. Duels were fought not only between people, but between ships. The whole country was seething with excitement.

Genet became bolder and bolder. At last he made statements, and wrote letters to the president that were considered insulting to Washington. At once Genet began to lose ground.

The American people would not tolerate abuse by a foreigner of the man they had elected president. Washington had already requested the French government to recall Genet; and in February his successor arrived. Thus Genet, in the ten months of his activities in this country, had aroused a vast amount of turmoil which caused Washington no end of anxiety, and which, but for his restraint and cool judgment, might have led the country into a disastrous war.

There were other causes besides sympathy for France that aroused strong feelings against Great Britain at this time. In the first place, she had never relinquished possession of the forts in the northwest as provided in the treaty of 1783. In the second place, her treatment of American ships and seamen was intolerable. England ordered her cruisers to seize every vessel laden with food, and to search every American ship for English-born sailors. The purpose of these orders was to recruit her own navy, and to prevent anything from going to France. When the year 1794 opened, hundreds of American vessels were in English hands. In the West Indies two hundred fifty seamen were shut up in a dingy prison ship for three days during which time they suffered terribly for lack of food and drink. Every petty governor of an island sat as a maritime judge on every vessel captured, and in no case was the vessel released. The blow fell not only on our shipping, but on our commodities as well. There was scarcely a household in the country that did not suffer directly or indirectly from the depredations on our commerce. Congress began to make preparations for war. There were rabid protests in Congress against England's aggressions. It was proposed that all intercourse with Great Britain should cease 'till she gave up her western posts and indemnified the country for the damages to her privateers. It was moved to call out eighty thousand militia to increase the regular army by twenty-five thousand troops, and to cancel all debts owed to subjects of King George.

Washington, however, was bent on peace. He decided to send an envoy-extraordinary to England to negotiate a treaty. For this office he desired Alexander Hamilton; but as soon as Hamilton's name was mentioned for the post, political clamor against the appointment arose to such an extent that Washington substituted John Jay, Chief Justice of the Supreme Court of the United States.

Party feeling ran so high at this time that Jay was vigorously denounced and his failure prognosticated before he had even arrived in England. The treaty was made, reached the President on March 7th, and the senate met to consider it in special session two months later.

It is probable that Jay's Treaty was the most unpopular measure of this kind ever ratified in the United States. The Senate endorsed it by a strict party vote of twenty to ten. So great was the outcry against it that the House of Representatives determined to assume the right of rejecting it. After days of debate Washington was requested to submit to the House all papers and dispatches relating to the treaty. Washington refused point blank. This added fuel to the flame, and he was personally denounced and vilified as an aristocrat and a tyrant. Jay was burned in effigy on the gallows. Riotous demonstrations took place in all parts of the country.

In due time the treaty was carried into effect. It was the best Jay could obtain from the British government, but not the best that someone else might have obtained. Jay was wined and dined by the British officials during the negotiations; and being of a pacific nature, without aggressiveness and self assertion, he was cajoled into accepting provisions that meant little to this country, and into leaving unmentioned many of the leading questions in controversy between the nations. It is now generally believed that if Alexander Hamilton had been the envoy as Washington desired, he would have rattled a saber, and his acute intellect have put forth unanswerable arguments, so that this country might have gained much more than she did by a treaty. In this case, as in many others since that time, partisan politics sacrificed the best interests of the country.

Washington was far from satisfied with Jay's treaty. Most reluctantly did he decide to accept it. His statesmanship was here displayed conspicuously. He knew that rejection of the treaty would involve us in still greater difficulties, probably in war. He knew that war would mean the destruction of the republic. He was therefore determined to keep the peace, however much the present situation might be unsatisfactory. In this contingency, as in his attitude toward the adoption of the Constitution, he was willing to accept what he could get rather than what he wanted, that the welfare of the country might not be jeopardized.

One of the most picturesque incidents of Washington's second administration was the Whiskey Insurrection in and near the city of Pittsburgh. In this part of the country whiskey circulated as money. A gallon of whiskey was accepted in every store or farm house as the equivalent of one shilling. The Federal Government, in order to raise revenue, imposed a tax of seven cents per gallon on the ordinary brand of whiskey, and as high as eighteen cents on the best brands. A tax of such proportions aroused a flood of protests among the distillers, who were numbered by the thousand. Agitators stirred up the people. Meetings were held throughout that part of the country to object to the tax, and to pledge resistance to its collection.

When the tax collectors arrived they were maltreated, ordered to leave the vicinity, expelled by force, or waylaid. Excitement grew so high that as many as six thousand men with nondescript arms were at one time gathered in form of an army.

When these reports reached the government at Philadelphia, the six thousand men had grown to sixty thousand. Washington at once issued a proclamation commanding the insurrectionists to disperse and keep the peace. This proclamation did not seem to carry three hundred and fifty miles. At any rate, it failed to quell the riots. Then Washington called on the Governors of Pennsylvania, New Jersey, Maryland and Virginia to furnish a total of twelve thousand, nine hundred militia to enforce obedience to the laws of the United States in Washington and Allegheny Counties. The soldiers were selected by draft. In Frederick, Martinsburg, Hagerstown, and other towns situated near the mountains, there was much criticism of the draft, the resistance thereto amounting in some cases to riots. Mass meetings against the draft were held in the cities mentioned, addressed in some instances by the people from the affected regions. They depicted a grievous situation, enhanced by what are nowadays called "tall stories." "One asserted that the government was taxing not only whiskey, but wheat and rye, and that he himself had paid four pence per bushel at Baltimore. Another said that this was not the worst; that flesh and blood were no better in the eyes of the odious law than sticks and stones, and that at Pittsburgh every boy at birth was taxed fifteen shillings and every girl ten. At this the crowd seemed so shocked that a third ventured to damn Congress and cry out 'God save King George!' He was tarred and feathered and marched to the county line." (McMaster, Vol. 2)

Meanwhile the Federal Army was marching one under the general command of Light Horse Harry Lee. General Daniel Morgan led the left wing composed largely of troops from Virginia. The march was slow, for the purpose was to overawe, and not to fight. Washington himself accompanied the troops west as far as Carlisle. Commissioners from the insurgents now arrived at this point to adjust matters. Negotiations failing, the troops proceeded to the disaffected districts, expelled some of the rioters, and arrested others. Peace was readily restored, though Morgan spent the winter in the vicinity with twenty-five hundred soldiers. The rest of the army went home, every returning soldier being toasted as a hero. The crossing of the Alleghenies by the army was said to have been an exploit greater than Hannibal's crossing of the Alps. Soon the whole affair took its place in history.

What was that place in history? It was the first serious test of the New Government. If the several states had refused to furnish their quota of troops to quell a revolt against the government in another state, the whole fabric of the Federal organization would have fallen to pieces. The Union would have been dissolved. The success of the Federal authority in uniting troops from various states for the national defense gave warning and warrant that this country could and would maintain its rights and preserve itself against internal revolt. Law and order were firmly established; and the United States rose to an advanced position of strength and dignity.

Large numbers of people in the country were still at this time unable to think nationally. They thought in terms of States and colonies. Washington on every suitable occasion tried to educate the people in the idea that this is one great country—a unity; that as such it must be clothed with dignity and power; that it must be respected as such by foreign nations, He would tolerate no interference in our internal affairs by other nations, neither would he permit the United States to become embroiled with the internal affairs of other nations. The principle of nationality was the rule of conduct that actuated Washington in his dealing with foreign as well as domestic situations.

This attitude of Washington led, in his second administration, to the formation of distinct political parties.

Before this time there had been opposition and criticism in regard to the federalist idea, but it had been individual and scattered. Now, however, the anti-federalist proponents became organized, and grew to substantial proportions. The troubles with England and France caused a radical division of sentiment. The federalists either favored England or neutrality with England. Others sympathized with France, and demanded an alliance with her in her contest with England. The whiskey insurrection showed the same divergence of opinion, the Federalists insisting on national self-preservation, while the opposition sympathized with the doctrines of the malcontents. The habit of opposition having been formed, there gradually developed two schools of thought, and those opposed to nationalism fought for the strengthening of the rights of the States, and against the party that stood for a strong central government. As Washington was a staunch Federalist, and indeed the leader of that school of thought, it was inevitable that the shafts of criticism should be aimed at him.

It is still thought by persons not well read in history that during the presidency of Washington everything was unanimous; that the vilification of the president, which has been a favorite indoor sport in recent years, did not exist in the first days of the republic; and that the press of today has greatly degenerated from the high plane it occupied at one time.

Let such persons read some of the pages of McMaster's *History of the People of the United States*, and they will become disillusioned. Knowing as we do now the noble character of Washington, it seems incredible that he should have been assailed by the press of his day in the meanest terms. Philip Freneau, the poet, and Benjamin Franklin Bache, a grandson of the great Franklin, opened their columns to the most virulent abuse of Washington. When the President had signed Jay's treaty with England, Freneau's paper, the *Aurora*, published in Philadelphia, declared that the President had violated the Constitution, and made a treaty with a nation abhorred by our people; that he answered the respectful remonstrances of Boston and New York as if he were the omnipotent director of a seraglio, and had thundered contempt upon the people with as much confidence as if he sat upon the throne of Hindustan.

Another writer claimed that Washington had overdrawn his salary in defiance of law, and had actually stolen in this way $4,750.00; and he went on to ask, "What will posterity say of the man who has done this thing? Will it not say that the mask of political hypocrisy has been worn by Caesar, by Cromwell, and by Washington?"

In February, 1796, the House of Representatives refused to adjourn on Washington's birthday for half an hour in order to fulfill the established custom of offering Washington congratulations on that day. When the last day of his second term arrived, the opposition papers let themselves loose blatantly. One article said: "His character can only be respectable while it is now known; he is arbitrary, avaricious, ostentatious; without skill as a soldier, he has crept into fame by the places he has held. His financial measures burdened the many to enrich the few. History will tear the pages devoted to his praise. France and his country gave him fame, and they will take that fame away."

Another thus relieved himself: "His glory has dissolved in mist, and he has sunk from the high level of Solon or Lycurgus to the mean rank of a Dutch Stadtholder or a Venetian Doge. Posterity will look in vain for any marks of wisdom in his administration."

On the day of Washington's retirement from the presidency, The *Aurora* said in part, "The man who is the source of all the misfortunes of our country is this day reduced to a level with his fellow-citizens, and is no longer possessed of power to multiply evils upon the United States. If ever there was a period for rejoicing, this is the moment. . . . This day ought to be a Jubilee in the United States."

These mendacious attacks did not, however, represent the heart of the American people; they only reflected the views of the most radical of the opposition party. Washington was besought by many to accept a third term; and during the administration of John

Adams, Washington was urged to succeed him. To all these requests Washington returned a polite but firm refusal. He had done with public life. He would not emerge from his retirement except in a crisis; and he lived his last years "first in the hearts of his countrymen."

The principles that guided Washington during the difficulties of his second administration are well set forth in a letter he wrote to Patrick Henry in 1795:

"My ardent desire is, and my aim has been as far as depended upon the executive department, to comply strictly with all our engagements, foreign and domestic; but to keep the United States free from political connection with every other country, to see them independent of all and under the influence of none. In a word, I want an *American* character, that the powers of Europe may be convinced that we act for *ourselves*, and not for others. This, in my judgment, is the only way to be respected abroad and happy at home; and not, by becoming partisans of Great Britain or France, create dissensions, disturb the public tranquility, and destroy, perhaps forever, the cement which binds the Union."

Later he wrote, when the difficulties with France were even more critical:

"The Executive has a plain road to pursue, to fulfill all the engagements which duty requires; be influenced beyond this by none of the contending parties; maintain a strict neutrality unless obliged by imperious circumstances to depart from it; do justice to all and never forget that we are America, the remembrance of which will convince us that we ought not to be French or English."

It thus appears that Washington's second administration showed a continuation of the policies of the first administration, but was tested with far greater difficulties. Not once did Washington deviate from his guiding principles. The infant nation must be permitted to grow undisturbed until it should become a strong and mighty power. All other considerations were with him secondary. Nothing was left undone that might make the country great, and all influences tending toward disruption met with his stern opposition.

The poet Longfellow many years afterward, without thought of Washington, expressed in beautiful lines the dream of Washington's life:

> "Thou, too, sail on, O Ship of State!
> Sail on, O Union, strong and great!
> Humanity with all its fears,
> With all its hopes of future years,
> Is hanging breathless on thy fate!
>
> Our hearts, our hopes, are all with thee;
> Our hearts, our hopes, our prayers, our tears,
> Our faith triumphant o'er our fears,
> Are all with thee,—are all with thee!

WASHINGTON AFTER HIS SECOND ADMINISTRATION

PROF. T. J. STUBBS

When I consented to give a paper on Washington's career from the close of his last administration, I did not realize that this period of his life was so uneventful. While I realize that anything about such a great man is interesting and perhaps important, yet, when compared with the stirring and sometimes thrilling events of his earlier life, we must confess that the life of a typical Virginia planter of that day comes somewhat as an anti-climax.

Washington had entered upon the presidency with great reluctance and at the sacrifice of all he considered pleasantest and best in life. He looked forward to the end of his second term with a feeling of intense relief, and after the election of John Adams began almost to count the days that intervened between him and retirement.

On the last day of his official career he gave a farewell dinner to the foreign ministers, their wives and the President and Vice-President elect. When the cloth was removed he filled his glass and said: "Ladies and gentlemen, this is the last time I shall drink your health as a public man. I do it with sincerity, wishing you all possible happiness." The gayety of the company was instantly checked. All felt the solemnity of the occasion and Mrs. Liston, wife of the British Minister, wept openly. Washington also appeared at the inauguration of Mr. Adams and was received with enthusiastic cheers. At the close of the ceremonies the people flocked around him to receive his farewell wave of the hand as he was too much affected to speak.

Thus, with the cheers and acclamations still ringing in his ears he went home again to Mount Vernon where he at once found plenty to occupy his time. An absence of eight years had not improved the property. He said he found himself in the situation of a beginner; almost everything about him required repairs and a house was to be immediately built for the reception and safe-keeping of his military, civil and private papers. He writes: "I am already surrounded by joiners, masons and painters, and such is my anxiety to be out of their hands that I have scarcely a room to put a friend into or to sit in myself without the music of hammers and odoriferous scent of paint. To make and sell a little flour annually; to repair houses going fast to ruin; and to amuse myself in agricultural and rural pursuits will constitute employment for the few years I have to remain on this terrestrial globe. If also I could now and then meet the friends I esteem it would fill the measure and add zest to my enjoyments; but if ever this happens it must be under my own vine and fig-tree, as I do not think it probable that I shall go beyond twenty-miles from them."

In a letter to James McHenry, Secretary of War, he furnishes a picture of his everyday life: "I begin my diurnal course with the sun; if my hirelings are not in their places at that time I send them messages of sorrow for their indisposition; having put these wheels in motion I examine the state of things further; the more they are probed the deeper I find the wounds which my buildings have sustained by the absence and neglect of eight years; by the time I have accomplished these matters, breakfast (a little after 7 o'clock) is ready; this being over I mount my horse and ride round my farms which employs me until it is time to dress for dinner at which I rarely miss seeing strange faces, come as they say out of respect to me. Pray, would not the word curiosity answer as well? And how different this from having a few social friends at a cheerful board! The usual time of sitting at table, a walk and tea bring me within the dawn of candle light; previous to which, if not prevented by company, I resolve that as soon as the glimmering taper supplies the place of the great luminary, I will retire to my writing table and acknowledge the letters I have received but when the lights are brought I feel tired and disinclined to engage in this work, conceiving that the next night will do as well. The next night comes and with it the same causes for postponement and so on. I have not looked into a book since I came home, nor shall I be able to do it until I have discharged my workmen; probably not before the nights grow longer when possibly I may be looking into Doomsday Book."

The influx of strange faces spoken of soon became overwhelming and Washington felt the necessity of having some one at hand to relieve him from a part of the self-imposed duties of Virginia hospitality. Accordingly, his nephew, Lawrence Lewis came to Mount Vernon and took most of the social burden from his shoulders.

The place at this time possessed attractions for young and old and was often enlivened by young company. One great attraction was Miss Nelly Custis, Mrs. Washington's granddaughter, who with her brother, George Washington Parke Custis, had been adopted by the General after the death of their father, and brought up by him with the most affectionate care. She was now maturing into a lovely and attractive woman and the attention she received began to trouble the General. So he gave her some excellent advice on the subject of matrimony. He was very much pleased when young Lewis fell in love with Nelly, although Mrs. Washington seemed to favor the suit of young Carroll of Carrollton, who had just returned from Europe with all the graces of foreign travel. Miss Nelly, however, became the wife of Lewis.

About this time young George Washington Lafayette who had been staying at Mount Vernon received news that his father and family had been liberated from prison and were preparing to come to America. Young Lafayette, in a great hurry, sailed for Europe only to find the report premature and the family was not united until some months later.

The highly prized retirement to Mount Vernon did not separate Washington from the affairs of the country. He continued to take a keen interest in all that went on, to correspond with his friends and to use his influence for what he thought wisest and best for the general welfare. These were stirring times too, and the progress of events brought him to take a more active part than he had over expected to play again. France having failed, thanks to his policy, to draw us either by fair words or trickery from our independent and neutral position, determined, apparently, to try the effect of force and ill usage. Working on the assumption that the Jay Treaty with England was a direct affront and accusing the United States of not living up to the terms of the treaties of 1778, she instituted retaliatory measures with the result that many American vessels were seized, their cargoes confiscated and hundreds of Americans imprisoned. Washington, before his retirement, had recalled James Monroe, Minister to France, and had appointed Charles Cotesworth Pinckney instead. When Pinckney arrived in France the Directory not only refused to receive him, but ordered him to leave the country, and when Adet, the French Minister, left America, diplomatic relations between the two countries were entirely suspended.

When Pinckney's treatment became known in the United States the extreme Federalists demanded drastic, retaliatory action, but President Adams urged a conciliatory program. He told Congress that France had treated the American people neither as allies nor as friends, nor as a sovereign state and condemned the Directory for attempting to distinguish between the American people and their government, and hoped the time would never come when Americans would fail to support their chosen representatives. He then urged adoption of measures of defense and expressed his intention of making a further attempt to reach an amicable understanding with France. A few days later he announced the appointment of a special commission to France composed of John Marshall of Virginia, and Elbridge Gerry, a Massachusetts Republican, to serve with C. C. Pinckney who was still in Holland.

Congress, in the meantime, made liberal provisions for the increase of the navy and fortifications of the harbors. It forbade the exportation of arms and gave the President authority to call out 80,000 militia.

Many months elapsed before the results of the American overtures to France were known. From October 1797 to March 1798 the Special Commission accomplished nothing except to make clear the actual character of the French policy. The Directory and also their gifted but unscrupulous Secretary for Foreign Affairs, Talleyrand, were notoriously corrupt. Although he refused to receive the United States representatives officially, Talleyrand allowed informal negotiations to proceed, working as a rule through three representations. After many delays these French agents demanded as an indispensable condition of friendly relations, the presentation of satisfactory apologies for certain of President Adams' remarks before Congress, the granting of a large government loan to France and the payment of a douceur to the Directory of approximately $240,000. After much sparring for time by the Americans, one of the French agents impatiently remarked, "Gentlemen, you do not speak to the point. It is money; we expect you to offer money." To a request for a definite answer the commission replied: "It is no, no, not a sixpence." The American reply soon received legendary embellishment and has gone down in history in the ringing words, "Millions for defense, but not a cent for tribute." After vainly attempting to reopen negotiations with Talleyrand, only to receive additional indignities, the Americans returned to the United States.

John Marshall, acting for the Commission, sent a detailed account of the negotiations to President Adams, who recounted the proceedings to Congress, substituting the letters X, Y and Z for the names of the three French agents. When the whole story of the attempted bribery came to public attention a wave of patriotic feeling went over the country. Adams informed Congress that he would never send another minister to France without assurances that he would be received, respected and honored as the representative of a free, powerful and independent nation. The response of Congress to the President's request for protective legislation was prompt and effective. It created a navy department; ordered the construction or purchase of twelve new vessels; a military force of 10,000 men, abrogated the treaties with France and gave merchant vessels the right to arm and defend themselves. The regular navy was given orders to capture French vessels interfering with United States commerce. Thus without a formal declaration the "naval war of 1798" began. Before its conclusion, two years and a half later, 85 armed French vessels, mostly privateers, had been captured with the loss of but a single American ship.

The whole country turned, as a matter of course, to one man to stand at the head of the national forces of the United States and Adams wrote Washington, asking him to take command of the provisional army. It was with a heavy heart that Washington found his dream of repose once more interrupted, but his strong fidelity to duty would not let him hesitate. He agreed, therefore to take command of the army provided that he should not be called into active service, except in the case of actual hostilities and that he should have the appointment of the General's staff. To these terms Adams, of course, acceded. But out of this apparently simple condition, relating to the appointment of officers, there grew a very serious trouble. There were to be three major-generals, the first of them to have also the rank of Inspector-General and to be the virtual Commander-in-Chief until the army was actually in the field. For these places Washington selected Hamilton, Pinckney and Knox, in the order named, going on the general principle that the army was to be organized *de novo* without reference to prior service. President Adams disliking Hamilton and knowing that there had been a conspiracy among his enemies to bring this very thing about, made up his mind to reverse the order and to send in Knox's name first. Now Hamilton had all his life firmly believed that he possessed military ability of a high order and here was a chance to show it. He was very much disturbed and angered by Adams' determination and appealed to Washington. At a distance from the center of action and possibly unaware of the growing differences within the party, Washington was not only surprised, but annoyed by the President's conduct, feeling that the conditions which he had made had been violated and that he had not been treated fairly. He therefore wrote Adams a plain but courteous letter stating these things and Adams gave way.

There was, however, another consequence of this affair which gave Washington much more pain than any differences with the president. His old friend and companion in arms, Knox, was profoundly hurt at the decision which placed Hamilton at the head of the army. One cannot be surprised at Knox's feeling, for he had been a distinguished officer and had outranked both Hamilton and Pinckney. He felt that he ought to command the army and that he was quite capable of doing so; and he did not relish being told in this official manner that he had grown old and that the time had come for younger and abler men to pass him. Hamilton and Washington both tried to soothe his wounded feelings but without result. On the other hand, Pinckney accepted service without a word of complaint although he had ranked Hamilton in the Revolution.

Early in November 1798, Washington, at the earnest request of the Secretary of War went to Philadelphia to consult with the Secretary and Generals Hamilton and Pinckney as to the arrangements for the forces about to be raised. After being closely engaged for nearly five weeks on these matters, their deliberations were reduced to form and given to the Secretary of War, and Washington returned to Mount Vernon.

As time went on recruiting was slow, there was delay in furnishing officers' commissions, and Washington, who did not know of cabinet friction, could not account for the apparent torpor of the administration.

The fact was that the military measures taken in America had really produced an effect on French policy. Efforts were being made by Talleyrand to induce an amicable overture on the part of the United States. He finally informed William Vans Murray, American Minister at the Hague, that an American Minister would be received with all the respect demanded by the president in his message to Congress. Accordingly, Murray, Oliver Ellsworth and William B. Davie were appointed as America's commissioners to France. They succeeded in negotiating a satisfactory treaty which superseded the treaties of 1778 and so terminated the embarrassing treaty of alliance.

The clouds of war were dissipated and Washington's hopes that he would continue to enjoy his retirement and repose unvexed by matters of state would seem now to be approaching realization.

He had for some time been occupied in making out a complete system on which his estate was to be managed for several years, specifying the cultivation of the several farms with tables for the rotation of the crops. It occupied thirty folio pages and is a valuable document showing the soundness and vigor of his mind at this stage of his life.

Washington was asked to become chancellor at the College of William and Mary.

"Griffin sent him an extract from the statute respecting the duties of the chancellor, which disclosed the fact that neither oath nor personal attendance was obligatory. The Bishop of London had been the last chancellor. Upon receipt of this information, General Washington replied:

"'Influenced by a heartfelt desire to promote the cause of science in general, and the prosperity of the College of William and Mary in particular, I accept the office of chancellor in the same; and request you will be pleased to give official notice thereof to the learned body, who have thought proper to honor me with the appointment. I confide fully in their strenuous endeavors for placing the system of education on such a basis, as will render it most beneficial to the State and the republic of letters, as well as to the more extensive interests of humanity and religion. In return, they will do me the justice to believe, that I shall not be too tardy in giving my cheerful concurrence to such measures, as may be best calculated for attainment of those desirable and important objects.'"

The morning of December 12th was overcast. He wrote Hamilton warmly approving the scheme for a military academy, and having finished this, which was probably the last letter he ever wrote, he mounted his horse and rode off for his usual round of duties. He noted in his diary that it began to snow about one o'clock, soon after to sleet and then turned to a settled cold rain. He stayed out for about two hours. On his return, Mr. Lear, his secretary, noted that snow was hanging in his hair and expressed the fear that he had gotten wet; but he replied that his great coat had kept him dry and sat down to dinner without changing his clothes. The next morning he complained of a sore throat which grew worse toward night, but he made light of it. In the night he had a severe chill followed by difficulty in breathing; and between two and three o'clock he awoke Mrs. Washington, but would not allow her to get up lest she should take cold. At daybreak, Mr. Lear was summoned and he found Washington breathing with difficulty and hardly able to speak. Dr. Craik, the friend and companion of many years was immediately summoned. While waiting for the doctor, the general was bled slightly by one of the overseers and external applications were made without relief. Dr. Craik arrived between eight and nine with two other physicians, Doctors Dick and Brown. Various remedies were tried and additional bleeding, but all of no avail. He then gave Mrs. Washington his will and gave Lear instructions as to his military letters, papers, farm accounts, asking him if he left out anything essential. At about 5 o'clock his old friend Doctor Craik came to his bedside. "Doctor," said the General, "I die hard, but I am not afraid to go."

About 10 o'clock he said to Mr. Lear, "I am just going. Have me decently buried, and do not let my body be put into the vault in less than three days after I am dead." A little later he died quietly without a struggle.

He was buried on December 18th in the old family vault on the estate. The obsequies were simple and modest according to his own wishes.

A deep sorrow spread over the nation on hearing of Washington's death. Congress, which was in session, immediately adjourned for the day. The next day a joint committee was appointed to consider on the most suitable manner of doing honor to the memory of America's greatest citizen. This committee selected General Harry Lee to deliver the oration, in the course of which he used those immortal words, ever since used to place Washington in the memories of all Americans— "First in war, first in peace, and first in the hearts of his fellow citizens."

I do not know whether or not it is a part of my task to present an estimate of Washington's career as a whole; however, I take the liberty of quoting to you the admirable estimate of a distinguished biographer of Washington, Henry Cabot Lodge, who said:

"For many years I have studied minutely the career of Washington, and with every step the greatness of the man has grown upon me, for analysis has failed to discover the act of his life which, under the conditions of the time, I could unhesitatingly pronounce to have been in error. . . . I see in Washington a great soldier who fought a trying war to a successful end impossible without him, a great statesman who did more than all other men to lay the foundations of a republic which has endured in prosperity for more than a century. I find in him a marvelous judgment which was never at fault, a penetrating vision which beheld the future of America when it was dim to other eyes, a great intellectual force, a will of iron, an unyielding grasp of facts, and an unequalled strength of patriotic purpose. I see in him, too, a pure and high-minded gentleman of dauntless courage and stainless honor, simple and stately of manner, kind and generous of heart. Such he was in truth. The historian and the biographer may fail to do him justice, but the instinct of mankind will not fail. The real hero needs not books to give him worshippers. George Washington will always receive the love and reverence of men because they see embodied in him the noblest possibilities of humanity."

"Where may the eye repose
When gazing on the Great;
Where neither guilty glory glows
Nor despicable state?
Yes—one, the first, the last, the best,
The Cincinnatus of the West
Whom envy dared not hate,
Bequeathed the name of Washington
To make man blush; there was but one."

SOME HEROINES OF THE AMERICAN REVOLUTION

W. T. Stauffer

I shall attempt in a few words to give you some idea of the heroism of American women during the Revolutionary var. This heroism was, for the most part, the inconspicuous heroism of the home. But here and there will be found women who, to a great extent, did a man's part in the conflict which brought us independence and freedom. I have selected for our consideration a few of these heroines, namely: Jennie M'Neal, Molly Pitcher, Mary Cochran Corbin, Deborah Samson, and Ann Trotter Bailey.

Jennie M'Neal

Paul Revere was a rider bold;
Well has his valorous deed been told;
Sheridan's ride was a glorious one;
Often has it been dwelt upon.
But why should men do all the deeds
On which the love of a patriot feeds?
Hearken to me while I reveal
The dashing ride of Jennie M'Neal.

On a spot as pretty as might be found
In the dangerous length of the neutral ground
In a cottage, cozy and all their own,
She and her mother lived alone.
Safe were the two, with their frugal store,
From all the many who passed their door:

For Jennie's mother was strange to fears
And Jennie was large for fifteen years;
With vim her eyes were glistening,
Her hair was the hue of the blackbird's wing.
And while the friends who knew her well
The sweetness of her heart could tell,
A gun that hung on the kitchen wall
Looked solemnly quick to heed her call;
And they who were evil-minded knew
Her nerve was strong and her aim was true.
So all kind words and acts did deal
To generous, black-eyed Jennie M'Neal.

One night, when the sun had crept to bed
And rain clouds lingered overhead
And sent their surly drops for proof
To drum a tune on the cottage roof
Close after a knock at the outer door
There entered a dozen dragoons or more.
Their red coats, stained by the muddy road,
That they were British soldiers showed.
The captain his hostess bent to greet,
Saying: "Madam, please give us a bit to eat;
We will pay you well, and, if may be,
This bright-eyed girl for pouring our tea,
Then we must dash ten miles ahead
To catch a rebel colonel abed;
He is visiting home, as doth appear;
We will make his pleasure cost him dear."
And they fell to the hasty supper with zeal
Close-watched the while by Jennie M'Neal.

For the gray-haired colonel they hovered near
Had been her true friend, kind and dear;
And oft, in her younger days, had he
Right proudly perched her upon his knee,

And told her stories, many a one
Concerning the French war lately done;
And oft together the two friends were,
And many the arts he had taught to her.
She had hunted by his fatherly side;
He had shown her how to fence and ride.
And once had said: "The time may be
Your skill and courage may stand by me."
So sorrow for him she could but feel
Brave, grateful-hearted Jennie M'Neal.

With never a thought or a moment more,
Bareheaded she slipped from the cottage door,
Ran down where the horses were left to feed,
Unhitched and mounted the captains steed.
And down the hilly and rock-strewn way,
She urged then fiery horse of gray.
Around her slender and cloak-less form
Pattered and moaned the ceaseless storm;
Secure and tight, a gloveless hand
Grasped the reins with a stern command;
And full and black her long hair streamed
Whenever the ragged lightning gleamed.
So on she rushed for the colonel's weal,
Brave, lioness-hearted Jennie M'Neal.

Hark! from the hills, a moment mute,
Came the clatter of hoofs in hot pursuit.
And a cry from the foremost trooper said,
"Halt or your blood be on your head."
She heeded it not, and not in vain
She lashed the horse with the bridle-rein.
So into the night the gray horse strode
His shoes hewed fire from the rock road.
And the high-born courage that never dies

Flashed from the rider's coal-black eyes.
The pebbles flew from the fearful race;
The rain-drops grasped at her glowing face.
"On, on! brave beast," with loud appeal
Cried eager, resolute Jennie M'Neal.

"Halt!" Once more come the voice of dread—
"Halt! or your blood be on your head!"
Then, no one answering to the calls,
Sped after her a volley of balls.
They passed her in her rapid flight—
They screamed to her left, they screamed to her right;
But, rushing still o'er the slippery track,
She sent no token of answer back,
Except a silverly laughter-peal,
Brave, merry-hearted Jennie M'Neal

Soon she rushed, at her own good will
Through woods and valley, o'er plain and hill;
The gray horse did his duty well,
Till all at once he stumbled and fell—
Himself escaping the nets of harm.
But flinging the girl with a broken arm,
Still undismayed by the numbing pain,
She clung to the horse's bridle-rein.
And, gently bidding him to stand;
Petted him with her able hand.
Then sprang again to the saddle-bow
And shouted, "One more trial now."
As if ashamed of his heedless fall,
He gathered his strength once more for all,
And, galloping down a hillside-steep,
Gained on the troopers at every leap;
No more the high-bred steed did reel,
But ran his best for Jennie M'Neal.

They were a furlong behind, or more,
When the girl burst through the colonel's door—
Her poor arm, helpless, hanging with pain,
And she all drabbled and drenched with rain,
But her cheeks as red as firebrands are,
And her eyes as bright as a blazing star—
And shouted, "Quick! Be quick I say!
They come! They come! Away! Away!"
Then sank on the rude white floor of deal,
Poor, brave, exhausted Jennie M'Neal.

The startled colonel sprang and pressed
His wife and children to his breast,
Then turned away from his fireside bright,
And glided into the stormy night;
And soon and safely made his way
To where the patriot army lay.
But first he bent in the dim firelight,
And kissed the forehead broad and white,
And blessed the girl who had ridden so well
To keep him out of a prison cell.
The girl roused up at the martial din,
Just as the troopers came rushing in,
And laughed, e'en in the midst of a moan,
Saying, "Good sirs, your bird has flown.
'Tis I who have scared him from the nest;
So deal with me now as you think best."
But the grand young captain bowed and said,
"Never you hold a moment's dread
Of womankind I must crown you queen,
So brave a girl I have never seen;
Wear this gold ring as your valor's due;
And when peace comes, I will come for you."
But Jennie's face an arch smile wore,
As she said, "There's a lad in Putnam's corps
Who told me the same, long time ago;

You two would never agree, I know,
I've promised my love to be true as steel,"
Said good, sure-hearted Jennie M'Neal.
—Will Carlton

Molly Pitcher

The character known to history as Molly Pitcher was Mary Ludwig, the daughter of a German farmer of New Jersey who married a Pennsylvania barber named John Hays. While Hays was enlisted in Capt. Francis Proctor's company of artillery, his wife, as was then allowable, went along as cook, dishwasher and seamstress to the soldiers. Many patriotic women of that time volunteered for these menial duties for the double purpose of being with their husbands and of contributing to the cause of independence. Mary always accompanied her husband into action and made herself useful by carrying water to the soldiers. Hence she got the nickname, Molly Pitcher. Mary took a deep interest in the field piece of which her husband was pointer, and had him instruct her in its mechanism and operation. At the battle of Monmouth, Proctor's artillery held an exposed position against which the British directed a murderous raking fire. Hays fell in the act of pointing the gun. As no more gun pointers were available, the captain was about to order the gun out of action, when Molly stepped up saying: "Here, I know as much about that piece as John did. You let me serve it." The officer left her in charge, and she served the piece throughout the rest of the action. She gained the personal encomium of Washington. The Congress made her a sergeant and voted her on retirement half pay for life. She died in 1832 aged 78 years.

Mary Cochran Corbin

For some unknown reason, history has given undue prominence to Molly Pitcher, though several other women saw harder service than she did. Indeed, one woman, now seldom heard of, duplicated Molly's act. This was Mary Cochran Corbin, who served a gun at

Fort Washington after her husband, a private in the First Pennsylvania Artillery, had been killed. She was wounded and disabled. The Congress granted her a vote of thanks and retired her on half pay for life. The State of Pennsylvania also granted her an annuity.

Deborah Samson

Deborah Samson was born in Massachusetts. When a small child, she was bound out getting nothing but her board and clothes, not even a rudimentary education. She picked up the art of reading by herself; and when, at the age of eighteen, she became free from her indenture, she worked in the home of a farmer half time for her board and clothes and attended district school for the other half of her time. She made remarkably rapid progress, and in a short time was able to teach school herself, managing thereby to save $12.00. With this she bought coarse fustian and made herself a boy's suit of clothes. Announcing that she was going where she could get a better salary, she disappeared from the community, donned her boy's clothes and presented herself to the nearest recruiting sergeant of the patriot army.

She was not a beautiful woman, but made a remarkably handsome boy, for her features were animated and pleasing; her figure, tall for a woman, was finely proportioned; and her whole appearance was prepossessing. The recruiting officer accepted her and she enlisted for the war as Robert Shirtliffe.

In active service no man was braver than this young woman. She served in some twenty battles, the most notable being White Plains and Yorktown. In addition she volunteered far extra-hazardous service a number of times. In 1773 she was made personal attendant to Gen. Patterson.

Shirtliffe was twice wounded. The first wound was a sword cut on the head and caused little worry. The second was a bullet in the thigh. Alarmed lest she be discovered, she dug the bullet out with a pen knife, bandaged the wound, and resolutely refused to go to the hospital. But, alas, she was seized with brain fever. Her case was considered hopeless and she received little attention from the nurses, who, therefore, learned nothing. She was in a hospital in Philadelphia. One morning Dr. Binney stopped at her bedside and inquired as to her condition. "The poor fellow is dead," was the reply. Detecting a feeble flutter of the pulse. Dr. Binney began a more thorough examination. Placing his hand over the heart, he found the breast tightly swathed with a bandage. Upon removing this, he found the sick soldier to be a woman.

The doctor kept the secret to himself, had the girt removed to his own home, and nursed her back to health. While Shirtliffe was convalescing, she made the acquaintance of Dr. Binney's niece, a young and beautiful woman and the heiress to considerable property. She fell desperately in love with the young soldier, much to Dr. Binney's secret amusement. Concluding that on account of the disparity in their positions, the soldier would not propose marriage, the niece herself proposed and offered to educate the soldier before marriage. Deborah afterward declared that the moment she learned she had unintentionally gained the poor girl's love was one of the most poignant anguish she had ever suffered.

As soon as her health was restored, Dr. Binney sent her with a letter to Gen. Washington. She delivered the letter with the utmost agitation, which Washington thought arose from diffidence and tried to dispel. Then he sent her into another room while he read the letter. She was soon recalled. In silence Washington handed her a discharge from the service and gave her a brief note of advice and enough money to take her back home. He spoke not a word for fear of adding to the girl's embarrassment, his eyes filled with tears, he was much moved. "How thankful," Deborah often said afterward, "was I to Gen. Washington for sparing my feelings. He saw me ready to sink with shame; one word from him just then would have crushed me. But he said nothing, and I blessed him for it."

Deborah afterward married Benjamin Gannett. During his presidency she visited Gen. Washington on invitation, and was rather lionized. The Congress granted her a pension as well as certain lands, and she was a guest at a number of functions given by leaders of official society.

Mad Ann Trotter Bailey

But the most extraordinary figure of the whole conflict was Mad Ann Trotter Bailey. According to her own account, she was born in Liverpool, England, in 1700, the daughter of a soldier named Sargent. At the age of nineteen she was kidnapped, brought to Virginia, and sold as a redemptioner. Having worked out her indenture, she married John Trotter in 1730. They removed to West Virginia where they lived quietly for more than forty years.

About this time began the Indian troubles preceding the Revolution. Trotter volunteered and was killed at the battle of Point Pleasant, his wife fighting at his side. Wild with rage, Mrs. Trotter offered herself to Col. William Clendennin for any service, the more dangerous the better, provided she could inflict a maximum of damage on the redskins. At this time she was 74 years old, short, stout, coarse featured, with a voice so gruff she frightened children, stronger than most men in their prime, masculine in every word and look and act. She was a crack shot, a splendid rider, and an expert in woodcraft. She rode a black stallion which she had broken herself and named Liverpool after her birthplace; a great, vicious beast, whom she alone could mount. He was the fleetest horse in the country and was dreaded more than a wild cat because of his murderous disposition. Some accounts say she used two horses, riding Liverpool and leading the other which was named Jennie Mann. Once Jennie Mann was stolen. She trailed the Indian thief and found him swimming New River with the animal. A well-aimed shot sent the Indian to the bottom and her familiar call brought Jennie Mann back to her. Mrs. Trotter was used as a spy, a scout, dispatch rider, and generally as an Indian killer. During the entire Revolution and afterwards until the Indians were pushed beyond the Ohio, she performed the most difficult and dangerous duties of every military expedition. The Indians regarded her as leading a charmed life and they feared her like a witch. Some of her reputation for possessing supernatural powers was due to the fact that she could beat the Indians at their own game of woodcraft; but most of it was due to her hardihood and recklessness.

Her greatest exploit was the relief of Fort Clendennin which was held by Col. Clendennin and was situated where Charleston, West Virginia, now stands. Word come to Clendennin that he might expect an Indian attack. This was serious news, as his stock of powder was low, and the nearest supply was at Port Union, where Lewisburg now is, 100 miles away. To send a few men for powder would be foolish as the country was infested by Indians; to send a sufficient force to beat off any attack by prowling bands would seriously weaken the garrison. Clendennin was in a quandary. Just then Mad Ann stepped up. "How much powder ye want?" she asked. "We'll have to have a keg," said Clendennin. "That is more than one person can carry." Mrs. Trotter grunted, picked up her smoothbore, gave a hitch to her buckskin trousers, took a big chew of tobacco, leaped on Liverpool and disappeared. On the third day she returned with a keg of powder slung across Jennie Mann's back, having covered 200 miles of hostile country in less than 60 hours.

At the age of 90 she married John Bailey, an old veteran. When he was murdered a few years later, she went to live with her son, John Trotter, a prosperous farmer in West Virginia. Some years later John removed to Gallia County, Ohio, where he became a land owner and leading citizen. Mrs. Bailey went with him, but in a few years tired of civilized life and turned back to the wild. Her son offered her a comfortable home, but she supported her declining years mainly with her smoothbore. She roamed the woods of Gallia and neighboring counties always clad in a slouch hat, a man's coat, and a pair of buckskins, over which she sometimes wore a woman's skirt. She was known for her kind heartedness no less than for her eccentricities. The game which she shot she divided with the sick and needy, often walking miles to present it. Her pioneer knowledge of herbs and simples made her a valued caller in the sick room. She died in 1825. If the date of her birth as she gave it can be trusted, she was then 125 years old. She "was active to the last." The post-mortem revealed no sickness of any sort. On the day before her death, she roamed the woods as usual. Returning at night, she simply wrapped herself in her blanket, lay down to sleep on the earthen floor of her rail cabin, and never woke up.

But the lives of the generality of patriot women did not take this turn of heroism. Theirs was the inconspicuous heroism of the home so well depicted in the anonymous poem:

THE BRAVE AT HOME

The maid who binds her warrior's sash,
With smile that well her grief dissembles,
The while beneath her drooping lash
One starry teardrop hangs and trembles,
Though Heaven alone record the tear,
And Fame shall never know her story,
Her heart doth shed a drop as dear
As ever dewed the field of glory.

The wife who girds her husband's sword,
'Mid little ones who weep and wonder,
And bravely speaks the cheering word,
What though her heart be rent asunder—
Doomed nightly in her dreams to hear
The bolts of war around him rattle,
hath shed as sacred blood as e'er
Was poured upon a field of battle.

The mother who conceals her grief,
When to her heart her son she presses,
Then breathes a few brave words and brief,
Kissing the patriot brow she blesses,
With no one but her secret God
To know the pain that weighs upon her
Sheds holy blood as o'er the sod,
Received on Freedom's field of honor.

WASHINGTON IN WILLIAMSBURG

J. Luther Kibler

Foreword

The story of Washington's occasional sojourns in Williamsburg, within a period of over thirty years, if an adequate account of his activities were given, would require the writing of a good-sized book. I can here give only a sketchy view of the available material.

The general public knows about just three important visits which George Washington made to Williamsburg prior to his election to the House of Burgesses in 1758. Other visits are generally overlooked. Virginians and people in other states know far too little about his associations in the Colonial Capital during the fifteen years of his membership in the House of Burgesses—his associations with its people in their homes and taverns, and with the leading men of the Colony whom he met here. Many incidents of his life in Williamsburg are a closed book to the public, and though they are, for a large portion of his sojourn period here, easily known—they were entirely neglected during the Bicentennial Year of his Birth by all the directors of that ten-month celebration. Only some of the "high spots" were noticed. But the whole story should be told—it needs to be—if the Williamsburg chapters of his life are to be complete as far as records have been preserved.

Some phases of this subject are presented in this paper, emphasizing historic landmarks which are really Washington shrines—still standing and visited by tourists who have never learned what they signify in the history of Washington's social life and public services here. The records reveal a remarkable story in scattered details. It is time to break the seal of silence regarding his temporary dwelling places in this "metropolis" as he called it, and give the world an opportunity to see how Washington spent his time during his frequent visits here!

Introduction

Through the greater part of the past year the people of the United States and in certain countries of the Old World honored the "Father of His Country" by celebrating, under the auspices and direction of the National and the State Governments, the Bicentennial of his birth; and less than two months ago, in 1932, the 133rd anniversary of his death and burial was memorialized as a fitting close to the multiform and inspiring commemoration of his name, character and achievements.

As the Thomas Nelson, Jr., Chapter, Sons of the American Revolution is in regular session tonight (February 10th, 1933) in the old Virginia Capital in this month of Washington's birth, the present is an appropriate time for us all to call to mind the many occasions of the great Virginian's presence in Williamsburg. His every visit here held something of interest for us today. The circumstances and incidents of George Washington's public and private life while a temporary resident of this historic capital is a subject prolific of information, entertainment, and patriotic appeal.

It is a matter of regret, as already indicated, that much of the material relating to his migratory residence in Williamsburg was overlooked in the Bicentennial story of his life. This neglected data is essential in presenting a full and satisfactory picture of Washington as he moved about the streets and among the people of the town. This long-buried data combined with what has already long been known to the public, presents Washington's various activities and pastime in their proper perspective; and its apt interpretation enables us to see more clearly *Washington the man* as an influential character and a real factor in the life of this city 150 to 175 years ago. Since a fairly satisfactory account of Washington's experiences in the Second Capital of Virginia would require a large volume to record it, in this brief paper I can touch upon only some of the more important features of such a story.

Washington's frontier experiences at the head of Virginia troops had placed him in line for civil honors, and he was chosen in 1758 to represent Frederick County in the House of Burgesses. His 15 years' experience as a Burgess in the General Assembly (the Governor's Council was the Upper House) which held its sessions in the *Old Capital* (now undergoing restoration) was, let us observe, a practical school of government which furnished a training in state craft for Washington. This experience, beyond a doubt, contributed very much in connection with his naturally sound judgment to the development of that type of statesmanship which our political mentors often recall today. The Washingtonian type of statesmanship we are often asked to regard and defend as one of the sheet-anchors of our Federal system of government, in the interpretation of the principles of our national constitution.

George Washington was the embodiment of and his name is today the shibboleth of this non-sectional American statesmanship. The roots of his governmental theories were imbedded in the experiences of his membership in the House of Burgesses and in the associations of his fellow-Virginians within the precincts of this historic center where constitutional government in America was first exemplified in Virginia's own first Plan or Government written by George Mason. Why, then, should a single Washington landmark or shrine that yet remains in Williamsburg remain unknown any longer to our school children or to pilgrims here from other states?

Hence, today, assembled as we are from patriotic motives, let us recall Washington's presence in this old seat of colonial government, for what inspiration we may receive as we envision him in his comings and goings about the old homes and public places in his earlier years when he was yet unable, perhaps, to foresee the ascendancy of his star of service and honor into the Revolution, through the presidency and afterwards to the end of his life.

Washington's various activities in Old Williamsburg, after his visit to William and Mary for his surveyor's license, may be grouped into three periods:

a) 1752 to 1758—before he became a burgess
b) 1759 to 1774—while he was a burgess
c) 1781—for the siege of Yorktown.

It affords one an interesting and satisfying experience in the study of *Washingtoniana* to find it possible to identify Washington's migratory dwelling-places in Williamsburg. It is like a revelation to be able to locate the historic shrines, the public buildings, and some of the sites of ancient structures where he found rest, sustenance and refreshment; sought diversion, or transacted public business. The list of these old landmarks which figured so prominently in his movements about this chartered little town-city, is a long one; some of them may never be definitely located. I now invite you to go with me to some of these more important places—(including the "unknown") and note

Where and How Washington Spent His Time in Williamsburg

Of course, such places as the College, the Church, the Capitol, the Palace and the Second Theatre, also the Raleigh Tavern are already well known as being inseparably associated with Washington's activities here within a period of 25 years. But there are other important landmarks, veritable highlights of history, in the whereabouts of Washington's comings and goings in the then Virginia metropolis that shall have our consideration at this time. Washington's visits to these other significant places, shrines hallowed by his associations with them, are recorded in his diary as far as that interesting journal of his has been preserved.

Circumstances surrounding Washington's entertainment as a guest in certain famous old homes and his patronage of various taverns here where the heart-beats of Virginia's social and political life were felt at their best, make such presence in these places a matter of unusual interest to us today, while they sometimes add much to the historic value and importance of these old landmarks, because the Washington phase of their history had not been until recently a matter of previous knowledge, even to the citizens of Williamsburg.

But let us now see Colonel Washington as he often made the journey on his way from Mount Vernon to Williamsburg, before we attempt further to visualize him on the dusty or muddy streets and unpaved sidewalks of this city-chartered town. In mental picture we see him journeying back and forth between his manor on the broad Potomac and the Virginia Peninsula, traveling in a jig or two-wheeled vehicle which he called his "chair," or in his family coach whenever Mrs. Washington accompanied him. I know you can visualize the Fairfax legislator on these trips, driving his two-horse "chair" from Mount Vernon direct south, or along the Maryland shore of the Potomac, crossing the river twice before reaching Fredericksburg, thence from the town of his boyhood on the Rappahannock down through Caroline County (where a century later "Stonewall" Jackson died), then through King and Queen and King William Counties, on ferries, crossing the Mattaponi and Pamunkey headwaters of the majestic York river into New Kent County, always stopping (when returning, too) at "Eltham," the mansion home of Colonel Burwell Bassett, his brother-in-law. These trips required four or five days each way, and the House of Burgesses usually allowed him ten day's traveling expenses.

Besides these periods spent in attending the General Assembly, Washington made a number of other trips to Williamsburg that were of unusual importance, and which still hold for many a romantic interest; three in particular, but several others, set in striking circumstances, are not so well known. Taken all together, these special journeys on particular missions foreshadowed the place in history which he was destined to fill; they formed a series of events like the links of a mighty chain.

Let us now be more specific: first, back in the vista of George Washington's youth, we see him here at William and Mary College standing the required test for his commission as a county surveyor, in 1749. There are no college records extant that might give us particulars of this epochal event that led to his appointment to a public office. The Culpepper County records show that on July 26, 1749, Washington presented to the Court his commission from the President and Masters of William and Mary College, and that he took several required oaths as a subject of the King, and as a county surveyor. Here he set his first "milestone" in the city.

Where Washington lodged and how long he remained in the 50-year old capital on this, his first visit to Williamsburg, can never be known. But this was his only educational connection with the College until April 30th, 1788, when he accepted the office of Chancellor of the institution, to which he was elected on January 18th, previous. But because of his interest in education, he was here in spirit until his death over 11 years later.

Scarcely three years after Washington became a licensed surveyor in 1752, he came to Williamsburg especially to see Governor Dinwiddie, a journey never mentioned in our school books This visit was made on his way home from the Barbados in February, 1752. He stopped here before going on to Mount Vernon with letters from his half-brother Lawrence, still in the West Indies for his health. When he arrived from the York River (and by what route did he come?) the Governor was at "Green Spring," Berkeley's old home. Washington waited for him at Dinwiddie's temporary residence, the Dinwiddie–Saunders House, now beautifully restored, on Palace Green.

This visit was an important one. Matters pertaining to the Ohio Company required consideration, for Lawrence Washington could not live long, and the Washingtons, the Lees and Dinwiddie himself were members of the Ohio Company. So here was Washington, at the age of 20, representing his brother's interests in this company with a grant of 200,000 to 500,000 acres of land along the Ohio River! Little has ever been written about this business conference young Washington had with the Scotch-born governor who later filled so large a place in his military life on the Virginia frontier. In a fragment of his diary he says that he was "received graciously" by the governor who "enquired kindly after the health of my brother and invited me to stay and dine" at the Dinwiddie–Saunders House as we now call it. Here and then Washington planted the second mile-stone in his public career. Here and then, no doubt, fate had chosen Washington for another but more momentous adventure. This call on the governor helps to explain why Dinwiddie chose him for that famous mission to the French in the Ohio Valley in the Fall of 1753, though neither the governor nor our young hero could yet divine the need for such a journey.

When Washington came in October, the Governor was occupying the Palace (recently enlarged and renovated) and he and Washington doubtless conferred together on the French danger in the Governor's office where Washington, we may believe, also received Dinwiddie's instructions. This office of the Governor's is a landmark that has been over-shadowed by the Palace itself in local history. It was a brick building with dormer-windows just east of the Palace, and has recently been restored. Here, no doubt, Washington reported in January 1754, first orally—with carefully made notes, however, in his possession; but he was required to present a written report within one day's time. This, his first "state-paper," is found in Marshall's *Life of Washington*. The document of twenty printed pages contains about 7500 words—a masterpiece for a youth of 21 revealing a faculty for observation and detailed presentation of the situation that was remarkable. This was the third mile-stone firmly set so near his second one.

Washington made another important journey to the seat of government here in 1758 to secure equipment and supplies for his regiment in the expedition headed by General Forbes against Ft. Duquesne. Momentous and far-reaching results hinged on this hurried trip. He had made a hasty visit to Williamsburg several years prior to this when he was sent from Braddock's army to get money to pay the Virginia troops on that historic march from Alexandria. But this time he no longer "counted" mile-stones—he had come to the great turning point in his life. The Assembly was not in session; Governor Dinwiddie had returned to England; and so Washington had to deal with the Colonial Council and John Blair, Sr., the President and Acting Governor. The situation compelled him to remain in the capital about two weeks. Meanwhile, he improved his waiting time by making several visits (no doubt) to the "White House" in New Kent County, the home of the wealthy and charming widow of Daniel Parke Custis, whom he had met at Poplar Grove plantation, the home of William Chamberlayne, where he tarried in his haste on his way to Williamsburg. His military expedition thus became also a romantic sojourn on the Peninsula. The whole story is too long for this occasion. The full account of this event of events in the life of Virginia's outstanding soldier is found in Irving's *Life of Washington*. Where Washington was entertained in this city until he succeeded in his mission no one knows; but one may surmise that he shared the hospitality of President Blair and other Councilors. And too, Williamsburg was always well supplied with taverns.

The sequel of this journey that marked the supreme turning point in his great career is well-known. Having won the heart of Martha Custis, Washington waited till his military campaign was ended before coming to claim her hand. He was present with General Forbes when Ft. Duquesne—now Pittsburgh—was captured. While yet in the army, at Cumberland, he was elected to the House of Burgesses by the people of Frederick County, whose tower of defense he had been against the Indians. On his way to occupy this post of political honor he married the widow Custis on January 6th, 1759.

The General Assembly met in the Capitol on Washington's birthday following. When the Colonel of the First Virginia Regiment appeared in the popular branch of the colonial legislature, he was given the opportunity to make his "maiden speech" forthwith! His attempt to reply to the vote of thanks by the Burgesses for his successful military services proved the eloquence of his embarrassment and lack of words to express his sentiments. But Speaker John Robinson came to his rescue: "Sit down, Mr. Washington; your modesty equals your valor, and that surpasses the power of any language that I possess." This story is a gem in American history.

At this session of the Burgesses Washington was made a member of the important committee on "Propositions and Grievances," and one reading the *Journal* of the ancient House of Burgesses will find that our colonial lawmakers had many "grievances" from their constituents to consider. The Council and Burgesses sat until the end of May, when Colonel and Mrs. Washington left the capital for their home that was waiting for them at Mount Vernon. The diary of Washington for this pivotal year of his life, unfortunately, is missing. But we are told by some writers that while in Williamsburg these three months Washington and his bride lived in Mrs. Washington's former home—the "Six-Chimney House." The Custis mansion has long since disappeared; only a little brick building remains on the premises, and is known as "Martha Washington's Kitchen." It stands in the eastern portion of the grounds of the Eastern State Hospital, in very bad repair, perhaps because it is State property! It certainly needs restoration. Fifty yards away stands the only yew tree in town, planted, tradition says, by Mrs. Daniel Parke Custis herself.

A new chapter in Washington's migratory residence in Williamsburg now begins. We have only fragmentary records telling about his presence in the city prior to 1768. His own record of a five-day business trip to the little metropolis in April, 1760, is most interesting. Because of the bad spring roads through Prince William and Stafford Counties, he crossed the Potomac at Posey's Ferry on April 19th. Shortly afterwards he broke his "chair"—about 11 o'clock, he wrote, and had to walk about six miles to Port Tobacco to get it mended. He had to remain in the neighborhood over night. His "repair bill" was 7/6, and other expenses, 9/9. He, of course, had to recross the Potomac into Virginia. On April 22nd he crossed the Pamunkey and visited his plantations in New Kent—formerly Mrs. Custis' estate. He "found the overseers much behind hand in their business." He lodged at Mrs. Washington's mother's home. The next two days he spent at Colonel Bassett's, coming to Williamsburg on the evening of the 24th. On the 25th, he waited upon the Governor, Francis Fauquier, at the Palace. On Saturday, he says, "I visited all the estates and my own quarters about Williamsburg." His own quarters—where were they? What were they? I do not know. But on Sunday, April 27th, he went to Bruton Church. On Monday he wrote that he had let his house in town to Col. Moore for 45 pounds per annum. This evidently was Mrs. Washington's former "Six-Chimney House" which he was to paint before giving possession in the fall.

Where he lodged and ate his meals during this stay he does not say. Note this though: "In the afternoon after collecting what money I could get I left town and reached Col. Basset's." This was on Monday April 28th, 1760.

Washington was doubtless active in the House of Burgesses in 1763, when an act was passed establishing his Dismal Swamp Land Company for draining the Swamp. This was about seven years before efforts were made to build a canal across Williamsburg to connect the York and the James Rivers, which enterprise, launched on the eve of the Revolution, never materialized.

The year 1765 is ever memorable in the annals of colonial Virginia. In May of this year Patrick Henry made his famous "Caesar–Brutus Speech" in the Old Capitol. Was George Washington present to hear the warning voice of the American Demosthenes? We are told that he was, though many members had already gone home. The report of Governor Fauquier giving an account of Henry's speech against the Stamp Act to the English Government describes Henry's supporters in a way that pays a peculiar compliment to the Mount Vernon member of the House of Burgesses; for Washington certainly entertained Henry's views. Fauquier called those who voted for Henry's resolutions "the young, hot and giddy members." But history refuses to accept Fauquier's epithet as justified.

Let us now take a view of Washington's migratory dwelling places in this one-time capital during the period of seven years, from 1768 to 1774, as covered by his diary. In this time he spent, altogether, approximately 230 days in Williamsburg; and counting two and one-half miles (a low estimate) daily as the distance he must have traveled in walking up and down and across the town as he went from place to place, four or five times a day, we have

575 miles traveled within the city, leaving behind him his footmarks on the records of time that can never be effaced. If not physically, yet historically this is most certainly true. Not once, according to his diary, did Washington spend an entire day, eating three meals at the same place. His frequent perambulations among the homes of the highest public officials place him in the limelight as very much of a peripatetic statesman, for all these visits to the homes of the great certainly were not for social reasons alone.

And into how many different homes was he welcomed, and what taverns and boarding-houses did he patronize? Of private homes there were at least eight, and of inns, taverns, etc., there were seven or eight more where he spent his time when not engaged at the Capitol. Of these eight colonial dwellings six are still standing, though one was used for many years in Washington's time as a tavern. But until quite recently only one of the eight had been positively identified as a Washington landmark. Even Williamsburg itself has been slow to find all its roots of history that give glamour and honor to her precious old homesteads. Yet, all the time, Washington's Diary pointed them out. An observation is apropos here: The restoration of the buildings of this historic town from their past means also the uncovering of much history relating to George Washington and other well-known characters that lay buried so long, like the ancient cities of that other hallowed region in the Near East of the Old World.

Therefore, if we can see Washington where he actually ate, drank, slept and conversed with his fellow-men here while rendering public service, we bring out in bold relief the circumstances under which he labored here in the then very heart of Virginia, in helping to lay the foundations for American liberty in that era of turmoil and travail when this city was made a shrine sacred to all people of our country today.

We will now allow Washington himself, as it were, to introduce us to this list of his stopping-places and private homes visited in 1768, as some of his "stepping-stones" to greatness when he and his Dismal Swamp Land Company associates made Williamsburg an objective on their trip to that "Dismal" region in Virginia and

North Carolina. On October 24th of this year he wrote: "Sent chairs and horses over James River and lodged in Williamsburg ourselves." But he leaves us in the dark as to where they lodged that night. On their return, October 30th, they again dined in Williamsburg—where we know not. But for October 31st, Washington is more specific: "Dined at the mayor's. Entertained of the Governor." (Botetourt was the new governor, but recently from England. But who was the mayor?)

During his stay in Williamsburg (till November 6th) Washington leads into two of the outstanding old landmarks in the city—the homes of two brothers: Peyton Randolph and John Randolph, sons of Sir John Randolph, distinguished Attorney-General for the Crown, before his two sons followed him in the same office. Peyton Randolph was Speaker of the House of Burgesses; John Randolph, the younger, was Attorney-General of the Colony. Washington's Diary reads: "November 1st, dined at the Speaker's with many gentlemen"—including, quite likely, members of the Dismal Swamp Land Company. The next day: "Dined at the Attorney-General's with Lord Botetourt (ye Governor) and many other gentlemen," probably his "Dismal Swamp" companions. The Speaker's home was the present "Peyton Randolph House," north of the Court House Green on Nicholson Street. Here Washington was a guest from 1768 to 1774 at least 28 times. The home of the Attorney-General was "Tazewell Hall" on South England Street, beyond the old "Powder Horn" and the new Court House. The first is private property; the second belongs to the Restoration.

The identity of Peyton Randolph's residence was established only three or four years ago, though it had been known as such in 1824 when Lafayette was entertained there. But the name was forgotten after Lafayette's visit led to its being called the "Peachy House" in honor of his hostess—Mrs. Mary Monro Peachy,

In November 1769, Washington dined with Mrs. Washington and her children—Jackie and Patsy Custis— "at Speaker Randolph's by candlelight and spent the evening there," he tells us. You can picture the scene of this family visit in the great parlor of this historic residence that had been the home of the only Virginian by birth who was ever knighted by the British Crown, and who died here in 1734. Here Count Rochambeau had his headquarters in September, 1781; and in this old home of the First President of the Continental Congress, General Lafayette was entertained by an all-night young people's ball about October 21st, 1824. Mrs. Peachy (already referred to) was herself a daughter of Wilson Miles Cary, a prominent figure in the Revolutionary War whose residence was at "Ceeley's," on Hampton Roads, at Kecoughtan within the city limits of Newport News. All these great names conclusively designate this ancient Randolph home as a real highlight among the patriotic shrines of Williamsburg, and as a *de facto* Washington memorial.

We can see Washington with his family also at "Tazewell Hall," built by John Randolph, the hospitable host of this famous mansion, about ten years before the Revolution came, when, as a conscientious Tory, he went to England where he died longing for his native Virginia. Pathos and glory mingle in the story of Washington's half a score of welcome visits to "Tazewell Hall," so named, however, as late as the 1790s. Two occasions call for our notice.

On December 1st, 1769, Mrs. Washington and children dined there while Washington himself dined with some officials and other gentlemen at one of the taverns. In the family at Tazewell Hall were three children: two girls and Edmund, afterwards United States Attorney-General and Secretary of State in Washington's cabinets. On May 23rd, 1774, Washington came to Williamsburg with Mrs. Washington and they dined at Tazewell Hall, remaining there to spend the evening. This old Randolph home was a literary and social center. Here often shone the brilliant lights of the best society, the host himself and his friend Thomas Jefferson vying with each other on the violin.

But the end to all these happy occasions came when Tory John Randolph departed for England in 1775, taking his family with him, all but Edmund whom Washington took into his own family and later made an aide in his army before Boston. These Washington–Randolph associations alone would make Tazewell Hall a famous patriotic shrine, though it was in future years that it was named after United States Senator Henry Tazewell, the father of Governor Littleton Waller Tazewell, the namesake of Tazewell County, Virginia.

But we must not leave Washington and his Dismal Swamp folks "stranded" in Williamsburg. Retracing our chronological journey to 1768, on November 4th we have a most interesting record. Christopher Ayescough had an inn near the Capitol. Washington mentions this place but twice. On this date, November 4th, 1768, he "dined with several gentlemen at Ayescough's. Col. Byrd's lottery began drawing," quoting his own words. Lotteries were common then; even the Virginia Assembly in the year of "Braddock's Defeat" had conducted a lottery to raise money for protecting Virginia against the Indians. On this occasion—at Ayescough's—Washington bought ten tickets, paying Peyton Randolph 50 pounds for his share of 100 that were sold. His "winnings" were seven prizes, or 560½ acres of land in Richmond building lots. Washington was a connoisseur of land—always looking out for the best investment in such property.

The Dinwiddie House on Palace Green, where Washington first met the Governor in 1752, is another old home where we find him in 1769. Councilor Robert Carter of "Nomini Hall," in Northumberland County, then lived here. On November 6th he says: "Came to Williamsburg. Dined at Mr. Carter's with Lord Botetourt, Governor Eden, etc." This was Sir Robert Eden, Governor of Maryland (1769–1776). Robert Carter had married in Maryland and held property there. Naturally Eden might be expected to visit Carter whom he had met in Maryland. This famous old landmark, standing near the Governor's Palace in restored beauty and completeness, has a wonderful architectural history and should be well-known as a Washington Shrine. It bears also the name of the sole President of William and Mary College who was born, lived, and died in Williamsburg—Robert Saunders, son of Robert Saunders, and a contemporary of John Tyler, President of the United States. An early scion of the Tyler family had lived here before the days of Dinwiddie. This "Dinwiddie–Saunders House" recalls another prominent colonial character, Robert Carter Nicholas, who owned the house after its temporary occupancy by Dinwiddie. He was Treasurer of the Colony. From him Robert Carter purchased the property and held it till after the Revolution, though he did not live here that long.

Washington often dined at the home of Treasurer Nicholas from 1769 to 1774. Nicholas, famous as a churchman as well as a statesman, was host to Washington fourteen times. But his home is no longer standing. It is probable that he lived in a house that stood on the site of the new "Restoration" Courthouse. A four-chimney residence here was the home of John Tyler before he moved to Bassett Hall. It was burned in 1871. A picture of it has been preserved. Perhaps this was the home of Robert Carter Nicholas where Washington was his guest so often. The old basement of the dwelling is under the new municipal building, below the Treasurer's office.

On March 6th, 1772, Washington says that he "dined at the Treasurers' and went to the ball given by the House of Burgesses to Lady Dunmore." For this ball Washington subscribed one pound, worth then about $3.33. It was the last of eight public balls which he says he attended, of course, in a very active capacity. Most of these balls were given in the Capitol.

This now takes us back to the Palace, originally called the "Governor's House." Here Washington was frequently the guest of Lord Dunmore, eleven times, to be exact. He had attended the "Queen's Birth Night" celebration there in 1769. This, no doubt, was another time he attended a ball, for the event was as brilliant as possible to be worthy of the occasion, doing honor to royalty.

On the day before the Burgesses' Ball in honor of Lady Dunmore, Washington had "Rid out with the Governor to his farm and breakfasted with him there." This was at "Porto Bello" on Queen's Creek, in York County. The house, though once ruined by fire, is still standing, but modernized. Now what must we think of Washington's friendship with Dunmore at this time? For the Governor, on the day before he and Washington rode out into the country five or six miles for breakfast, had dissolved the House of Burgesses because its members had passed resolutions of sympathy for Boston, and had set June 1st for a Day of Fasting and Prayer—the day for the Boston Port Bill to go into effect. Let us surmise this: Washington and Dunmore did not permit political differences to destroy their personal friendship. But did they never discuss affairs of government on any of these eleven occasions while the gulf between Virginia and England was growing wider and wider? Doubtless they did. In general, it may be believed that Washington's associations with all the government officials, already named, was turned to good account by informing himself on matters that were discussed from time to time at the Capitol. When June 1st came, Washington went to church and fasted all day. But his diary records few times he was at Bruton Parish Church. He frequently spent the week-end with Colonel Bassett at "Eltham" in New Kent.

One more old home where Colonel Washington was often a tavern guest stands conspicuous on Duke of Gloucester Street. It is the Richard Bland House, nearly opposite Raleigh Tavern. Here in 1710, was born Richard Bland, a member of the Continental Congress and known as "The Great Virginia Patriot." In this house of Patrick Henry's forerunner, Washington must have been a frequent guest. It was the home for twenty years or more after 1738 of Henry Wetherburn who kept the Ordinary at the Raleigh Tavern where his "Arrack Punch" became known throughout Virginia. This old-fashioned house—private property today—was used as a tavern long after Wetherburn's day by James Barrett Southall and Robert Anderson. Southall took charge of the Raleigh Tavern, succeeding Anthony Hay in March 1771, and Anderson succeeded Southall at the Richard Bland House.

Washington mentions the Raleigh Tavern by name infrequently, preferring to use the name of Hay fourteen times and Southall also many times, instead. His reference to dining, supping and spending the evening at Southall's prior to 1771 evidently places his visits at the Bland House. From this year on he made twelve visits to Anderson's tavern here. But whether at Southall's or at Anderson's as keepers of this Bland House Inn, we may picture Washington here with other public men on many occasions, seated at the table in the large "Bull Head" Dining Room in the west end, so called by Wetherburn, and still bearing this name.

A brief observation here: What is more fitting in the sequence of history than that Bland, who first proclaimed England and Virginia two separate dominions under one crown, should be associated through this house of his birth with Washington who actually accomplished the definite separation of these two "dominions"! Virginia history is full of just such coincidences. To name one other that should be mentioned in this paper: In 1770 and 1771, Washington was twice the guest of John Blair, Sr., in the John Blair House, a block east of the College. Little could he then divine that in the not distant future he would appoint Father Blair's son, John, an associate Justice of the U. S Supreme Court! And pardon me if I go a little further to say that this same John Blair House was one time the property of our beloved Governor, Dr. John Garland Pollard. How securely all these places enshrine the name of George Washington.

So much for the old homes. There were several other places, inns, taverns, and boarding-houses which Washington freely patronized. Where they all stood no one knows to a certainty. The sites of several may never be identified—because of records destroyed. This is one of the historical "shortcomings" or misfortunes of Williamsburg. Would that some mysterious alchemist could bring back to us these ancient tomes from the scattered ashes of the silent past, where they are saved from utter oblivion only by our keen regret for "what might have been." Nevertheless, a few locations are indicated, though indefinitely. The names of these places will suffice for our purpose.

The one most conspicuous in Washington's Diary was Mrs. Christian Campbell's, for a while at least just west of the Richard Bland House at the southwest corner of Botetourt and Duke of Gloucester streets, where 100 yards from the "Raleigh" old foundations of a large brick house have been unearthed. Washington mentions Mrs. Campbell's place 75 times, besides naming her tavern as the same place where he "Went to the Club," a social group with its own room there. Anyone familiar with the customs of colonial times can surmise at once the "program" for the pastime of this "Club" which Washington frequented 33 times in five or six years.

Where he lodged cannot be definitely determined; he refers to his "own room" or "lodgings," but never directly indicates where such place was. He once paid a large amount for lodging and meals for himself and family to Richard Charlton, a tavernkeeper, but does not refer to him in this connection in his diary of that date. He once paid Mrs. Campbell an amount that appears too large for meals only for the time stated.

In 1772 and 1773 we find him half a score times at the Coffee House, a hostel that stood near the Capitol close to the present large brick house where McClellan had his headquarters in 1862. Among the more famous tavernkeepers in the town in Washington's day was Jane Vobe. She owned two or three places or public entertainment, one of which was quite a "swell place" for aristocratic young gentlemen. But Washington seems to have visited Mrs. Vobe's tavern only four times within four years. There is preserved an original merchandise account Jane Vobe had with Matthews Wills, a man of many businesses and occupations, living at Mulberry Island. Her purchases for 1773 amounted to £9–12s–3½d. In January 1774, she paid this amount of pounds, shillings and pence in cash, loaf sugar, and four gallons of rum.

Mrs. Dawson, a widow, also conducted a boarding-house which Washington patronized every year from 1768 to 1774, in all 35 times. Mrs. Dawson was Mrs. Pricilla Bassett Dawson, sister of Colonel Burwell Bassett of "Eltham," and Washington's own sister-in-law. She was the widow of Rev. Thomas Dawson, D.D., a president of William and Mary College and also a rector of Bruton Parish Church.

Colonel Washington as a visitor with this family at a private residence must not be overlooked. In 1770, Mrs. Ambler, formerly of Jamestown Island, visited her sister, Sally Cary Fairfax, at "Belvoir," and Mrs. Washington, at Mount Vernon. The Washingtons, in time, "returned the visit" in those hospitable days of long journeys in 1772, when Washington and his family, four of them, were guests of Mrs. Ambler in Williamsburg. And four times does Washington mention Mrs. Ambler's place, the home of Mary Cary Ambler, widow of Edward Ambler, who had died at Jamestown in 1767. Mrs. Ambler herself died in Hanover County in May 1781.

In addition to all these visits to the homes of prominent people and to the inns, taverns and boarding-houses for his "daily bread," George Washington was sometimes the guest of the Governor's Council at semiofficial or social dinners. First, in 1769 on his arrival in town, and last, in 1774 at the Raleigh, where, perhaps, five other dinners were given with Washington present. These Councilors formed the aristocratic branch of the General Assembly, though in this day the Burgesses were more powerful. But shall we not judge Washington as the equal in his own personality and character of any of his host of twelve gentlemen, for we know who these Councilors were? Washington, the Burgess, was the peer of any man in His Majesty's Council. Here he came directly, under the influence of those members of the Assembly whose chief concern was to guard the prerogatives of the Crown, but they could not determine the course or the popular political current. And Washington was a figure not to be left out of the picture, for though counted among the "aristocrats," he had that universality of viewpoint that made him capable of adapting the "class" attitude to the conditions and needs of his fellowmen, regardless of the social standing of any of them. A question: How much did this contact with the Councilors influence Washington and in what way? And how much did he influence them?

Washington had also his diversions. These, besides those of his "Club" as you know, were provided by balls and plays, the plays at the Second Theatre, east of the Capitol. The First Theatre of 1716 had become a Town Hall in 1745. This second one erected in 1751, on Waller Street, Washington attended at least twenty-two times, noting in his diary that he "went to the play," as he always wrote it and principally in 1770–1772. The Hallams, (Lewis, Jr., and his sister, Sarah) conducted this theatre in this period of the '70s. Sometimes Washington went alone, sometimes with a party of friends. He always bought a "box" ticket—price 7/6. Once, when he had a theatre party, he paid one pound for tickets.

His attendance at balls he notes six times, the first at the Capitol on December 13, 1769. The Council gave a ball at the Capitol on June 4, 1770; and the Burgesses gave another one on March 18, 1772, also at the Capitol. On November 1, 1772, he attended "Mr. Baylor's Ball." This was John Baylor a relative of George Baylor, of Revolutionary fame. On the 13th of the same month Washington was present at a Terpsichorean in the Apollo Room at the Raleigh where Jefferson had, years before, danced with his fair "Belinda"—Rebecca Burwell, of Carter's Grove. (See his famous letter to John Page.) Once he mentions the Daphne, the Ladies Social Room at the Raleigh, next to the Apollo.

But Washington's chief interests in Williamsburg centered at the Capitol, though some of his important work here had the Raleigh Tavern for its locale. This historic inn is known in history as "Virginia's Cradle of Liberty"—duplicating Fanueil Hall in Boston. And George Washington helped to give it this significant name. The affairs with which he was closely identified at these two historic landmarks—the vital centers of political thought in Virginia—were those matters of public concern that served to evolve the legislator into the broader sphere of the statesman, who can originate and execute as well as legislate.

It was Washington who had persuaded Dinwiddie to offer a land bonus in addition to army pay to secure volunteers for recruiting his regiment in 1754, because men were disinclined to enlist. But for Washington, these claims, held legitimate by the veterans, would have been obliterated entirely. He got settlement, including the survey of the lands on the Ohio frontier, finally in 1772. When the Non-Importation Agreement was first formed following Botetourt's dissolution of the House of Burgesses in 1769, it was Washington who presented, at the Raleigh Tavern, George Mason's resolutions which were signed by 88 of the Burgesses and Richard Clarke, the Clerk. Mason was Washington's neighbor, but not a member of the House of Burgesses at the time. Washington's name stands number six on this roster of eminent names; those of

Randolph, the Speaker, and of Nicholas, the Treasurer heading the list as it is also embronzed on the memorial marker-stone of the Old Capitol, erected over forty years ago by the A. P. V. A.

Now when it became necessary to reorganize the Non-Importation Association and include the merchants with the burgesses, Washington seems to have been in the forefront of the movement. He attended four different meetings of the reorganizing committee at the Capitol in May 1770, sitting for hours at a time.

The climax of Washington's services in Williamsburg came in 1774, after Dunmore's dissolution of the House of Burgesses. He was one of the 25 burgesses who tarried in the Capital, met at the Raleigh, and arranged for calling the First Revolutionary Convention in August. He left Williamsburg on June 18th, returned to the convention on August 1st, and was chosen one of the six delegates to the Continental Congress which met in Philadelphia in September following. Washington's share of the expenses of the delegates, which he paid here in Williamsburg, was 90 pounds, 13 shillings and 9 pence. He also brought to this convention the famous declaration: "I will raise one thousand men, subsist them at my own expense, and march at their head for the relief of Boston." Here the widening horizon of his sympathies almost anticipated Patrick Henry's famous statement at Philadelphia a few weeks later: "I am no longer a Virginian; I am an American." (This according to Tyler: Richmond has also claimed this patriotic outburst of Washington, as spoken at St. John's Church.)

While at this historic first Revolutionary Convention, Washington dined at each one of his favorite places of entertainment: At the homes of the Speaker, the Treasurer, and the Attorney-General, and at Mrs. Davison's and Mrs. Campbell's boarding-houses, spending the evenings in his own lodgings. At nine o'clock on August 7th, we see him drive out of Williamsburg—not to return again until after seven long years of courageous battling for American freedom.

He then appears again with the victory of Independence for the 13 colony states within his grasp as he rides into Lafayette's camp west of Williamsburg at four o'clock on September 14th, 1781. He then promptly makes the George Wythe House his headquarters, while he plans the details for the Siege of Yorktown, a period of two weeks. Meanwhile, General Thomas Nelson, Jr.., successor to Jefferson as governor, occupied his gubernatorial chair in the camps of the several armies while he provisioned the troops. Washington's own command was encamped east of Williamsburg until the march on Yorktown began, September 28th.

For seven days Washington and several subordinate officers were with De Grasse at Lynnhaven Bay, aboard his flagship, the *Ville de Paris*, conferring with the admiral of the French fleet. A storm prevented their earlier return.

Three times in 1769 Washington had been the guest of George Wythe, dining with him as with other distinguished men. But his presence here in September, 1781, gives the Wythe House a radiant halo of its own, marking it as atypical, a real Washington shrine. Adding to this George Wythe home, which enshrines also college, church and Revolutionary associations: also these: The Blair, the Dinwiddie, the Bland, the Peyton Randolph, and the "Tazewell Hall" colonial houses as Washington landmarks, in this city we have (including the humble little Custis Kitchen) one dozen intact Washington shrines, restored where patriots from every State in the Union may receive inspiration from what the Father of His Country did or said here for the good of his fellowman while yet a novitiate in statecraft.

The success of all his efforts was signalized by his triumphant march from Yorktown after the fall of Cornwallis and the surrender of the British falchion, and the acclaim accorded him and his troops as they passed through this ancient capital city—even then no longer the Capital of Virginia; but already a shrine of liberty and memorialized through all the years until now as the very "Cradle of the Revolution" and the "Cradle of the Constitutional Government."

By his activities here in many of his earlier years, Washington helped to make Williamsburg great in the eyes of the world, and largely through Williamsburg, Virginia gave to the nation her own first warrior and her preeminent leader in state-craft—the patriot of lofty vision, uniting talent and service in his fatherhood of a future free country. His lifework is today the study of patriotic minds and the inspiration of future citizens, in their youth celebrating his birth from year to year, even as this antique city-chartered town is now the cynosure of a wondering world, in its colonial habiliments restored.

And when history beckons us to contemplate the past of these ancient homes and public buildings and men ask the reason why, like an echo from this hallowed ground itself comes the impressive reply: Great men dwelt and sojourned in service here, among whom stood foremost the forechosen chief of a nation yet unborn; and these memorial landmarks enshrine forever the honored name of the great and noble Washington. Inextricably and forever interwoven in the very woof and warp of Williamsburg's history is the name of Washington. And laden with the enduring power of his matchless name, may this ancient new-made city's Revolutionary atmosphere, as we breathe it today, inspire us all to unselfish deeds of public service, and may we thus truly honor the memory of Washington in Williamsburg.

JACK JOUETT'S RIDE

PROF. T. J. STUBBS, JR.

It was not until the beginning of 1781 that Virginia felt the pressure of actual invasion. Hitherto she had escaped it, although her seacoast was undefended, the country without military posts and population nearly drained of fighting material.

In 1779 Jefferson had succeeded Patrick Henry as Governor and in 1781 came the last scenes of the Revolution on the soil of Virginia.

It is difficult to convey an impression of the gloom and despondency of the country at this time. Never had the American cause been in a more desperate condition. Its resources had been drained almost completely; the army was in a wretched condition, poorly clothed, badly fed, and worse paid, exposed to cold, snow and wind, with no protection but old worn out coats and sometimes with but one blanket to three men. Such was the state of affairs when the British determined to invade Virginia. It is singular that they had not done so before. The state was defenseless and unprotected except by the militia composed of old men and boys.

The first expedition was under Benedict Arnold who had captured Richmond, ravaged the surrounding territory and then retired to Portsmouth. In the spring came Cornwallis up from the Carolinas. He had hoped by capturing and devastating the great rebel province to end the war victoriously. He was opposed by Lafayette who had been sent by Washington to defend Virginia with about 1500 men. Lafayette steadily refusing battle, retired toward the Rappahannock with Cornwallis following. Cornwallis learning that the Governor and the Legislature had assembled in Charlottesville, detached the famous Colonel Tarleton and sent him with about 250 men to capture them.

Tarleton was hunting big game, for the Governor was Jefferson and among the Legislators were Patrick Henry of "Give me liberty or death" fame; Richard Henry Lee who had introduced in the Continental Congress the resolutions which led to the Declaration of Independence; Benjamin Harrison, ancestor of two presidents; and Thomas Nelson, Jr., who had advocated armed opposition in 1775 and later spent his large fortune in equipping soldiers for the Continental Army. Jefferson had, of course, drafted the Declaration of Independence and Lee, Harrison and Nelson had signed it.

Tarleton having enjoined strict secrecy on his men and, moving cautiously was able to conceal his movements until he reached Cuckoo Tavern, Louisa County, between 9 and 10 o'clock at night on June 3rd.

It is here that Captain Jack Jouett, Jr., injected himself into the picture.

John Jouett, known to posterity as "Jack" was born in Albermarle County, Virginia, December 7th, 1754. He was the second son of Captain John and Mourning Jouett who owned the Swan Tavern at the county seat. The family was of Huguenot origin. Jack served in the Revolution as Captain in the State Militia, as did his father and three brothers, one of whom, Mathew, was killed at Brandywine. Why Jack happened to be in the neighborhood when the British Cavalrymen came we do not know, nor is it known how he found out or guessed their errand. One version of the story has it that several of the troopers entered the inn for a dram and that he overheard their plans from a rear room. Another says that he captured a dragoon and extracted from him the information that they were headed for Charlottesville. The latter version might easily have been true as he was a young Hercules and could have easily subdued any one man in the British troop. At any rate he determined to outride Tarleton and warn the Governor and Legislature. Fortunately, he was thoroughly familiar with the region and so could proceed by a different route from that taken by the British, which made him cut across country. He probably got under way about ten o'clock on his thoroughbred, which was said to be the best and fleetest of foot of any nag in seven counties. He had to go through what was a virtual wilderness, his progress being impeded by matted under-growth, tangled brush, overhanging vines, ravines and gullies. His face bore to the grave the scars left by the tree branches and low-hanging limbs. It is likely that it was moonlight, because if the night had been dark, he would probably have broken his neck and killed his horse at the speed he was riding. He must have rested several times on his forty-mile ride as no horse or rider could have covered so great a distance without stopping for a breath.

Dawn was breaking as he drew near Monticello at 4:30. The raiders were still far behind. Mr. Jefferson was aroused and told of his danger, after which he gave Jouett several glasses of his old ante-Volstead Madeira. Jack then hastened on to Charlottesville and warned the legislature. He had beaten the British by about three hours. Paul Revere's fifteen-mile jaunt over fairly good roads in the moonlight seems like the morning gallop of a school girl just learning to ride in comparison. Jouett, however, lacked a Longfellow.

Despite his timely warning, Mr. Jefferson came within a hair's breadth of being captured. He and his guests, some members of the Legislature, breakfasted at leisure, after which his guests joined the other legislators in town. Jefferson directed his wife and children to prepare to go to "Blenheim," the Carter home, some miles away and then spent nearly two hours gathering together his important papers. Being warned again by a neighbor, he sent his family off to Blenheim. He had directed his horse to be stationed at a point between Monticello and Carter's Mountain, which adjoins it. After a short while he took his telescope and walked a few rods up Carter's Mountain, but could see no enemies in Charlottesville, nor could he hear any approaching. Thinking he still had time to go back to the house he walked toward it, but soon missed his sword cane which had fallen from its sheath. Returning to the point whence he had surveyed the town a short while before, he found the sword and took another look through the telescope. This time he saw the troopers swarming through the streets. He instantly plunged through the woods and joined his family at Blenheim. He was not a moment too soon for Tarleton's men were already at Monticello. If he had not dropped the sword and gone back for it he would have walked straight into their hands. As the British did not know where to look for him they gave up the chase.

On the arrival of the raiders at Monticello an amusing incident occurred. Two faithful negro servants were busily engaged in hiding the silver and other valuables when the troopers reached the house. Martin, Jefferson's body servant, was handing the articles to Caesar through a trap door in the floor of the portico. When the soldiers loomed up before him, Martin dropped the trap door, shutting Caesar up in total darkness where he remained quaking until they left eighteen hours later.

In spite of the stories we have been brought up on about the ruin and devastation wreaked by Tarleton, he allowed nothing to be disturbed at Monticello. He could scarcely have been blamed had he chosen to confiscate the possessions of the man who had written the Declaration of Independence. Jefferson himself told a friend later that Tarleton "had behaved very genteelly with him."

The Legislature, warned by Jouett, hastily convened and as hastily adjourned to meet three days later in Staunton, forty miles to the west. Jouett went along to Staunton in company with General Stevens, a member of the Legislature, who had been recuperating from a wound received at the battle of Guilford Courthouse. As he was on leave from the army he was dressed as a farmer. Jack wore a scarlet coat and plumed hat, which was his eccentric custom. Tarleton's men in pursuit thought, naturally, that Jouett was an officer of high rank, and Stevens no officer at all. They therefore ignored the General who escaped into the woods and tried to capture Jouett, but he was too swift for them and galloped gaily away.

In recognition of his valuable services to the Governor, the Assembly and the Continental Army, the members of the Virginia Legislature voted Captain Jouett an "elegant" sword and a pair of pistols. The pistols were presented in 1783, but the sword was not delivered until 1803, nearly twenty-two years after the ride.

Jouett moved the next year to Mercer County, Kentucky. While *en route* from Virginia an amusing incident took place. Jouett and his companions passed a lonely cabin from which there came the cries of a woman. Jack rushed inside and found a man beating his wife. Thinking she was in need of help he knocked the man down. The lady, thereupon, picked up a long handled frying pan and smote Jouett such a hard blow on the head that the bottom was knocked out and the rim was driven down around his neck. Finding that it was not healthy to interfere on such occasions, Jack departed quickly and wore his strange necklace for thirty miles until he could find a blacksmith to file it off.

Two years after he arrived in Mercer County he married Sally Robards, sister-in-law of Mrs. Lewis Robards, who afterwards became Mrs. Andrew Jackson. He served in the Virginia Legislature for two terms and in the Kentucky Legislature for four terms. While in the Kentucky Legislature he was largely responsible for Kentucky's becoming a great live-stock raising state, leading the way in importing cattle and horses from England. He was serving his second term in the Virginia Legislature when Lewis Robards applied for a divorce and was mainly responsible for the passage of an act authorizing the courts to determine whether grounds for the divorce existed. Andrew Jackson, who had known Mrs. Robards for some years, being wrongly informed that an absolute divorce had been granted, married her not long afterwards. The divorce was not granted until two years later, after which the Jacksons had a second marriage performed.

Jouett entertained lavishly and was a close friend of many of the most eminent men of the day, including Andrew Jackson and Henry Clay.

Jouett died in Bath County, Kentucky, 1882, aged 67, and is supposed to have been buried there.

Several of Jouett's descendants are better known to the present generation than he. One was Matthew Harris Jouett, a noted portrait painter and a Captain in the War of 1812. Matthew had three sons who achieved military or naval distinctions. Among them was James Edward, ("Fighting Jim") who fought through the Mexican War and was particularly distinguished for his naval career in the War between the States. He was the officer at Mobile Bay to whom Farragut issued his famous order: "Damn the torpedoes, full speed ahead, Jouett!"

It is interesting to speculate as to how the history of America might have been affected had Tarleton succeeded in his mission. What would have been the fate of Jefferson, Henry, Lee and Nelson had they been captured? Jefferson, at least, might have been taken to England, tried as a traitor and hanged. It is certainly safe to assume that these prominent leaders in the Revolutionary movement would have been treated as harshly as any civilian Americans who could have fallen into the British hands. If the career of Jefferson alone had been cut short or materially altered at this period of his life, the history of the United States would have been profoundly affected. The capture of the author of the Declaration of Independence, three of its signers, and Patrick Henry would have been a severe blow to the struggling colonies when their fortunes were at such a low ebb.

Yet, the name of the man who prevented such a calamity is unknown to perhaps ninety percent of his fellow Virginians. We are glad to note, however, that his exploit is becoming better known each year.

If any of you feels burning within you the spark of poetic fire, here is at your hand material for a saga or a ballad which might make his name ring through the length and breadth of this land.

JOHN PAUL JONES, NAVAL GENIUS

Capt. George A. Mallison, USN, Retired

On October 3rd, 1779, John Paul Jones arrived in the roads off Texel on the ship *Serapis*, formerly of the British Navy, and news was given to the world of the sea battle between this vessel and the *Bon Homme Richard* in which the latter, though the victor, could not survive the wounds of battle and was of necessity abandoned one hour before she plunged beneath the surface and sank to her last resting place at the bottom of the North Sea.

It is, generally speaking, upon this sea battle, a remarkable one within itself, together with his operations on the *Ranger*, during which he made the Whitehaven raid and captured the British Sloop of War *Drake*, that his reputation as a seaman and fighter rests. These alone are sufficient to place him in the highest rank within this class, but, while it is freely admitted that he was a great seaman and fighter, the real life work of the man is so little known and understood, that with this admission usually comes the declaration to the effect that, after all, Jones was somewhat of a pirate.

An examination of biographies that seem to exhaust sources of information, with the exception of a few that may possibly be developed in the future, discloses a character, who, if not touched with genius, deserves a place professionally among the most exalted naval heroes. It discloses a man kindly considerate of others, punctilious where his own honor or that of his adopted country is concerned, yet candid and forgiving to his enemies, He had the capacity to plan in large matters and the daring to execute.

When once embarked in a campaign with a definite object in view he would cling tenaciously to the necessary plans for accomplishment, modified by contingencies, irrespective of criticisms in regard to rashness or timidity that may have been hurled at him. Timidity had no place in his character and this charge arose in the Russian campaign as the result of an intrigue to destroy his reputation. His sense of proportion was not distorted by personal considerations when he was engaged in naval operations.

On June 14, 1777, Congress adopted the national flag and appointed Jones to command of the *Ranger*. On September 6th, 1777, he was directed to sail for a French port and report to the Commissioners (one of whom was Franklin) on his arrival. He was to be given command of the frigate *Indien* being built in Amsterdam under the direction of Silas Deane. On November 2nd, 1777, he hoisted the Stars and Strips on the *Ranger* and sailed for France, arriving in the River Loire near Nantes on December 2nd, 1777, just too late to be the first to give the news of Burgoyne's surrender.

The British learning that the *Indien* was being built for America, the Dutch turned the ship over to France to avoid trouble, and on January 16th, 1778, the Commissioners ordered Jones to cruise in the *Ranger*. When off Quiberon Bay on February 13th, he sent a boat in to ask the Admiral if he would return his salute. "He answered that he would return to me as the Senior American Continental Officer in Europe the same salute which he was authorized by his Court to return to an Admiral of Holland, or of any other Republic, which was four guns less than the salute given. I hesitated at this, for I had demanded gun for gun, but after a very particular inquiry, on the 14th, finding that he had really told the truth, I was induced to accept his offer; the more so as it was in fact an acknowledgment of America's independence." (De Koven, Vol. 1, p. 263.)

Owing to contrary winds the *Ranger* did not get in until after sunset when he saluted *La Motte Picquet* with 13 guns which he returned with nine. To clinch the matter, he went in the following day in the *Independence*, saluted the Admiral and was in turn saluted with nine guns.

This was the first salute to the American Flag and the French Admiral had at the time no knowledge of the treaty which had been concluded at Paris on the 6th of the month.

On April 22nd he made his descent on Whitehaven. Leaving a party at the landing to burn the shipping, the party with him surprised and secured the sentries and spiked the guns at the two forts. When he returned to the landing just about daylight, he found the other party had done nothing. So securing a light from a nearby house he set fire to a large ship and reembarked on his own vessel.

Immediately after the Whitehaven raid he sailed to the entrance of Kircudbright Bay and landed a party at the gardens of Saint Mary's Isle for the purpose of capturing Selkirk. Finding him absent he wished to withdraw, but compromised with the plundering spirit of his officers and men to the extent of permitting them to take the plate, provided nothing else was taken and they conducted themselves with propriety.

Jones purchased this plate and it was finally returned to Selkirk. "A very brief letter from Lord Daer to his father (Selkirk), written from Paris in the year 1791, relates his meeting with Jones at the house of the American envoy to Paris, with an expression of surprise that the black-browed marauder was in reality so quiet and estimable an individual." (De Koven, Vol. 1, p. 324.)

His First Lieutenant, Simpson, was mutinous and caused so much trouble that Jones was compelled to so maneuver his ship as to invite an action on the part of the British Sloop of War *Drake* and thus force his crow to fight in self-defense. On April 24th, about an hour before sunset, he fought this ship and captured her.

The two vessels were repaired and Simpson placed in command of the *Drake*, but he was shortly afterward suspended for deliberate disobedience of orders and replaced by Second Lieutenant Elijah Hall. The ships arrived off Brest with two hundred prisoners. Jones' draft on the Commissioners for 24,000 livres was dishonored due to the machinations of Arthur Lee, the friend of the mutinous Simpson. He was, however, enabled to care for his crew and prisoners because of money borrowed from his French friends on his own personal credit.

Jones was again promised the *Indien* but the strained relations between the English and the French caused the Dutch to put obstacles in the way of her completion and delivery, and as he was about to return to America the French Court asked the Commissioners to keep him in Europe. He suggested plans for operations against England which, though approved, came to naught because of too much publicity. He was promised a French frigate only to be again disappointed when she was given to Frenchmen, and permission to sail with D'Orvilliers on a cruise arrived too late to be availed of. Through the contrivances of Arthur Lee, the *Ranger* was given to the mutinous Simpson who, on arriving in the United States with the ship, was relieved if his command and was not subsequently employed in the navy. Thus Jones found himself without a ship and unemployed, and the attempt was made by his enemies to produce the impression that he no longer enjoyed the confidence of the Commissioners or the Court.

Although in these days harsh and extreme penalties were imposed when action was taken in the name of discipline, the orderly discipline with which we are familiar did not then exist, and the spirit of unrest amid insubordination was manifest as the result of long-continued wars and as a harbinger of the Revolution to break in the not far distant future, Under the circumstances the French Minister of Marine did not dare give him a French ship. Even an expedition proposed by Jones against the English Baltic fleet, and which he was to carry out, was hastily organized and attempted under French auspices and resulted in a total failure.

In recognition of his merit, and realizing that he had been badly treated, it was determined that a command should be had for him even if it were necessary to purchase a vessel for that purpose. Unfortunately French finances were in a very straitened condition and the individual who had the money for the enterprise was accepted as sponsor for the expedition. There was in contemplation a squadron composed of several vessels to be commanded by Jones, who was to be accompanied by Lafayette with a body of troops to be used in landing expeditions on the coasts of Britain. It was the intention to harass the English Coast, destroy her commerce and strike at the Baltic Merchant Fleet.

The squadron actually consisted of the flagship *Bon Homme Richard*, so named for Jones' friend Franklin, one of the commissioners, the *Alliance*, the *Vengeance*, the *Pallas* and the *Cerf*.

The *Richard* was an old converted Indianman with rotten timbers and equipped with such odds and ends of ordnance as Jones could pick up here and there. Four-fifths of the ship's crew was composed of a collection of Portuguese, Malays, and Swedes with about one hundred English prisoners. Fortunately he was able to enlist a number of American seamen from prisoners arriving in France from Britain, among whom was Richard Dale who was made First Lieutenant. Lafayette had been withdrawn from the expedition and ordered to join his regiment, but the Minister of Marine sent on board a force of marines under two officers recommended by Lafayette.

The *Alliance* was an excellent new ship of her class which had been given to Landais, a Frenchman, to command in compliment to France. It developed that Landais was a French naval officer who had been cashiered. The *Alliance* brought Lafayette to Europe. Lafayette wrote in regard to Landais, that "he considered it inadvisable that any military should be put upon the *Alliance*, for he had had a full experience of Landais' eccentricities during his passage across the Atlantic, and he gave as his reason that he feared that Captain Landais would get into trouble with his officers." (De Koven, Vol. 1, p. 405.) Whatever ill-balance mentally Landais may have suffered prior thereto, he was unquestionably insane when he was forcibly removed from command during his return voyage to America.

The *Vengeance* was a small brig; the *Pallas*, a merchant ship purchased by M. de Chaumont and fitted with 32 12-pounders; and the *Cerf* was a cutter.

The remarkable cruise in which these vessels took part began on August 14, 1779. Just before sailing, the generalissimo of the expedition, Chaumont, required all the captains to sign what was called the "Concordat"; the captains acted under the brevet of the

United States, "but were in no manner required to yield obedience to their commander, except as it suited their discretion." (De Koven, Vol. 1, p. 425). Unquestionably Jones pocketed his pride and acquiesced in these humiliating conditions in the hope that he would he able to prevail upon the commanders of his consorts to cooperate with him in a great measure, if not completely. The only alternative was an abandonment of the expedition.

On August 23rd Jones' barge, which was towing a prize to keep her off the rocks, cut the hawser and deserted. A second boat, manned with Americans, sent to chase the first boat was lost in the fog, fired upon by the *Cerf* which had been sent out to look for her, and was eventually captured. The *Cerf* deserted and returned to France two days later. In the meantime, Landais on the *Alliance* ignored Jones entirely and disappeared when his whims prompted.

Jones determined to attack at Leith, Frith of Fourth, but when he had convinced the captains of the *Pallas* and *Vengeance* of the feasibility of the enterprise, adverse weather conditions prevented, and the people of Edinburgh having taken measures for their protection, thus eliminating the element of surprise, the attack was abandoned and Jones made for the last rendezvous off Flamborough Head, arriving there September 22nd, 1779. On the morning of the 23rd, while giving chase to a brigantine, he sighted a larger ship to which he gave chase, sending an aimed boat under second Lieutenant Henry Lunt after the brigantine. It turned out that he had come in contact with the Baltic fleet of 41 sail under convoy of the *Serapis* and the *Countess of Scarborough*. The merchant ships made for harbor. The Englishman Pearson was not loath to fight and soon the slow-sailing *Richard* was within hailing distance of the *Serapis*. Landais with the *Alliance* was beyond range of the guns to the windward and the *Vengeance* and *Pallas* were near the *Countess of Scarborough*.

At the first discharge of a broadside two of the 18-pounders on the *Richard* burst, wrecking a part of the main deck above, blowing a hole in the ship's side, and killing nearly all the men near the guns. The *Serapis* having been maneuvered into a position to rake the *Richard*, the bow of the latter struck the former and Jones attempted to tie up to the *Serapis* and board her, but he was repulsed and his grapnels went overboard, The gun deck between the mainmast and the stern was completely shattered, all guns were silenced but three 9-pounders on the quarterdeck, and the ship was practically a wreck at the end of an hour. The *Serapis* maneuvering for a position of advantage, Jones so held the *Richard* that the jib-boom of the *Serapis* fouled his main rigging. The *Serapis* dropped anchor expecting the headway of the *Richard* to clear the ships, but Jones lashed her jib-boom to the rigging and finally the ships swung to wind and tide, side to side, bow to stern, and yards interlocked, the fluke of the *Serapis'* anchor hooking into the *Richard's* quarter. The men in the tops of the *Richard* swept the decks of the *Serapis*, driving their men to the gundeck where they were firing through the *Richard* with broadside guns. Fires were started on both ships and during this confusion the Master-at-Arms, understanding Jones and Dale had been killed, came up to haul down the flag, but was driven below by Jones. It was at this time Pearson asked: "If he had struck," and Jones replied, "I have not yet begun to fight."

The men had been dislodged from the maintop of the *Serapis* and it had been occupied by our men. About this time Landais passed in the *Alliance* and gave the Richard a full broadside. The Master-at-Arms, convinced that the ship was sinking, released the English prisoners who were met by Jones and put at the pumps of the *Richard* under Dale. Shortly afterward an American, crawling out on the main yard of the *Richard*, dropped a hand-grenade down the main hatch of the *Serapis*, resulting in an explosion which caused the loss of 20 lives and produced a panic which was added to when Landais again appeared and poured a discharge of grape into both ships. The *Serapis* struck at 10:30 o'clock P.M.

The *Pallas* alone captured the *Countess of Scarborough*.

The boat that had been sent out to chase the brigantine did not rejoin the ship until after the engagement, thus Jones was deprived of the services of the Americans in this boat, Henry Lunt its officer, and his brother, Cutting Lunt, who had been captured in the boat lost on the west coast of Britain.

Jones introduced an innovation in sea-fighting, which was subsequently adopted by Nelson. It was the use of a great number of riflemen aloft and a plentiful expenditure of hand-grenades. It was to the extended use of the rifle and hand-grenade that he owed his victory in this instance.

It was Jones' wish to return to a French port, but in obedience to orders from the Commissioners, he made for Texel where he arrived safely on October 3rd, 1779. Here he was to meet with new disappointments and be subjected to further attempts to humiliate him, but he bore up bravely under adversity, as was usual with him, and in the end brought some good to America by his visit.

The Commissioners had three objects in view in sending Jones to Texel—(1) to convoy 100 vessels loaded with military supplies to the French fleet at Brest, (2) to claim the long-promised *Indien*, and (3) by presence of the squadron, to force the Dutch to take sides with the colonies.

Chaumont, the generalissimo of the expedition, again talked too much, and in consequence the British Ambassador became aware of the proposal to carry supplies to the French fleet and with the backing of a British fleet in the offing, made demands in regard to the surrender to him of the prisoners and prizes taken by Jones.

Diplomatic complications arose and the final outcome was that Franklin directed Jones to turn over the prisoners and prizes to the French Government and assume command of the *Alliance*. This ship had been left by Landais, who had been relieved of command, in a deplorable condition from the point of view of both materiel and personnel, but Jones had other troubles. Official Holland had become hostile to him and the States-General authorized the Dutch naval officer at Texel to use force in driving him to sea. It seems that official Holland at this time not only refused to do anything that might be construed as a recognition of the Colonies, but went out of its way to heap indignities on Jones as its representative, so the Dutch Admiral asked Jones to show his commission from his majesty, hoist the French colors and fire a salute. Jones told him he would fly the American colors until directed to do otherwise by Franklin. The French Minister of Marine offered to supply him with a French letter of marque, and Jones was asked to represent that this was issued at the beginning of the cruise. Jones indignantly refused and defied both England and Holland.

In a letter to his friend Williams, Jones said, "They are not rich enough to buy the 'Pirate' Paul Jones." (De Koven, Vol. II, p. 49.) With all Americans on the *Alliance*, he received peremptory orders from the Dutch Admiral to depart. He replied he would go when the pilot thought proper to carry him out and that he was indignant at daily threats and annoyances and that if he met the Admiral at sea, "he should force him to answer for his insults and menaces" (De Koven, Vol. II, p. 54.)

On December 27th, 1779, with a gale off shore he dashed out of the harbor and escaped, the English ships having been driven off shore. With ships looking for him everywhere in nearby waters, he went through the English Channel "in full sight of Downs, took a good look at the English fleet anchored at Portsmouth, and so out to the ocean." (De Koven, II, p. 56.)

On January 16, 1780, the *Alliance* being in need of repairs, he entered the Spanish port of Corunna.

What he did at Texel and his popularity with the Dutch "was the direct cause of involving the Dutch Government in the general war with England, and of forcing the Dutch Government's ultimate acknowledgment of American independence." (De Koven, II, p. 59.) On February 10th, 1780, the *Alliance* arrived at L'Orient.

"In a letter, of May 30th (1780) to the President of Congress, M. de Sartine thus communicates his sovereign's desires (to invest Jones with the Cross of Military Merit, never before given to one not a subject, and with title of Chevalier) to the American Government, with the express statement that his Majesty would be ready to approve any of Jones' projects which should be supported by Congress." (De Koven, II, p. 79.)

In spite of the fact that Franklin was desirous of having Landais sent home quietly for court-martial and thus avoid the washing of dirty linen for the amusement of Paris gossips, Arthur Lee contrived, by misrepresenting to the crew of the *Alliance* that they would not get their prize money unless they returned to America with their old captain, to make it possible for Landais to seize the *Alliance*. This he did while Jones was absent in an effort to get prize money for the crew. The French stood ready to fire on the ship and sink her, if necessary, in order to obtain custody of Landais whom they were anxious to punish for loss of French lives when he fired on the *Richard*. However, they deferred to Jones who would not give the order to fire. Finally, July 8, 1780, the *Alliance* sailed "with the loyal men of the *Richard* who had refused to obey Landais' orders confined in the hold in irons and with Mr. Lee's carriage and personal effects, although war material and stores on board had to be removed for this purpose." (De Koven).

Jones finally set sail on December 8th, 1780, in the *Ariel* loaded with much needed stores, arrived in Delaware Bay February 4th, 1781, and was in Philadelphia on the 18th of the same month.

February 27th, 1781, Congress passed a Resolution commendatory of Jones and authorized his acceptance of the Order of Military Merit. This was done two days before Maryland adopted the Articles of Confederation by which Articles, then becoming effective, the acceptance of such an Order would have been forbidden. On April 14th, 1781, after due investigation of his conduct of affairs in Europe, Jones was given a vote of thanks by Congress. On June 26th, 1781, Congress gave him command of the *America*, the largest 74-gun ship in the world, and he proceeded to Portsmouth to complete her and fit her out. The French fleet under the Marquis de Vaudreuil having lost the ship *Magnifique* on the rocks while entering Boston harbor, Congress in their generosity gave the *America* to the French. Jones, again disappointed, delivered her to Chevalier de Martigne on November 5th, 1781, the day she was launched. An effort was again made to get the *Indien* for him but failed. The ship was finally captured by the enemy, and thus for all time disposed of so far as Jones was concerned. He was authorized by Congress to take service with the French fleet under Vaudreuil. He joined the *Triomphante*, but the operations in the

West Indies came to naught. Congress having announced a cessation of hostilities, he took the first vessel sailing for America and arrived in Philadelphia May 18, 1782.

Congress by Resolution on November 1, 1783, appointed Jones agent to France to collect the prize money for prizes taken by the officers and crews under his command. The *Washington* was purchased to take him to France and he sailed from Philadelphia on November 10, 1783. He successfully concluded the prize negotiations with France, and on September 5, 1785, the money was paid into Jones' hands, but the Board of Treasury through Jefferson, who had taken the place of Franklin, directed this amount to be retained in Europe for diplomatic missions. Jones' commission of 5% which Congress had allowed him was to be replaced by his claim for expenses and even this was not paid him.

Jones had to go to America for funds. Congress approved his accounts on October 11, 1787, allowing the full amount, and on the 16th of the same month awarded him a gold medal.

Henry Sherburne (2nd edition—*Life of Paul Jones*) in collecting letters, was astonished to learn in 1837 what Jefferson and the Board of Treasury had done with the prize money. Nothing had been paid to the officers and men. Bills passed in 1846 and 1848 for payment were not finally carried out until 1861. (De Koven, II, p. 265.)

Negotiations with Denmark, against which country there was a claim in connection with prizes taken into her ports, were transferred to diplomatic channels at Paris and Jones took service with Catherine of Russia. He arrived at Prince Potemkin's headquarters on June 1st, 1788, and was given command of a squadron for service against the Turks in the Black Sea. The success of the operations here was due to Jones who carried on under most adverse conditions. The jealousy and treachery of his associates, culminating in false reports in regard to his operations, resulted in his being recalled to St. Petersburg ostensibly for an independent command in the Baltic. He was kept waiting in St. Petersburg and during this time a final plot to destroy his character took form and he was dismissed from Catherine's service, though it was given out that he was on leave of absence. He was finally saved from the stigma of this plot against his character through the efforts of the French Ambassador to St. Petersburg, who uncovered the plot against Jones and laid bare the falseness of the accusations against him.

Jones died in Paris on July 18th, 1792. He appended to his will the signature, "Paul Jones, a citizen of the United States." (De Koven, II, p. 428.)

Jones' place of birth, Kircudbright, near the Irish Sea, and his early surroundings, were such that it was not unnatural he should have drifted into the life of an adventurer upon the sea. Born John Paul, at the age of 12 or 14 years he was apprenticed to a Mr. Younger and made his first voyage on the *Friendship* to Virginia. He subsequently received an appointment as a midshipman in the British Navy in which position he served for several years, but finding that promotion did not depend upon merit alone, he resigned. He began his career on reentering the merchant service as third mate on a slaver and subsequently served as chief mate on another slaver. The slave trades though unquestionably very lucrative, proved distasteful to John Paul, who severed his connection with it and in consequence found himself in Jamaica in 1768 without employment. Here for a time he was a player in the theatrical company of John Moody.

He engaged passage to Scotland on the *John of Kircudbright*. During the voyage the captain and first officer died of fever and he brought the ship in safely. His management of affairs so appealed to the owners that he was given command of the vessel.

He was rapidly progressing in his commercial ventures when two incidents occurred that had a marked effect on his subsequent career. On the second voyage of the *John*, while at Tobago, he had occasion to flog a member of the crew. This man and John Paul were from the same neighborhood in Scotland. On a subsequent voyage this man died of fever, but malicious tongues, without the slightest justification, attributed his death to flogging. Subsequently, at the same island, in his own ship (he had a partnership with Archibald Stuart, Esq., planter in the island,) he killed a mutinous seaman in self-defense. He had by deferring payment of the crew until completion of the return voyage antagonized the crew and incited a spirit of mutiny, but the killing of the drunken, mutinous leader was forced on John Paul and was a last resort in self- defense. On the advice of his friends (these seem to have included the Lieutenant Governor and the Judge) he left the island. This was some time about or just subsequent to April 1773.

His next appearance is at Martha's Vineyard in September 1773, where he put into Holmes' Hole for the burial of an officer of the vessel he commanded, evidently a Spanish corsair or something of the kind. At this time John Paul appears under the name of Jones. After leaving this ship he made his way to Edenton, N. C., looking for James Smith with whom he had been associated during this period of his career. James was the brother of Robert Smith who was an associate of Joseph Hewes. In Halifax, N. C., early in 1775, Jones met Willie Jones, who befriended him and introduced him to Hewes.

John Paul seems to have retained the name Jones, which he adopted as an alias in his troubles, in compliment to Willie Jones, his benefactor, and after he found it was agreeable to him that he should do so. It seems probable that Jones disclosed to Willie Jones and Joseph Hughes, if not to Franklin, substantial information in regard to the one and a half years of his life about which so little is known.

Through the influence of Joseph Hughes, member of the Continental Congress and one of the Naval Committee, Jones secured an appointment as Lieutenant in the Navy in December 1775. He modestly thought that service in a subordinate position under competent officers would fit him for future command. Service under the incompetent Hopkins and association with others must soon have convinced him there were few from whom he could learn. He was commissioned captain of the *Providence* by Hopkins on May 10, 1776, and Hancock, President of the Continental Congress, issued to him a regular captain's commission, dated August 8, 1776, the first granted subsequent to the Declaration of Independence.

He performed many valuable services before he assumed command of the *Ranger*, capturing many prizes, among them store ships with supplies and equipment much needed by our army, and he inflicted heavy damage on the fisheries off Newfoundland.

The career of privateer was so much more lucrative than service in the Navy, on account of the small pay and small share of prize money given in the latter, that it was difficult to enlist crews for the Naval service. In order to secure a crew for the *Ranger* Jones personally made provision for the families of the men to the extent of one-half of their wages monthly and made personally to them certain advances for themselves.

In the disturbed conditions of the day there were adventurers operating upon the sea whose activities would now be considered beyond the pale of the law. There were operations carried on at that time partaking of the nature of war. In so far as depredations upon commerce were concerned, with all shades of gradation from complete authorization of a national government to that character of plain piracy which was even then beyond the pale of the law.

It is absolutely inconsistent that a man of the character of John Paul Jones should ever have been a pirate in the modern sense, either in spirit or in deed, and a proper clarification of this phase of his life should be undertaken by some competent person as a final tribute to a character deserving of the highest respect and praise.

BENEDICT ARNOLD

Hon. John Weymouth

Some months ago when a member of your organization invited me to address you on the subject of one of Washington's general's, I surprised him, perhaps, as well as myself, by choosing Benedict Arnold as my theme. There were many reasons for this choice—first, he was pictured in my mind as only a traitor. Whatever I may have learned about his earlier career in my youth had been clouded by the events of his later years, so I wanted an excuse to find out more about him. Second, he was certainly the most picturesque figure of his time, not excepting Anthony Wayne or Ethan Allen, or General Putnam, who are chiefly remembered because of certain more or less isolated heroic events. No one of them, however, was as consistently heroic a figure as Arnold. Whatever may be said about him, wherever he was there was action, energy, glamour.

Sometimes it appears that our methods of arriving at moral and spiritual values are all wrong. A little late repentance apparently outweighs so much sin; a little late sinning outweighs so much of fine straight living. A man lives a fine, clean life for forty or fifty years; but suddenly through indiscretion or impulse or the stress of a great emotion, he commits an evil deed and all of the noble things of his life are forgotten. On the other hand, a man may live beyond the pale of respectable society for forty or fifty years; and by virtue of a belated, and often times, a thoroughly scared repentance, die amid the saints. It is not altogether fair; and it is also not a bit understandable. But I am not apologizing for Arnold. I am simply thinking out loud.

Perhaps the Captain captured by Arnold in his Virginia raid was nearly just when he was asked by Arnold what would happen to him if he (Arnold) were ever captured, and replied: "They would cut off the leg that was wounded at Quebec and Saratoga, and bury it with the honors of war, and the rest of you they would hang on a gibbet."

Among the authorities which I have consulted is Headley's *Washington and His Generals*. While the story of Arnold is both well and sympathetically written, I fear this historian falls into the same inexcusable error that many others do, that is, attempting to prove that all that a man subsequently develops into may be attributed to certain boyish traits or events which inevitably pointed the way. Parson Weems used this method of accounting for Washington's greatness by the cherry tree incident. (I never took much stock in that story. In the first place, the manner of its telling made the boy an insufferable little prig; and furthermore, there was nothing unusual or remarkable about it. Nearly all the boys I have known would have refused to lie about cutting the tree.) Headley proceeds upon this thesis—Arnold, when a boy, would rob bird's nests of their young and then torture the young birds; he would scatter broken glass where the school children passed barefooted; and he would grab a water wheel at the grist mill and go around with it—ergo he betrayed his country at forty. Well, it doesn't happen so. I have seen too many sanctimonious boys grow up into rascals, and too many mischievous scamps grow up into useful men to believe that it is true. Yet, it may be that the "germs of all moral evil are in all human hearts."

Arnold evidently possessed a temper that he could not govern, as well as a restless energy that swept him along with the force of a torrent. He was a reckless, daring soldier of fortune, with a love of adventure who cared not where his adventures led him. If he did not possess all of the positive qualities of leadership, he at least had something that impelled men to follow where he led.

He was born in Norwich, Connecticut, May 3, 1740; and was therefore a mature man of 35 when the Battle of Bunker Hill was fought. He had a good education, and had been apprenticed to a druggist, and at sixteen enlisted in the army. Later he left the army and commenced business as an apothecary in New Haven. He prospered in business and accumulated property. This he later lost and was forced to go through bankruptcy. Then the Revolutionary War came on—at which time Arnold was the Captain of a militia company in New Haven called the Governor's Guards. When news came of the Battles of Lexington and Concord, Arnold made a fiery speech, called for volunteers and without waiting for higher authority, forced the selectmen to deliver the keys to the magazine, where his company helped themselves to ammunition and marched to Cambridge. He there waited on the Committee of Safety, proposed to head an expedition to Ticonderoga, obtained permission to do so, and raised 400 men; but an expedition had already started under Ethan Allen. Arnold wanted to take charge of this expedition, and claimed authority for so doing, but he decided not to press his claims; and he and Allen entered the Fort together. When Allen was appointed Commander in Chief of the Garrison, Arnold became enraged and complained to the legislature of Massachusetts. His energy was resistless. With 50 men he moved forward upon St. John's, sailing down the lake with one schooner, he seized a British sloop, destroyed five batteries and captured four others.

At this time he ran into the first of the series of charges and investigations which pursued him throughout his career. It would appear that this proceeding, which was instituted by the Legislature of Massachusetts, was rather irregular, and he was rightfully indignant over it. He had borne himself bravely; there was nothing in his conduct to justify it and he had spent more than a hundred pounds out of his own funds for the public good, as he expressed it. He thereupon resigned his command and hastened to Cambridge. Soon after his arrival at Cambridge, Washington decided to send an Army through the forests of Maine and New Hampshire to Quebec. This expedition was placed under the command of Arnold with the rank of Colonel. It was no inconsiderable undertaking—but Arnold jumped at it. Morgan, with his Virginia riflemen was in the party—likewise Aaron Burr. Looking back upon this expedition in the light of all that happened, it may seem foolhardy;

but Quebec was defenseless, and the capture of such a position would have tremendous moral effect. Time does not permit us to detail an account of this hazardous journey. Sufficient it is to say that it tested the moral and physical qualities of those who participated in it as few things could have done. Paths must be cut; long and tedious portages made; the rigors of a north country winter endured. As an example of the hardships they suffered, I quote: (Headley pages 106 and 107):

"Again the tents were struck, and the disordered line pressed forward; but scarcely had it got under way before it began to rain. Dark and angry clouds swept the heavens pouring an incessant torrent on the drenched and toil-worn army, while the tree-tops swayed and groaned in the blast, making the somber wilderness ten-fold gloomier than before. For three days and nights it rained without cessation, till the Dead River began to show signs of life and energy. The swollen waters went surging by, but still the boats were urged on and upward. But one night, just as the wearied soldiers had landed and lain down on the wet leaves to rest, a roar like that of the ocean was heard, and the next moment the sudden flood swept over the whole ground of the encampment. Instantly all was confusion; men hurried about in the storm and darkness, and anxious orders and shouts and cries mingled in with the roar of the torrent. When daylight broke over the scone, it was enough to fill the bravest heart with discouragement. Boats had drifted into the forest, and as far as the eye could reach the level ground was one broad lake, out of which rose the dark stems of the trees, like an endless succession of columns, while shattered trunks and logs went floundering by on the turbid waters, which had risen eight feet perpendicular in the last nine hours. But Arnold could not wait for the stream to subside, for provisions were getting short and so he launched his army upon its turbulent bosom. Through the half submerged forest they pulled and shoved their boats until at length seven, caught in the eddying waters, were upset at once, and all they contained lost. This disaster reduced still further the scanty supply of provisions, while thirty miles more across the mountain were yet to be traversed to reach the head of the

Chaudiere River. They had not yet get on the northern slope, and only twelve days provisions remained."

As has been truly said—men may do such things in a retreat, but seldom in advancing after an enemy. The march to Quebec is a monument to the American Soldier, and to Arnold, the leader. The sequel—well, the attack upon Quebec failed. The gallant Montgomery was killed; Arnold received a shattered leg. For his gallant conduct Congress promoted him to Brigadier General.

In the meantime the British had constructed a fleet at St. John's with which to advance on Crown Point and Ticonderoga. After some difficulty a small fleet consisting of one sloop, three schooners, and five galleys were manned and placed under Arnold's command. With this fleet he set sail in August 1776, and after looking about finally chose Valcour Island in the northern part of Lake Champlain as the place to make a stand. This island was about parallel with the shore, with a deep channel opening towards the south. In the upper end of this Channel Arnold moored his ships. He had no way of getting out except through the English ships, though he could not be flanked. The British fleet approached. It contained in all 73 boats, with 700 seamen and 93 guns. Nothing daunted—Arnold gave battle; and there followed one of the most heroic, as well as the most dramatic, naval engagements over recorded in the history of man.

I quote from Headley (pages 113, 114, 116):

"The light clouds trooping over the sky—the quiet nook in which the fleet lay at anchor—the embosoming forest—the crowds of shouting, swarthy savages on the shore, all added strange interest to the scene; and that October sun, as it rolled towards the western hills, looked down on as brave a battle as was ever fought. The smoke, lifted by the north wind, rolled sluggishly up the lake, leaving open and unobscured the contending fleets as they thus lay and vomited forth fire on each other. The *Congress* and *Washington* galleys received the weight of the shock. Arnold, in the former, with two eighteen-pounders, two twelves, and six sixes, fought like a desperado. Seeing the dreadful odds against him, and maddened at the thought of defeat, he seemed to scoff at death. Cheering his men on by his thrilling words, and still more by his fierce courage, he maintained the fight hour after hour with a tenacity that nothing seemed able to shake. With his vessel riddled through and through, and filled with the dead, he still maintained his ground. Having no good engineers, he pointed his own guns, and multiplied himself with the dangers that encompassed him. Now casting his stern eye along his line of shattered boats, and now along his heated cannon, to make the shots tell—blackened with powder and smoke, he bore up for five mortal hours in the driving tempest. The water was churned into foam around him by the raining balls—his mainmast had been struck twice, his rigging was cut into fragments—he had received seven shots between wind and water, and been hulled twelve times; yet, still he refused to stir and seemed resolved to sink at his anchors A more gallant crew never rallied around a brave commander and though thinned and wasted, stood ready to go down at their post." . . .

"Thus hour after hour he struggled in this unequal contest, until at length other boats of the enemy arrived, and advanced to the attack. With seven vessels around him, hemming him in and pouring in broadside after broadside, he still disdained to surrender. In the very center of this fleet, covering him with a cloud of canvas, and drawing their circle of fire nearer and nearer every moment, he stood like a tiger at bay. For four terrible hours he had continued this unusual combat, and now a perfect wreck, he saw his vessel must inevitably be lost. But scorning to fall into the hands of the enemy, he put forth one of those great and desperate efforts for which he was remarkable, and breaking fiercely through the ships, run his galley and four gondolas ashore in a small creek and set fire to them. He then ordered the marines to leap overboard, musket in hand, and wade to the beach, and there fire at the small boats if they ventured to approach. For himself, he remained all alone aboard his burning galley, with his flags flying over his head. Enveloped in smoke, he stood and watched the fierce flames as they gained on the vessel, until they be advanced too far to be extinguished, and then sprung into the water and joined his men on shore."

As a leader and a fighting man, he was amphibious. Given the opportunity, he did the rest. Arnold passed the winter of 1777 at Providence, make preparations to raise militia to attack Rhode Island. At this time, in spite of his proven military valor and experience, Congress created five new Major Generals (Sterling, Mifflin, St. Clair, Stephen and Lincoln) without including him in the number; and all of them were his juniors—one of them from the militia. It was an act of the grossest injustice—Washington was astonished and distressed when he heard it and wrote Arnold, begging him not to do anything hastily. Arnold replied in a dignified vein: "Congress undoubtedly have a right of promoting those whom, from their abilities and their long and arduous services, they esteem most deserving. Their promoting junior officers to the rank of major-generals I view as a very civil way of requesting my resignation, as unqualified for the office I hold. My commission was conferred unsolicited, and received with pleasure only as a means of serving my country. With equal pleasure I resign it when I can no longer serve my country with honor. The person who, void of the nice feelings of honor, will tamely condescend to give up his right, and retain a commission at the expense of his reputation, I hold as a disgrace to the army, and unworthy of the glorious cause in which we are engaged."

Arnold unquestionably had sufficient and justifiable reasons for resigning from the army and surrendering his commission. Washington requested an explanation from Congress, but no sufficient reason was forthcoming, and Washington practically told Arnold so—so Arnold determined to seek redress from Congress in person. On his way to Philadelphia he passed through Connecticut just after Governor Tryon had burned Danbury. Immediately he forgot his wrongs at the prospect of a fight and joined General Silliman and Wooster who were following the enemy. Wooster was mortally wounded early in the combat, and Arnold really took command. He made a stand at Ridgefield at a place in a narrow road, threw up a barricade of carts, wagons and logs and made his stand behind this barricade. The little band was overwhelmed—500 against 2000—but it put up a gallant fight. Arnold's horse was shot under him. A British soldier rushed upon Arnold as he was down, rushed upon him with the bayonet. Arnold watched him approach coolly, took out his pistol, made sure of his aim and killed him instantly.

Congress with rare consistence, conferred upon him the rank of Major General; but still kept him under his five juniors. Washington gave him command of the army on the North River. The Board of War gave him a hearing, and pronounced all the accusations against him false, and declared that he had been "cruelly end groundlessly aspersed." Congress confirmed this report, but refused to restore his rank.

He was then placed in command of the army around Philadelphia. He still withheld his resignation, though his lost appointment placed him under a man whom he really should have ranked. Congress refused to restore his rank, and he asked permission of General Schuyler to retire from the Army—both Schuyler and Washington urged him to continue, which he agreed to do until the immediate danger was over.

He joined the army of Gates just before the Battle of Saratoga. Arnold commanded the left division of the Army; Gates the right. Burgoyne's army approached. Arnold urged Gates to advance and give battle, which the latter finally reluctantly consented to do. Arnold directed the battle, inspired the troops, and was everywhere on the field, threatening to cut the English lines in two. Gates was never on the field of battle at any time; and in his report to Congress refrained from saying one word in praise of Arnold or his division. General Burgoyne, however, in his testimony given afterwards, before the House of Commons, maintained that his plan of attack had been utterly defeated by the bold and skillful tactics of "Mr." Arnold. They had it hot and heavy. Then Gates took Arnold's division away from him and gave it to General Lincoln. In the fighting of October 7th he was without a command. He heard the roar of the guns; he chafed under his restraint; and at last, when he could no longer endure it, he ordered his horse and rode headlong into the battle. Gates learned that he had gone and sent Colonel Armstrong after him; but Colonel Armstrong could not travel fast enough to catch up with him. He was at once in the thick of the fight, giving orders which were readily obeyed by the troops. Once when he found it necessary to go from one end of the line to the other, instead of passing in the rear, he boldly rode the length of the line between the warring lines of troops. He conducted the whole battle; he rallied the men; he handled himself with a wild courage, a reckless daring and a skill that was marvelous. Towards the end of the day he fell on the very ground of the enemy with a shattered leg—the same one which had been broken at the storming of Quebec. This was his last battle for his native country.

All the ensuing winter he lay in Albany recovering from his wounds. Congress relented and gave him his rank. When Philadelphia was evacuated he was appointed to the command of the city. He was not popular in Philadelphia, became involved with the President and Council of Pennsylvania, and charges were brought against him which were in brief; that he abused his power, invaded the rights of citizens, and interfered with the government of the State. Congress referred the charges to a Committee who in their report absolved Arnold from blame. This report was pigeon-holed, and Congress would not act, so Washington convened a court-martial to hear the charges, which trial lasted over a month. The charges were not sustained, but a general verdict was rendered against him, in which the finding was that he had acted imprudently and unwisely, and he was sentenced to be reprimanded by the Commander-in-Chief. Washington performed his part of this in a most considerate manner, but Arnold was thoroughly angry and wounded.

Here was a soldier—a bit arrogant perhaps—and inclined to over assert his authority; but a born leader and strategist, who always possessed the courage and the daring to execute a plan he had formed, no matter how grave the danger that intervened. Taking him at his best he had many qualities of Theodore Roosevelt. He had distinguished himself at Ticonderoga, Valcour Island, Ridgefield, Quebec, Stanwix, Bemis Heights, Saratoga, Freeman's Farm, and on a score of other fields. It is the general opinion that for military genius he was not surpassed in the army save by

Washington, and even so far as Washington was concerned, the difference in their ability as soldiers was in effect the difference between Lee and Jackson. Washington planned and fought deliberately; Arnold planned and fought impulsively. Fiske expresses it succinctly and charitably when he said that Arnold lacked "moral robustness." And going still farther stated— "both Arnold and Morgan were persecuted and insulted by political enemies until the weaker nature sinks and is ruined, while the stronger endures to the end."

Persecution followed Arnold persistently. Unless Washington was grossly deceived and misled, Arnold was treated shamefully, for Washington took sides with him in all of his controversies. It may be said that Washington did not want to lose the services of a valuable fighter, but it went deeper than that.

Supposedly at this time Arnold reached a determination to betray his country. Various historians have attempted to furnish an explanation, or a motive, for his rash cause. Aaron Bancroft in his history of Washington, in his introduction to the account of Arnold's treason, states, "His enterprising spirit, his invincible fortitude, his heroic and persevering ardor in battle, had exalted his military character in his own country and in Europe." In the same breath the same historian, after telling of Arnold's appointment as Commandant in Philadelphia after the evacuation, and of his getting hopelessly into debt on account of extravagant living, says that "*being hollow at heart* he had recourse to fraud and peculation."

On the 3rd day of April 1779, Arnold had married Miss Margaret Shippen, the reigning belle of Philadelphia, the daughter of a gentleman, as Fiske expresses it, "of moderate Tory sympathies, who some years later became Chief Justice of Pennsylvania." She was 20 years of age, he 35, a widower with three sons. No historian of standing has ever attempted to implicate Arnold's wife in his treasonable acts. She was evidently a woman of unusually high character, loyal, perhaps to the mother country; but of too fine a quality either to enter into or to have had any part in his plans. Fiske says it is in the highest degree probable that down to the final catastrophe, Mrs. Arnold knew nothing whatever of what was going on.

Up to this time it seems that Arnold's anger had been directed chiefly toward the authorities at Philadelphia; but when Congress dilly-dallied and refused to act upon the report of its Committee, he became incensed at the whole party who had been constantly slighting him; and so in April 1779—this date approximately coinciding with Arnold's marriage—he wrote a letter to Sir Henry Clinton in a disguised handwriting, describing himself as an officer of high rank who being disgusted with the French Alliance, and other recent proceedings of Congress, might be persuaded to go over to the British. The correspondence was kept up for some time—the replies of Sir Henry Clinton being written by Major John André, Clinton's adjutant General, over the signature of "John Anderson." André was of Swiss descent, a polished gentleman, an accomplished soldier, a brave man. General Knox had met him previously, as had Alexander Hamilton; both spoke most highly of him. The historian, Fiske, is of the opinion that nothing appears to have been in Arnold's mind in the beginning beyond his own personal desertion to the enemy. The betrayal of a fortress was a later development. Then too, it may be supposed that Arnold was, as Fiske writes, "merely playing with fire, while he awaited the result of the court-martial."

I can do no better than quote Fiske here, because Fiske is the only historian to whom I have had access who works out a reasonable motive (from Arnold's point of view, of course) for his treasonable acts. After referring to Washington's considerate reprimand, he says:

"It was too late, however. The damage was done. Arnold had long felt persecuted and insulted. He had already dallied with temptation, and the poison was now working in his veins. His sense of public duty was utterly distorted by the keener sense of his private injuries. We may imagine his brooding over some memorable incidents in the careers of Monk, of the great Montrose and the greater Marlborough, until he persuaded himself that to change sides in a civil war was not so heinous a crime after all. Especially the example of Monk, which had already led Charles Lee to disgrace, seems to have riveted the attention of Arnold, although only the most shallow scrutiny could discover any resemblance between what the great English general had done and what Arnold proposed to do. There was not a more scrupulously honorable soldier in his day than Geo. Monk, Arnolds thoughts may have run somewhat as follows: He would not become an ordinary deserter, a villain on a small scale. He would not sell himself cheaply to the devil; but he would play as signal a part in his new career as he had played in the old one. He would overwhelm his blundering Congress, and triumphantly carry the country back to its old allegiance. To play such a part, however, would require the blackest treachery. Fancy George Monk, "honest old George," asking for the command of a fortress in order to betray it to the enemy!"

It is unnecessary to go into the sordid details of the treason or the various steps taken to accomplish it. The story is familiar to every schoolboy. In spite of his tragic end, and of the manifest justice of his execution, André emerges as a pathetic and tragic figure. All American historians agree that there was but one decision which could have been reached by the court-martial that tried André. He made valiant, but ineffectual efforts to save himself, and every effort was made by Sir Henry Clinton to save him. It may be interesting in this connection, however, to give you some idea of how this whole proceeding has been treated by at least one English historian, Percy Greg. (It may also be of interest to say parenthetically that about 1892 there appeared the first American Edition, or reprint, of a history of the United States written by this Englishman. It contained two volumes condensed into one. Because of the fact that the second volume took a most positive side with the Southern Confederacy in the Civil War, the American edition contained a foreword and a recommendation by General Wade Hampton, and was widely purchased throughout the south. Whether General Hampton read the book through before he penned his preface, I do no know, but had he read that portion dealing with the Revolutionary War and marked the contempt with which the author held Washington, and particularly Washington's handling of the André court-martial, I doubt if that gallant old soldier who followed Lee so loyally would have loaned his name and fame to such a book.)

Greg says that it was, of course, Clinton's duty to profit by the treason of an enemy; but it would have been folly to trust the traitor. He also states that André was prevailed on to remain on shore until the following night—negotiations not having been completed the first day; and that he was led without his knowledge within the American lines. The original plan had been that Arnold should meet André on board the *Vulture* anchored in the Hudson River; but Arnold's nerve apparently failed him. Smith, the agent who had brought André from the *Vulture*, had instructions to put him back on board as soon as darkness fell, but when darkness arrived, Smith failed to fulfill his commander's promise, and his own instructions. Smith, according to Greg, furnished André with a disguise and persuaded him to adopt it; and then Greg goes on to accuse Smith of a treacherous design to entrap André. Greg further says that André having reached neutral ground, Smith left his companion and André having gone about ten miles farther, "a rebel bandit dressed in the uniform of a royalist, and therefore by strict military law himself a spy, sprang upon him, and the latter deceived, declared himself a British Officer." (The fact is that the American soldier, Paulding, had been imprisoned in the North Dutch Church and afterwards in the noted Sugar House in New York, and his captor stripped him of his garment, and forced on him his own refugee coat. This accounted for the royalist garment.) Greg asserts that Washington determined from the first that André should die; and that no officer could thereafter have acquitted André without inflicting a stinging rebuke upon his chief, and placing himself in direct and flagrant antagonism to that "cold, unforgiving, implacable spirit." Greg writes:

"The nomination of the court-martial fixes a clear and paramount responsibility upon the Commander-in-Chief. Its president was his devoted creature, General Greene, a brave and capable commander, but a man utterly devoid of education, literary or social, a blacksmith till called by the outbreak of war from the forge to the field; necessarily as ignorant as any British private of the distinctions and even of the principles of military law; the last man, moreover, in the American army who would have wished or ventured, by acquitting the prisoner, indirectly to censure the superior who had condemned him by anticipation. Baron Steuben's professional knowledge was neutralised by his practical ignorance of the English language. Lafayette, a gentleman by birth and feeling, had entered the American service as a schoolboy, without a tincture of professional education; and was so completely devoted to and dominated by Washington that a knowledge equal to Steuben's would hardly have given him the will or the courage to oppose his chief. Of their eleven colleagues perhaps the best known was the self-styled Lord Stirling and the dashing partisan St Clair. The prosecution was conducted by a skillful Judge-advocate; the prisoner was without counsel. No evidence was called. The verdict and sentence of death were founded solely upon André's own confession, which, of course, no legal advises would have permitted him to make, which an English court-martial would have stopped at the first word. He had landed under a flag of truce and a pass granted by the American General in command at the place; but this obvious and conclusive advantage he was adroitly induced to forego.

"Clinton of course remonstrated with passionate indignation against the death sentence eagerly confirmed by Washington.

"He reminded Washington that his own spies, of whose guilt there was no question, had been spared at his instance. He neither denied the fact nor the unquestionable inference that he was bound in honour to requite Sir Henry Clinton's generosity. He would not and dared not argue the point. He was too shrewd not to see that neither on technical nor moral grounds could he make out his case. Technically, André was protected by a flag of truce and the passport of the American Major-General in local command. Technically, therefore, he was no spy. Morally, it might be urged that Arnold's treason, known to André, divested him of the character of an American officer and rendered his protection worthless. But morally, upon the showing of Washington's most thoroughgoing advocates, André was wholly innocent. His passage through the American lines was no voluntary act. He was led through them not only in ignorance, but in violation of his own express stipulation and of Arnold's promise. His disguise was forced upon him; and finally, he was arrested on neutral ground. His was not—as American writers have not shamed to represent it—the case of an ordinary spy, like their own favourite Hale, caught *in flagrante delicto* and hanged, of course. Technically, André was an envoy; morally, he was an involuntary trespasser within the hostile lines. Only by shifting backwards and forwards from technical to moral ground, by denying the technical excuse as morally valid and straining to the technical answer to the moral vindication, could even the shadow of a case be made out for a determined judicial murder.

"American writers plead that Washington acted under a solemn, even had it been mistaken, sense of duty; that he felt himself in conscience bound to take his prisoner's life. Washington himself has supplied a complete and crushing answer to such plea. He transmitted to Clinton an offer which placed him on a level with Arnold himself. He would spare André's life if Arnold were betrayed into his hands. The infamous proposal was of course instantly and scornfully rejected, and only served to refute absolutely and forever the "Tyrant's plea of necessity." So far from being compelled to make a deterrent example by the execution of the alleged "spy," Washington was willing to forego that advantage if he could but gratify his army with the spectacle of Arnold's death. In further determining that a soldier and gentleman in every respect at least his equal should die on the gallows, Washington clenched the accumulated proof which placed his motives beyond doubt or excuse. Few soldiers but would prefer the heroic death of André to the conscience of his executioner."

It may be noted that Nathan Hale was brutally refused the use of a Bible and his captors destroyed a letter he had written to his mother on the eve of his execution.

Arnold's subsequent career seems to have been a case of Saint Paul reversed. The same energy, the same impetuosity, the same zeal, with which he had fought for his country, he now used against her. The sordid, pathetic aspects of his treason and his apostasy are things we should like to forget. It is doubtless true that he never saw a happy moment after his betrayal of his country. It is perhaps equally true that he never saw many happy moments before that. Men of Arnold's disposition do not have happy moments. Life is to them a swiftly moving kaleidoscopic series of actions and events, revolving around themselves. The know only the job of combat, of strife, of movement.

From on board the *Vulture*, Arnold wrote a letter to Washington, which appears entirely inconsistent with his then recent acts:

"On Board the *Vulture*
Sept. 25, 1780

"Sir:

The heart which is conscious of its own rectitude cannot attempt to palliate a step which the world may censure as wrong. I have ever acted from a principle of love to my country, since the commencement of the present unhappy contest between Great Britain and the Colonies; the same principle of love to my country actuates my present conduct, however it may appear inconsistent to the world, who very seldom judge right of any man's actions.

"I have no favor to ask for myself. I have too often experienced the ingratitude of my country to attempt it; but from the known humanity of your Excellency, I am induced to ask your protection for Mrs. Arnold, from every insult and injury that the mistaken vengeance of my country may expose her to. It ought to fall only on me; she is as good and as innocent as an angel, and is incapable of doing wrong. I beg she may be permitted to return to her friends in Philadelphia, or to come to me as she may choose; from your Excellency I have no fears on her account, but she may suffer from the mistaken fury of the country.

"I have to request that the enclosed letter may be delivered to Mrs. Arnold, and she permitted to write me.

"I have also to ask that my clothes and baggage, which are of little consequence, may be sent to me; if required, their value shall be paid in money.

"I have the honor to be, with great regard and esteem, your Excellency's most obedient humble servant,

B. Arnold."

"His Excellency, General Washington."

"N.B. In justice to the gentlemen of my family, Col. Varrick and Major Franks, I think myself in honor bound to declare, that they, as well as Joshua Smith, Esq., (who I know are suspected) are totally ignorant of any transactions of mine, that they had reason to believe were injurious to the public."

As an example of the humor of the times, I quote from Niles' *Principles of the Revolution*, a description of the burning of Arnold in effigy in Philadelphia, in September 1780:

"A stage raised on the body of a cart, on which was an effigy of General sitting; this was dressed in regimentals, had two faces, emblematical of his traitorous conduct, a mask in his left hand, and a letter in his right from Beelzebub, telling him that he had done all the mischief he could do, and now he must hang himself.

"At the back of the general was a figure of the devil dressed in black robes, shaking a purse of money at the general's left ear, and in his right hand a pitchfork, ready to drive him into hell, as the reward due for the many crimes which his thirst of gold had made him commit.

"In the front of the stage, and before General Arnold, was placed a large lantern of transparent paper, with the consequences of his crimes thus delineated, i.e., on one part General Arnold on his knees before the devil, who is pulling him into the flames—a label from the general's mouth with these words, 'My dear sir, I have served you faithfully,' to which the devil replies, 'And I'll reward you.' On another side, two figures hanging, inscribed 'The Traitor's Reward,' and wrote underneath, 'The Adjutant General of the British army, and Joe Smith, the first hanged as a spy, and the other as a traitor to his country.' And on the front of the lantern was written the following:

"'Major General Benedict Arnold, late commander of the Fort West Point. The crime of this man is high treason

"'He has deserted the important post, West Point, on Hudson's river, committed to his charge by his Excellency the Commander-in-Chief, and is gone off to the enemy at New York.

"'His design to have given up this fortress to our enemies has been discovered by the goodness of the Omniscient Creator, who has not only prevented him from carrying it into execution, but has thrown into our hands André, the Adjutant General of their army, who was detected in the infamous character of a spy.

"'The treachery of the ungrateful general is held up to public view, for the exposition of infamy; and to proclaim, with joyful acclamation, another instance of the interposition of the bounteous Providence.

"'The effigy of this ingrate is therefore hanged (for want of his body) as a traitor to his native country, and a betrayer of the laws of honor.'

"The procession began about four o'clock, in the following order:

Several gentlemen mounted on horseback.
A line of continental officers.
Sundry gentlemen in a line.
A guard of the city infantry.
Just before the cart, drums and fifes playing the Rogues march.
Guards on each side.

The procession was attended with a numerous concourse of people, who, after expressing their abhorrence of the treason and the traitor, committed him to the flames, and left both the effigy and the original to sink into ashes and oblivion."

In spite of all the obloquy heaped upon Arnold by his contemporaries and by historians and people of a later day, one thing stands out above all others as indicating that he possessed unusual military skill and inspired confidence. It is the faith that General Washington had in him. Until the overt act of treason was committed, Washington believed in him, trusted him, relied on his skill as a soldier, and defended him against the attacks of his enemies.

General Schuyler a gentleman, a soldier and a patriot, likewise had confidence in Arnold. Gates and Arnold naturally could not get along. One was a military genius, a fighter, a man of unquestioned bravery; the other, a braggart who lacked courage, both physical and moral, and who always fought his battles in a bombproof and waxed courageous when the fight was over. Dastardly as was Arnold's treason, even though it had succeeded, the effect of it, in my opinion, would have been no more disastrous than the results would have been if Gates had succeeded in his machinations and supplanted Washington as Commander-in-Chief of the American forces. Both men failed in their treasonable designs. Arnold was guilty of black, vile actual treason; Gates of no more than a trace of it from a legal standpoint; for as Fiske expresses it, "with all his faults Gates never incurred the odium which belongs to a *public traitor*"; but had the latter succeeded the calamity could have been farther reaching than the surrender of West Point, because George Washington was the life, the soul of the American Revolution, and in my humble opinion it is due almost to him alone that success came to American arms.

Benedict Arnold—a bundle of inexplicable contradictions, a brave soldier, a bold and skillful leader, a strategist of high order, an accomplished gentleman, a considerate husband, a kind father, a keen intellect, a man who could and did endure hardships; at times a merciful man, as witness the incident of forbidding one of his men to kill the soldier who had wounded him at Saratoga; a man whose behavior at Quebec has been declared by Jefferson to be equal to Xenophous' retreat; and whose game fight against odds at Valcour Island has been likened to Thermopylae; a man of whom it was said— "He did not say 'Go on Boys,' but 'Come on Boys'"; a man who when he heard of the children of General Warren, the hero of Bunker Hill, being in distress, sent them five hundred dollars, with promise of future assistance if needed; a man who deserved better of his country than he received; and whose country deserved better of him then he gave.

GENTLEMAN JOHNNY BURGOYNE

Col. C. E. Lester

There are so many sources of information available to the searcher concerning this handsome, somewhat pompous though affable and likeable English gentleman, who had such a variegated and romantic career that it has been difficult to select, segregate and put into a short paper correlated and interesting incidents and general information pertaining to his life in the short time that I have had since being assigned to the subject. The result is that you will hear a somewhat disconnected, disjointed summary with a multitude of missing things that goes to make a talk worth listening to. I have selected some of the major events in his life of which much has been written pro and con. I have examined many volumes wherein he is mentioned and have quoted copiously from his biographer, Huddleston, who wrote most entertainingly of his career, adventures and misadventures in his volume— "Gentleman Johnny Burgoyne." Of his adventures and misadventures on this continent much centers around Saratoga and the events leading up to and succeeding it. The greater part of this paper is devoted to Saratoga and to related things. Of the many prominent characters of history whose lives are entwined with Burgoyne's are those of Lord George Sackville, Gen. Guy Carleton, Gen. and Mme. de Riedesel on the side of His Brittanic Majesty and those of Gates, Schuyler, Arnold and Heath on the side of the Colonists are intimately associated with his adventures on this continent.

The two who played the most conspicuous part in the humiliating affair at Saratoga and associated events were Sir Wm. Howe and Lord Sackville who later changed his title to Lord Germain.

In 1760 there was held a trial of Lord Geo. Sackville who was charged with disobedience of orders while he commanded the British Horse in Germany. This was at the battle of Minden. The court-martial decision was: "It is the opinion of this Court that the said Geo. Sackville is, and is hereby adjudged to be unfit to serve His Majesty in any military capacity whatsoever." Yet in 1775 this same man blossoms out as Secretary of State for the American Colonies and the American War.

Huddleston of the British War College says that Washington won the War in spite of Congress and that the loss of the Colonies was due not so much to the incapacity of British Officers as the stupid bungling of Lord George Germain.

It is a fact not generally known that until 1931, Sir Wm. Howe, who opposed Washington in all but two of his major engagements, never had a biographer, when Bellamy Partridge wrote his most entertaining account of Sir Billy Howe. Much of this material is new, so to speak, and has been gleaned from the Clinton, Gage, Knox and Germain original papers now housed in the Clement Library at the University of Michigan. The question has been raised, and with considerable merit, in view of the discovery of these original documents as to whether the generally accepted American viewpoint of many Revolutionary events may not be erroneous.

Burgoyne was born in London in 1722 and entered the Army at 22. He eloped with and married Lady Charlotte Stanley not long after. Our hero was not indifferent to feminine charms as his life shows, still he loved his wife dearly and was a kind and considerate husband. He left the Army in 1747 and settled with his wife in France. In 1756 he rejoined the Army and thanks to his wife's family connections, was made Captain of the 11th Dragoons. As a Captain he saw service in France, at St. Malo, Belle Isle and Cherbourg. In 1759 he was given command of the Regiment of the 16th Dragoons. He was most successful at recruiting his regiment. His recruiting advertisement ran as follows: "You will be mounted on the finest horses in the world with superb clothing and richest accoutrements, allowance and privileges will equal 2 guineas a week, you are everywhere respected; your society is courted; you are admired by the fair; which together with the chance to get switched to a buxom widow or brushing with a rich heiress renders the situation truly enviable and desirable." Later after returning from Portugal, George III gave the regiment the title of the Queen's Light Dragoons and reviewed it regularly. Burgoyne was then and later a most popular commander with the rank and file.

The "point of honor" was (after women) Burgoyne's lode star. In 1762 England declared war against Spain and Burgoyne went to the Peninsula with his Dragoons and was made a Brigadier General. He and his regiment distinguished themselves in the surprise and capture of Valencia d'Alcanatara. Later Burgoyne captured Villa Velha. This was greatly due to a certain Col. Charles Lee whom we meet again later in America. It is a strange coup of fate that this officer who so gallantly led Burgoyne's troops here was captured by the same troops near Trenton in 1776. Burgoyne returned to England in 1763, and not having got the permanent promotion he thought that he deserved, he wrote the Secretary of War quite a hot letter. He got his promotion.

H was elected to Parliament from Midhurst in 1761 and took his seat after his return from the war. In 1765 he toured the Continent to see the foreign armies. A letter of thanks to Lord Chatham for a letter of introduction ends in the 18th century grand eloquent manner and is quoted for its style: "I have the honor to be, with the most profound respect, attachment and sense of obligation, your Lordship's most obedient sand humble servant, John Burgoyne."

He was present incognito at the maneuvers of the Army of the Emperor of Austria. He reported at considerable length on what he saw there. He wrote that the Infantry was the best he had ever seen. The Cavalry was not so good, and the general officers of whom there were no less than 338, were very knowing, devilish sly, in fact. He pays great tribute to the Irish. He wrote: "In the Austrian service many of the most distinguished characters will be found among men of Irish extraction, and the lower ranks of the Army swarm with sons of the best Catholic families of the country." He regrets that the Roman Catholic Irish were not allowed to serve as officers in the British Army. Though this was winked at later in the 18th century, it was not until about 1800 that Catholics were admitted to the army with the knowledge of the Crown.

We find Burgoyne Governor-General of Ft. William in 1768 and standing for Preston in the General Election. This election must have been quite spirited and the affair must have had the aspect of some of our not far distant large city elections, as there was much rioting. Burgoyne was fined 1000 pounds and others fined and imprisoned, as an aftermath of the election.

In the events leading up to the Revolution, sentiment in the Mother Country was much divided Admiral Keppel said he would not draw his sword against the Colonies. Howe did not want to serve against them and when appointed to a command asked if it were a proposal or a command. The Earl of Effingham threw up his commission. Jeffery Amhurst refused to serve. James Wilson, a member of Parliament, asked to be relieved of his commission.

The Colonial Society of Cornhill raised 100 pounds for the "relief of widows and orphans murdered by the king's troops at Cambridge and Concord." Burgoyne, however, said: "I look upon America as our child which has been spoiled by too much indulgence." He did a lot of wire pulling and saw everyone that he thought could help him to get a command in America for the impending conflict. His efforts were successful and he sailed for America with Howe and Clinton. He did not like his station in Boston under Gage and he wrote Lord North suggesting that he be given a sort of a roving commission to endeavor to reconcile the rebels. He also wrote Gen. Harvey at the Horse Guards, criticizing Gage, the Quartermaster-General, and the Adjutant General and also the home authorities.

After Bunker Hill Burgoyne wrote Lord Rochefort a review of the situation and his impressions, since his arrival, Gates hadn't done many essential things. He grumbled that his rank as a junior Major-General left him a useless spectator. He wrote at length on the courage of the British Officers at Bunker Hill and the fact that they were illy supported by the privates. He wrote that Gage was not equal to the occasion. However, in addition to his destructive criticism he offered a constructive campaign and other suggestions of value.

We find Gentleman Johnny a little later in correspondence with the Colonial General Charles Lee with plans of his own for ending the conflict. However, the Provincial Congress in a diplomatically worded letter to Gen. Lee gave him a hint that caused him to drop the correspondence. Burgoyne later writes to Lord North and alludes to Gene Lee as "late half pay Major and incendiary in the King's service and by a very strange progression for a man of his temper—Major General and demagogue in the rebel army in the blockade of Boston."

Shortly before he left for home in December 1775, Gen. Lee wrote him a lengthy letter—I quote but two paragraphs: "The whole British Empire stands tottering on the brink of ruin and you have it in your power to avoid the fatal catastrophe. For heavens sake avail yourself of the precious moment; put an end to the delusion; exert the voice of a brave and virtuous citizen and tell the people at home that they must immediately rescind all their impolitic, iniquitous, tyrannical and murderous acts; that they must overturn the whole party system or they are undone." History does not relate that Johnny followed Lee's importunities.

While home, the situation in Canada being not too favorable, Burgoyne was called in to advise and drew up his "Reflections on the War in America." It was his suggestion that two armies should advance, one from the north and one from the south and cut the Colonies in half. He was appointed second in command to Gen. Carleton in Canada in March 1776. The general scheme adopted by the ministry for offensive operations seems to have been a plan for Burgoyne in command of the main Canadian offensive; to work up Lake Champlain—take Ticonderoga and drive through to Albany. St. Leger was to advance via Oswego and the Mohawk Valley and join Burgoyne. In the meantime Howe was to force the Hudson to Albany thereby cutting the colonies in half and separating New England from the rest of the Colonies. Burgoyne stresses in two paragraphs of his "Thoughts on the Conduct of the War" that the chief purpose was the junction of the Canadian and Howe's Army. King George approved in principle and wrote: "As Sir Wm. Howe does not think of acting from Rhode Island into Massachusetts, the force from Canada must join him at Albany." Germain, the bungler, wrote to Carleton a very critical letter and in it said: "highly necessary that the most speedy junction of the two armies be affected," and "I shall write to Sir Wm. Howe by the first packet." Carleton, a very competent and energetic officer was bitterly resentful of many things in the letter and rightly so, and came back at Germain with a very warm letter in which he stated that without reason he had been treated with slight disregard, and. censure which he attributes to Germain's private enmity. Later when Howe pulled out with his army for the Delaware, Washington wrote Gates: "Gen Howe's, in a manner, abandoning Gen. Burgoyne is so unaccountable that, 'till I am fully advised it is so, I cannot help casting my eyes continually behind me."

It is unquestionably a fact that Germain's orders to Howe to move up the Hudson to meet Burgoyne were never sent due to Germain's particular aversion to being put out of his way on any occasion, and his refusal to wait a few minutes to sign them. The details are elaborated upon at considerable length in Fitzmaurice's *Life of Lord Shelburne* and in the Knox Manuscripts. Knox was Under-Secretary for the Colonial Department. It may be observed that the triple plan for the two invasions in conjunction with the operations of Gen. Howe's Army carried with it many dangers in spite of the fact that looking at a map, it looks comparatively simple. Of course the plan of holding the entire line of the Hudson and the Lake George and Champlain country carried with it many dangers in the immobilizing and isolating of many small detachments subject to attack by the Colonials, as is witnessed by Col. Brown's operations in Burgoyne's rear after he left it most vulnerable. A better plan suggested was that the Canadian army be transported by sea to join Howe. However, there were in New England many thousands of men who would not join the Colonial regular army that would and did promptly join the militia for short periods of duty not far from home. It is quite possible that the invasion *from* Canada prevented an invasion *of* Canada. It is a prime military principle that a force operating upon interior lines has a decided advantage over a force operating upon exterior lines and scattered bodies of troops. As might have been foreseen, the three British commands were forced to act more or less independently of one another due to lack of means of communication. No modification of plans so far as it affected either of the two other units could be made, as St. Leger was practically isolated and it would take Howe and Burgoyne about three months to send and receive any answer to despatches even if they were not intercepted, as they were frequently.

Burgoyne arrived in Quebec May 6th, 1777. The force he was about to command was about 8,000, of which about 4,000 were British, 3,000 Germans, about 150 Canadians and 500 Indians. The Germans were Hessians and Brunswickers in command of Gen. De Riedesel, a Brunswicker, and Col. Breyman, a Hessian. According to *Letters and Memoirs of Madam de Riedesel* (translated from the original German) she arrived in Quebec June 10th in preparation to follow her husband through the campaign. She followed and joined him at Ft. Edward and was with him to the end. She wrote very entertainingly a review of events as well as very pithy comments on the lives of the habitants, conduct of the campaign as well as intimate views of those of the military and their lady friends of whom she heard and with whom she occasionally came in contact. She did not like Burgoyne—she didn't approve of his philanderings and probably had some feeling due to the fact that Gen. de Riedesel felt that he was not accorded the prestige that he should have had.

An abstract of a memoir of his complains that he never was permitted to take part in the deliberations held by the British Officers. However, Burgoyne wrote very highly of him in a report laid before the House of Commons in 1780.

The expedition under St. Leger failed to take Ft. Stanwix—the key to the Mohawk. The battle of Oriskany was a draw. Dame rumor got in some good work for the Colonists and St. Leger got scared out and beat it back for Montreal, completely failing in his mission.

Burgoyne with his invading army reached Crown Point late in June and menaced Ticonderoga under the command of St. Clair. Ticonderoga had been a key position against an invasion from the north. Schuyler and St. Clair had asked in vain for reinforcements to hold the position, but the States and their Representatives in Congress had failed to give them sufficient men to hold the position. Congress had been deaf to all of Schuyler's calls for help. Suffice it to say that St. Clair was forced to evacuate and Burgoyne pursued. A number of batteau was overtaken at Skenesboro and destroyed. After battles at Ft. Anne and Hubbardstown with varying fortunes on both sides, St. Clair finally reached Ft. Edward with about 2000 men.

Schuyler continued to fall back, impeding the advance of the British by destroying bridges and felling trees across the roads, making Burgoyne's progress most difficult, he not reaching Ft. Edward until late in July. Schuyler made a stand in August at Stillwater

On July 11th Burgoyne asked Carleton to garrison Ticonderoga. Carleton couldn't see his way clear to do so and Burgoyne was forced to detach 900 men that he could illy spare for this purpose and as he wrote, "leaves my position a little difficult."

Bennington, Vermont, had been reported to Burgoyne by a fellow named Skene as a good source of supplies and horses for de Riedesel, who needed them badly. Col. Baum was sent with his Brunswickers "to try the affection of the country, disconcert the councils of the enemy, to mount de Riedesel's dragoons and to obtain large supplies of horses, carriages and cattle." To make a long story short, poor Col. Baum with his dragoons and the reinforcements sent him was badly defeated. Picture if you can a soldier wearing high jack boots, leather breeches, huge gauntlets and a hat heavy with feathers, and from the back of his head a long peruke protruding. He carried a broad sword weighing twelve pounds, on his shoulder a carbine and other minor impedimenta. Imagine men thus equipped fighting in the woods with men in their shirt sleeves. Horace Walpole wrote, "Gen. Burgoyne has had very bad sport in the woods." The facts were that Col. Skene, who was next to Germain, Burgoyne's evil genius, wanted and got a road through his property at public expense.

Burgoyne as getting very uneasy. He wrote Germain on August 20th that "Ft. Stanwix still held out that the Royalists were not rising as expected and, what was more worrying, that wherever the King's forces pointed, militia to the number of three or four thousand assembled in 24 hours," and brought their own sandwiches, so to speak, and when things quieted down a bit, they went back to the farm. It must have been very disconcerting to Johnny to find such an entire disregard for etiquette and the ethics of war. His opponents just would not play according to the rules. Other than that he had had but one letter from Howe, and that had contained the very disconcerting information that Howe intended to go to Pennsylvania, not to Albany. Poor Burgoyne goes on: "No operation, My Lord has yet been taken in my favor. The highlands have not even been threatened. . . . Had I a latitude in my orders, I should think it my duty to stay in this position or, even back as far as Ft. Edward where my communication with Lake George would be perfectly secure till some event happened to assist my movement forward." He had not foreseen, he continued that he "was to be left to pursue his way through the forests and hosts of the enemy without cooperation from Howe." His army was as astounded as he. Everyone knew that the object of the expedition had been to join Howe at Albany. Germain wrote to Knox, "I am sorry to find that Burgoyne's campaign is totally ruined. The best I can wish for him is that he has returned to Ticonderoga without much loss. . . . What alarms me most is that he thinks his orders positive to go to Albany to force a junction with Howe."

Huddleston says of this letter: "This scoundrel is already preparing his defense. He could not prove for he would have told any lie, that Howe had been instructed to go north and meet Burgoyne, so, in place of this he is going to plead, of necessity, that Burgoyne had totally misunderstood his instructions." Why *did* Howe go south? Huddleston says of him that it was characteristic of the man to never go anywhere except calling on the ladies. As referred to in an earlier paper of mine on Washington (a book called the *Treason of Charles Lee*), a plan for the defeat of the Colonies by sending troops up the Potomac and Delaware, gives very plausible reasons for Howe moving south instead of north. On September 14th Burgoyne and his army crossed the Hudson and camped near Saratoga. The Americans were yet at Stillwater. On August 19th Gates had arrived and succeeded Schuyler as Commander-in-Chief of the Northern Department. Arnold arrived about the same time. As is now well known, Gates got his command through intrigue and took the place of a much superior officer—General Schuyler. Burgoyne's troops were beginning to get in a bad way. Food and forage were getting short and they had no heavy clothing.

The battle of Bemis Heights was fought on September 19th with Burgoyne bravely in the thickest of it. Beyond a doubt, Gates, who had determined on a defensive battle, would have been defeated had it not been for Arnold, and Burgoyne would have been in Albany in another day. Burgoyne was in a bad way also. Had Gates attacked the next day as Arnold wanted—the surrender probably would have been dated a month earlier. After this battle Burgoyne delayed, hoping for cooperation from Clinton. On October 6th he attempted a reconnaissance in force, which finally developed into the general engagement of Saratoga in which he was defeated, chiefly due to Arnold. His losses were heavy, Clark, Frazer and Ackland being mortally wounded.

On October 12th he called a council of war to determine plans of action. They were practically surrounded with four possible plans of action. (1) To await favorable action, (2) to attack, (3) to retreat with the artillery, and (4) to retreat leaving artillery and baggage. The retreat plans, the fourth, proposed by de Riedesel, was accepted and details decided upon. However, the order for the distribution of rations for six days to be carried, for some reason had not been carried out. The commissariat was directed to no longer delay distribution and the retreat as to start about 10:30. However, when that time came, the exterior situation had so changed that Burgoyne decided it was too late to make the attempt.

Another council of war was called and Gen. Burgoyne laid the following queries before the body: (1) Whether military history offered precedents of any army capitulating in such a situation? (2) Whether a capitulation under the circumstances would be dishonorable? (3) Whether the army was really in such circumstances as to be obliged to capitulate? It was generally answered in reply to the first query—that the situation of the Saxon Army at Pirna, of Gen. Fink at Waxen, and of Prince Maurice of Saxony had been less unfortunate than their own case and that nobody could blame generals who capitulated at such a time to save their army. Gen. the Baron de Riedesel was authority for the examples. As answer to the second query the answer to the first sufficed. In answer to the third all officers declared themselves ready to sacrifice their lives in any possible attempt of successfully attacking the enemy, but that the army's position was untenable, and they thought it advisable to capitulate. Burgoyne decided to surrender.

There was considerable correspondence and intercourse between the commanders of the opposing armies, Burgoyne and Gates and their envoys, on terms and conditions. However an agreement was arrived at and the conditions of the treaty were fulfilled at Saratoga October 17th. There were 13 Articles of the Convention covering the several phases of the situation. The 2nd Article, providing for the return of the British troops to England by way of Boston, was quite a victory for Johnny at this time, however it proved a sort of a boomerang and caused him no end of trouble later.

Burgoyne and Mme de Riedesel commented very favorably on the most courteous reception and attention accorded them by Gates and Schuyler after the surrender. Burgoyne, the soul of kindness and courtesy, appreciated these qualities in others. Later in Parliament he said that Gen. Schuler was one of the first persons he met in the American camp, and when he attempted to make some excuse for the destruction of Schuyler's property the general begged him not to think of it as the occasion had demanded it. He did more, Burgoyne added: "He sent an aide to conduct me to Albany, in order, as he said, to procure better quarters for me than a stranger would be able to find. The gentleman conducted me to a very elegant house and to my great surprise presented me to Mrs. Schuyler and her family. In that house I remained during my whole stay at Albany with a table of more than 20 covers for me and my friends and every other demonstration of hospitality." Burgoyne's surrender naturally created a great furor of excitement in London. Lord Shelburne speaking in the House of Lords said: "The issue of Burgoyne's expedition is too melancholy to be made a subject of conversation," and savagely attacked Germain.

The Duke of Richmond was most contemptuous of the strategy of the campaign, he said, "supposing, which is improbable, Burgoyne had got through to New York, what has he affected? He has lost several thousand men and he might have arrived at New York two years ago without any loss at all." On December 3rd, Col. Barre in the House of Commons called upon Germain to declare upon his honor what had become of Burgoyne and his army. Germain shuffled about and hoped that the House would suspend judgment on both the General and the minister until news was authenticated. Barre rose again and said that he was shocked at the easy manner in which the noble Lord related the fate of the brave Burgoyne. Nobody could say that Burgoyne had failed through his own misconduct. The minister who had planned the expedition was all to blame and it was an inconsistent and impractical scheme unworthy of a British minister and rather too absurd for an Indian Chief. Edmund Burke said that the failure as due to the ignorance of the Minister for the American Department. Fox attacked as follows: "An army of 10,000 men destroyed through the ignorance, the obstinate willful ignorance of the noble Lord calls loudly for vengeance." "A gallant general sent like a victim to be slaughtered where his own skill and bravery would have won him laurels, if he had not been under the direction of a blunderer." The House of Lords was equally emphatic in their denunciations. Lord Chatham paid Burgoyne many compliments. Lord Shelburne said: "Mr. Burgoyne is directed to march to New York or to effect a function with Mr. Howe. Mr. Howe goes aboard his ships and after beating to the southward gets on the other side of Philadelphia. If

I do not hear full and sufficient reasons for this extraordinary conduct, I protest, I think Mr. Howe would deserve to be brought home in chains."

Huddleston devotes a chapter to Burgoyne's apology and he asks very tritely why did Burgoyne fail? "Well in the first place the whole plan of the campaign was crazy. A lover in an old play made a modest request of the gods to annihilate but space and time. Could that have been done, Burgoyne, Howe and St. Leger might have met at the same date at Albany. But as things are in this world, British ministers were banking on the impossible."

General John Glover had been appointed by Gates to conduct Burgoyne and his troops to Cambridge and it is recorded in *Historic Hadley* by Alice Walker and *A History of Old Kinderhook* by Collier that the captives were well treated on the trip and that there were many courtesies extended Burgoyne that endeared the donors to him. Burgoyne also made many favorable comments.

Things were not so good in Cambridge. General Heath in command there wrote in his memoirs that the capture of Gen. Burgoyne and their housing in Cambridge "opened a new, important and delicate field" for him. Times were very trying there, and many unfortunate incidents happened. It was not to be expected that the inhabitants and the captive soldiers would have much love for one another. General Heath was hard put to keep things going decently, keep himself out of hot water and keep the trouble at even a decently low ebb. Congress would not ratify the conditions of the Convention entered into between Gates and Burgoyne, and there was endless conversations, correspondence and trouble concerning it. Burgoyne was most anxious to get home to defend his action, character, and honor. He finally got permission from Congress to go. Gates wrote him: "If courage, perseverance and a faithful attachment to your Prince could have prevailed *I* might have been *your* prisoner." Washington with his natural sagacity wrote him a most kindly and courteous letter (in reply to a letter from Burgoyne); among other things he wrote, "I am ever ready to do justice to the gentleman and the soldier and to esteem, where esteem is due, however the idea of a public enemy may interpose.

You will not think it the language of unmeaning ceremony if I add that sentiments of personal respect are reciprocal. Viewing you in the light of an officer contending against what I believe to be the rights of my country, the reverses of fortune you experienced in the field cannot be unacceptable to me, but abstracted from consideration of national advantage, I can sincerely sympathize with your feelings as a soldier the unavoidable difficulties of whose situation, forbid his success; and as a man whose lot combine the calamity of ill heat, the anxieties of captivity, and the painful sensibility of a reputation exposed where he most values it to the assaults of malice and detraction." Burgoyne's biographer writes very highly of Gen. Wm. Heath. He says particularly, that "he may have cut no great figure in the field, but if there *was* a courtly and kind-hearted gentleman on either side in this war, it was this Roxbury farmer." He hopes that "in Massachusetts somewhere there is a very corpulent and bald-headed statue to him." "Among those generals who have done what they could to preserve what used to be called the Amenities of War, Wm. Heath takes a very high place."

Burgoyne, on parole, arrived home in May 1778 and at once demanded a court-martial. The tricky Germain, in a carefully devised plot, arranged things so it would appear that Burgoyne was getting a square deal. He arranged the order for the court-martial and probably packed the court, and pending trial, etiquette demanded, as he casually remarked to Burgoyne, that Burgoyne could not appear at Court or see the King while awaiting trial. The Court met and decided that inasmuch as Congress had a lien, as it were, upon Burgoyne, *they* could not begin any inquiry to restrain or affect his person. The Board was discharged and Burgoyne notified. There not having been any inquiry he could not see the King. Germain kept busy and put the Law Officers of the Crown on the job of trying to prove, so to speak, that Burgoyne did not exist.

He failed in this and then got the Secretary of War busy, who wrote Burgoyne to the effect that His Majesty thought his presence material to the troops still held prisoners in New England and ordered him back to Boston soon as his health permitted.

Burgoyne replied, citing his still unwell condition and the inadvisability of it from the viewpoint of the troops. Barrington, a little later again ordered him back to America. Nothing happened until late in September when the new Secretary of War, Jenkinson, wrote Burgoyne as follows: "I am commanded by the King to acquaint you that your not returning to America is considered as a neglect of duty and disobedience of orders."

Burgoyne wrote a very indignant reply in which he made one very good point. He had been deprived of a court-martial because he was not amenable to the law, but he is found amenable to the law when he is ordered to return to America. Germain had slipped a bit here.

Burgoyne continued that "my enemies are systematically desirous of burying my innocence and their guilt in the prisons of the enemy and in the removing of my person to the other side of the Atlantic, destroying the means of renewing parliamentary proceedings which they have reason to dread." He therefore felt constrained, if still denied a court-martial, to resign his appointment on the American staff, his Colonelcy of the Queen's Dragoons, and the Governorship of Ft. William, but he desired to keep his rank of Lt. Colonel in the Army so he could still be amenable to a possible court-martial and to fulfill his personal faith should he be required by the enemy to do so. His resignation was accepted, and he was told that a court-martial was out of the question. He was sacrificed for Germain. In April 1781 Congress passed a Resolution recalling Burgoyne. This led to an exchange of letters between Edmond Burke and Benj. Franklin which had the desired effect, and in February 1782 Burgoyne was exchanged for 1047 officers rank and file. After the close of the war there was the usual changes and the scramble for posts and Burgoyne as a panacea was given the post of C. on C. in Ireland and was made a Privy Councilor. He was unhappy in Ireland, and resigned in 1784. He was again elected from Preston in 1787 and died in 1792.

May I quote in conclusion Huddleson's opinion of him as a man: "One cannot spend five or six evenings a week with a man without forming a pretty definite opinion of him. I have spent that surrounded with all the books and material that I could lay hold of about him, and I have grown to like him tremendously.

"He was pompous, he was a gambler, in morals a latidenarian, and worst of all a politician. He was both a comic and tragic figure. As a soldier, though of unimpeachable courage, he was not a success in the field. He was not a great dramatist and he was not a great general. He was, though, a courteous and polished man about town. He loved his profession and his soldiers loved him. He always gave his men the credit due them, a little formality which some great generals have neglected. Regarding his morals it must be remembered that the 18th century was an immoral age, or perhaps one should say, less hypocritical. Burgoyne owned up to his weakness for women like a man. There has never been in British military history a soldier so shockingly let down by the minister at home because there has never been in military history a war minister so casual, so incompetent, so mean, so contemptible, so cowardly as that 'man' Germain."

GENERAL NICHOLAS HERKIMER

W. T. Stauffer

Like Warren, Montgomery and Mercer, General Nicholas Herkimer gave his life for his country on the field of battle. Unlike Mercer, but like Warren and Montgomery, he was in independent command on the field where he met his death; but like Mercer the conflict in which he died was a turning point in the American Revolution.

In his scheme for the settlement of Pennsylvania, William Penn induced Mennonite refugees of Crefeld, Germany, to settle in his province. They founded Germantown, and by their skill in weaving made Philadelphia the great weaving center of the colonies. Their successful settlement turned the attention of German-speaking people toward America and especially toward Pennsylvania. I use the term German-speaking, since these early settlers were not as a rule German in the sense in which we now use that term. At least half of them were Swiss; a great part of the remainder were Dutch, Huguenot or Alsatian. As many came from the Palatinate, they were, in the language of the day, called Palatines, a term which I still use in referring to them. Once started, this Palatine migration grew by leaps and bounds. The height of this migration was reached in 1709, when some thirty-two thousand made their way to London en route to America. There was not sufficient shipping to carry them to America. They camped in London and taxed to the utmost the generosity of Queen Anne. Seven thousand returned to their old homes along the Rhine. Six-hundred and fifty, who were

Swiss, under Count Graffenried, settled in New Berne, North Carolina. A portion came to Virginia and settled at Spottsylvania. Three thousand were sent to Ireland, where their descendants were gathered into the Methodist Church. Two descendants of these German Irishmen, Phillip Embury and Mrs. Barbara Heck, became the founders of the Methodist Church in the United States, while the well-known London preacher, Frank B. Meyer, was also a descendant of this Palatine colony in Ireland. In 1710, between three and four thousand of these same Palatines were sent to New York and were settled by Governor Hunter along the Hudson River, whence many of then migrated, taking up land in the neighborhood of Schoharie, New York, and farther west. Later Palatine immigrants to New York were attracted to this nucleus. These settlements produced not only Nicholas Herkimer and his heroes, but also Conrad Weiser who later migrated to Pennsylvania and negotiated every Indian treaty from 1732 to the close of the French and Indian War. The Palatines have been said to be "the most virile race which ever set its foot on the American continent." They became the farmers par excellence of the United States, if not of the world. They were honest, frugal, thrifty and stubborn. The last mentioned quality made them conquerors on the field of Oriskany and accounts for the fact that, though often attacked by the public enemy, they have never been passed in foreign war or domestic strife. I have gone somewhat a-field so that you may realize the stuff that the heroes of Oriskany were made of.

Among the Palatine immigrants in 1721 were John Jost Herkimer (Hergesheimer), his father, George, his mother, Madeline, and his wife Catharine. John Jost joined the Palatine settlements and took up lands on the Mohawk between German Flats (Herkimer) and Frankfort. He was a man of sagacity and ability, and accumulated wealth in lands, chattels and slaves. His family, next to that of Sir William Johnson, became the most prominent in the Mohawk Valley. His large stone mansion with the church fifty rods away became Fort Herkimer in the French and Indian War. His oldest daughter married into the celebrated Schuyler family.

Nicholas Herkimer, the oldest son of John Jost, was born about 1728. He was educated in German, that being the language then in general use in the Valley. He was a hardy, ambitious, wide-awake youth and was familiar with woodcraft and Indian craft; and the customs and ways of the redskins were well-known to him. He was twice married. His first wife was Lany Tygert, and his second was her niece, Myra Tygert. He had no children. Herkimer was a man of sterling qualities and was much beloved by his friends. In 1758, he was appointed Lieutenant of militia by Lieut.-Gov. James Delancy and commanded at Fort Herkimer. During an attack on this fort by the French and Indians, many Palatine settlements were destroyed, many Palatines were slain, and about 100 were carried into captivity. In 1772 Nicholas Herkimer represented the Canajoharie district on the Committee of Safety. He was an early advocate of the rights of the colonies as were the rest of his family except his brother, John Jost. In 1775 he became colonel of the First Battalion, Tryon County Militia, and in September 1776, was commissioned Brigadier General in the same militia.

Before the Revolution, by far the most influential family in the Mohawk Valley and western New York was the knightly family of Johnson. This family was founded by William Johnson, a native of Ireland. He was connected with the wealthy and powerful Delancy family of New York, which had large estates along the Mohawk. Johnson was sent to manage one of these Delancy estates held by his uncle, Admiral Sir Peter Warren, in right of his wife who was a Delancy. Johnson opened a successful trade with the Indians; gained their confidence and respect; and was elected Sachem of the Mohawk tribe. During the French and Indian War, he was appointed Indian Commissioner of New York, was instrumental in keeping the Iroquois true to the British cause, and was a prominent general in that war. For his services he was created a baronet and received a royal patent of 100,000 acres of land. By his treaty with the Iroquois in 1768, he established the frontier at the Allegheny and the Ohio, thus giving Kentucky to Virginia. After the war he retired to his estate, built a magnificent mansion, known as Johnson Hall, where Johnstown, New York, now stands, and lived the life of a baronial landlord with a host of tenant retainers. On his death in 1774 his son, John Johnson, became the head of the family and succeeded to the baronetcy and the estate. This influential family held not only the English-speaking people of the Mohawk Valley and western New York, but also the Indians and even some of the Palatines true to the British Crown. Sir William Johnson had married Catharine Weisenberg, a Palatine, and General Herkimer's own brother, John Jost, was a Tory and died in Canada after his property had been confiscated by the patriots. At the beginning of the Revolution, Sir John Johnson gathered his tenants and savage followers at Johnson Hall and the fate of the settlements in the Mohawk Valley could not be doubted. Schuyler hastened from Albany and with militia under Herkimer, then Colonel, surrounded the place on the night of January 19, 1776, and forced its surrender with arms and stores. Sir John was released on parole, was accused of breaking faith and fled to Canada. His immense estates were confiscated and sold. From his dispossessed tenants and others deprived and expelled, he raised the Queen's Royal Greens of bloody memory.

The British plan to split the colonies in two was to sweep the lower Hudson, the upper Hudson and the Mohawk by three expeditions under Howe, Burgoyne and St. Leger, all meeting at Albany. St. Leger was to move with a small force by the St. Lawrence and Lake Ontario to Oswego, join hands with the Johnsons, the Tories and the Indians, capture Fort Stanwix and move eastward through the Mohawk Valley to Albany.

In June 1777, General Herkimer at the head of 300 local militia and 150 men of Col. Van Schaick's regiment had sought an interview with Joseph Brant, who had been on the Susquehanna collecting an Indian force, had made no hostile attacks, but had unequivocally expressed his own feelings. Brant was an Indian, the brother of one of Sir William Johnson's many Indian mistresses. He was educated in the English language by Sir William and became a brave, active and artful Mohawk Sachem. Though an Indian, he was as humane as Sir John Johnson, and compared to Walter Butler, was chivalry itself. Herkimer and. Brant had been friends and neighbors before Brant went to Canada. Some Mohawk Indians had agreed to remain neutral in 1775, and Herkimer endeavored to hold Brant neutral also. Herkimer has unjustly been accused of treacherous intent on this occasion.

On July 17, 1777, General Herkimer issued a spirited and patriotic proclamation to the people of Tryon County, notifying them of the assembling of the enemy at Oswego and calling on the male population to repair *en masse* to the field on a moment's notice, armed and equipped to meet the invading foe, those from sixteen to sixty to take the field; those over sixty to assemble in proper places to protect the women and children.

Meanwhile St. Leger with 650 British and German Regulars, Tories and Canadian militia had landed at Oswego. He was soon joined by 75 of Col. John Butler's Rangers and Brant with 300 Indians. The British took for granted that everything from Johnson Hall west was Tory through the immense Johnson influence. They had not counted the Palatines and the new owners of the vast Johnson estates. The patriots had repaired old Fort Stanwix on the site of Rome, New York, and had renamed it Fort Schuyler. It commanded the chief trade route between the Hudson and the Lakes. On August 2nd, St. Leger invested Fort Schuyler garrisoned with about 600 men under Col. Peter Gansevoort with Col. Marinus Willett second in command. The British had expected to find the usual ill-manned Indian fort and were disconcerted to find a strong work requiring a regular siege for which they had no heavy artillery. The people of Tryon County now awoke and gathered to the colors with the Palatines and the new owners of the Johnson estates in the van.

General Herkimer ordered the militia of his brigade to rendezvous at Fort Dayton, a defense erected in the western part of Herkimer village. He had about 700 men in three regiments commanded by Klock, Cox and Vischer. On August 4 he left Fort Dayton to relieve Fort Schuyler and on August 5 encamped near Oriskany. He sent Adam Helmer with a message to Fort Schuyler to arrange concerted action. Helmer did not arrive until next day due to the vigilance of the British and Indians. Herkimer expressed doubt as to the expediency of a further forward movement until reinforcements arrived. He was denounced to his face as a Tory and a coward. He replied stating that their safety was in his hands and that he desired to avoid all difficulties which could not be surmounted by bravery and good conduct. He told them that they were rather noisy and liberal with accusations against his fidelity and courage and that they would be the first to run, a prophecy which was soon fulfilled. St. Leger's force now consisted of nearly 2000 British and Indians led by Sir John Johnson and Brant Herkimer knew this and knew also that a superior force could be sent against him, which could select its own battleground. But noisy insubordination prevailed and precipitated the little band of patriots into the jaws of death. Smarting and irritated, the General gave orders to march, having thrown out the usual advance and flanking parties. In the meantime, Indian scouts had reported the advance and St. Leger had sent Johnson with 50 Greens and 30 Rangers and Brant with 400 Indians to intercept them.

On August 6th at ten o'clock in the morning, the main body of troops, two-thirds of the whole, in rather disorderly exultation, passed over a causeway on a marshy ravine, the advance having already commenced the ascent of the westerly slope. Suddenly a fire was opened on this band from front and both sides accompanied by a terrible Indian war whoop. Johnson held the front while Brant and the Indians attacked from the sides. The Causeway was blocked up with heavy teams and retreat become impossible. The rear commanded by the officers who had taunted Herkimer with cowardice, turned and fled, but were followed by the Indians and suffered worse slaughter than if they had stood. The baggage and ammunition wagons were cut off from the main body. "The van suffered awful carnage from the hidden rifles and the knives and tomahawks of the screeching fiends who leaped out to dispatch the wounded; but nerved by desperation, the patriots braced themselves for the fight and scattered to cover. A volley killed Herkimer's horse and shattered his leg, but he had himself propped up in his saddle and gave orders as before. Whenever a patriot fired, Indians would rush upon him and tomahawk him before he could reload. Then behind the trees the militia fought in couples, one reserving fire for the rush, and punishing it until the savages grew weary. Gradually the ambushers crept closer, stalking the patriots from the side or behind." But Herkimer formed his doughty troops into circular squads among the trees and resistance became effective. The British charged with bayonets, but were met with brave hearts and strong arms. "The battle raged until a terrific thunderstorm broke—a godsend to the patriots, whose only powder was in their belts. For over an hour the British drew off to closer coverts to keep their powder dry. Herkimer chose for his men a spot so defensible that it seems strange the enemy should have left it for them—the north end of their field, a steep knoll sloping to the flats beyond and gullies on all its sides, easily assailable only from the south. Here his men formed into one great circle. As the sky cleared the allies approached once more; but now the patriots had the vantage in turn, and the enemy began to shrink back. Just then Watts came on the scene with a fresh detachment of Royal Greens, sent from the camp on the news from Indian runners of the check sustained. He evidently had fighting blood in him, and for the first time there seems to have been something like a real battle in which he has desperately wounded." The Royal Greens were brought face to face with their former neighbors. Mutual hate and revenge made the conflict more of a death struggle than ever. "Not long afterward the boom of cannon from the fort came to their ears. The crafty Butler at once turned it to account for a well-nigh fatal ruse, disguising a body of Greens by homespun over-garments and sending them from the west to the patriot lines as reinforcements; but a keen eye detected the uniforms and several were shot down. Gansevoort noticing that St. Leger's lines had been thinned and suspecting that a detachment had been sent to intercept Herkimer, sent Col. Willett on a sortie against St. Leger to draw attention in that direction. Soon the Indian retreating sign, "Oonah," was heard and the flight began. Johnson's Greens and Butler's Rangers followed, abandoning the dead and wounded. Somewhat over two hundred able-bodied patriots were left after the struggle, but they were so exhausted that they were unable to follow and were glad to escape and carry their wounded back to Oriskany. From the character of the combatants, the surprise and the disadvantage under which the patriots labored during this six-hour conflict, the proportions of killed and wounded was far beyond what ordinarily occurs in the hardest action. Two hundred patriots were killed and as many wounded and captured. The British loss was probably as great. The Indians, exasperated at the defeat, murdered and scalped not only the prisoners, but also many of the British.

Col. Willett's sortie was a signal success. Immediately after the thunder-storm with 250 men and one cannon, he drove the investing Tories into the river and Indians into the woods, carted the camp stores into the fort in three journeys of seven loaded wagons and returned without losing a man, though St. Leger sent one force to cut him off and another to harass him. The spoils included Johnson's papers—plans of campaigns, maps, orderly books and letters—full of valuable information. The Stars and Stripes first fluttered in the breeze in the face of an enemy at Fort Schuyler. The flag, improvised from the blue of an old coat, the white from a shirt and the red from the petticoat of a soldier's wife, was unfurled by Col. Gansevoort above the five British colors which Willett had captured.

The garrison did not know what had become of Herkimer. Provisions soon became scarce. Willett and a lieutenant, by a notable feat of daring and labor, floating over the river on a log and crawling on their hands and knees through the swamps, made their way to Schuyler's headquarters. Gansevoort declared that, rather than surrender, he would cut his way out through St. Leger's forces. Schuyler, in the face of insinuations against his motives and overruling a council of war, determined to relieve the fort and asked for volunteers. Arnold instantly responded. With over a thousand men he marched up the valley to Fort Dayton. His council of war voted to ask Gates for heavy reinforcements but Arnold, knowing that every day was precious, resolved to march on despite the council and was on his way when he received a message from Gansevoort that the siege had been raised and the enemy had fled. A half-witted Tory boy, who had been taken prisoner and was condemned to death, was promised his freedom if he would spread the news among the

British that a large body of Americans was close at hand. His brother was held as a hostage and a friendly Oneida was sent with him. His coat having been shot full of holes, he ran breathless into the British camp, showing the bullet holes and describing his narrow escape from the enemy. When asked their number, he mysteriously pointed to the leaves of the trees. The Indians, who looked upon those stricken by the Great Spirit with awe, fled precipitately, followed by the British who left their tents and artillery behind.

Throughout the conflict at Oriskany, General Herkimer with his leg broken by a musket ball rested on his saddle against a beech tree, smoked his pipe, and coolly directed the battle. In vain his soldiers begged for permission to remove him from the place of danger and shelter him during the storm. The sturdy soldier's only reply was: "I will face the enemy." His calmness and deliberation infused into his men a spirit of unconquerable resistance. After the battle he was carried on a litter to Fort Herkimer and thence to his home at Little Falls. His leg was unskillfully amputated. The flesh and bone were cut off square without taking up or tying the large blood vessels. He died ten days after the battle of a hemorrhage, possessed of a large property which he disposed of by will among his friends and relatives. He signed his will "Nicholas Herckheimer." The Congress passed an appropriation of $500.00 for a monument to his memory. But it was not until 1884 that the Congress of the United States, with the help of the State of New York, erected a monument.

The battle of Oriskany was a small conflict heroically fought. In its immediate effect it was perhaps a draw, unless the fact that the patriots held the field should class it as an American victory. But in its ultimate consequences, it was an American victory of the first importance. It gave Gansevoort and Willett a chance to bag the British camp stores and the invaluable Johnson Papers and to revictual Fort Schuyler. It caused the desertion of St. Leger's Indians and the consequent abandonment of his campaign, which Arnold might not have been able to compel; and it assured Burgoyne's destruction. In the words of Washington, "Herkimer first reversed the gloomy scene of national campaign."

GENERAL JOHN STARK

PROF. H. C. KREBS

Early in the month of August in the year 1777, there was anxiety in the mind of General Burgoyne, commander of the British army invading the State of New York. He had thus far conducted a memorable campaign. Starting at Montreal on May 14 with an army exceeding 8,000 men and with an immense train of artillery, he had marched southward to Plattsburg, and a week later landed by boats at the other end of Lake Champlain. Three days later he appeared in the vicinity of Fort Ticonderoga, the barrier in this valley to invasion from the north. Through the neglect of the American commander, St. Clair, to possess and fortify the hills commanding the fort, and the enterprise of the British in seizing them, this formidable military protection was taken with little fighting, and the Americans retreated, leaving behind them 128 pieces of heavy artillery.

Encouraged by this unexpected success. Burgoyne pushed up Lake George, and using the same tactics as at Fort Ticonderoga, compelled the Americans to retreat to Fort Edward on the Hudson River, a few miles south of Lake George. Burgoyne continued to advance, cutting his way through dense woods, a distance of 22 miles, in 20 days taking possession of Fort Edward, which Schuyler, the American commander, had evacuated. On August 14th Burgoyne had moved down the east bank of the Hudson to the present city at Schuylerville, near Saratoga, and had built a bridge across the Hudson at this point.

Burgoyne now began to feel the result of the great defect in his campaign, namely, the long distance between his army and its base of supplies at Montreal. Food and munitions had to be transported two hundred miles by wagon-train and boat through rough, wooded country. This long line was subject to raiding parties of irregular militia, and the interruption of occasional thunderstorms. Little in the way of supplies was to be gathered in his immediate vicinity, because General Schuyler had destroyed them on his retreat. Therefore some means had to be found to feed his army without relying on his usual source.

Information had reached Burgoyne that at Bennington, in the present State of Vermont, there had been established a great depot of corn, flour, and cattle, and that this place was guarded by only a few militia. He was also told that the people living in that vicinity were "the most active and rebellious race on the continent." Burgoyne thereupon determined to capture the supplies at Bennington, secure horses for his unmounted Hessian dragoons, and strike terror into the hearts of the rebels. For this expedition he selected 600 men to be commanded by Colonel Baume, consisting of these unmounted dragoons, Captain Fraser's sharpshooters, some Tory militia, and 2 field guns.

It may well be imagined that the people of Vermont had long watched the progress of Burgoyne's invasion with great apprehension. This large body of hostile troops moving along its western boundary would certainly in due time harass their country with fire and sword. Committees of Safety implored their people to shoulder arms and join the militia; and they appealed to neighboring colonies to come to their assistance. Citizens of property sacrificed everything to raise money for the defense of the country; and to inspirit martial ardor, it was announced by the Assembly that the troops would be under the tried and trusted leadership of their old friend General Stark.

It is now necessary to introduce on the stage of events the man of the hour. In 1720 there came to America Archibald Stark who had been born in Glasgow, Scotland. He had lived for some years as a member of a Presbyterian colony in Northern Ireland, and then had decided to cast his fortunes in the new world. His party was refused a landing in Boston because of the prevalence of smallpox there; so they spent the first winter in Maine, and the next at Nutfield, now Londonderry, in what afterwards became New Hampshire. Here John Stark was born in 1728, the second of four sons. In 1736 the family moved to Derryfield, now Manchester.

At the age of 24 John Stark, now a brave and hardy young man, while on a hunting expedition with three others, was taken prisoner by a band of Indians. It was while a captive that he accomplished his famous feat of running the gauntlet; when his turn came for the ordeal, he snatched a club from the nearest Indian and laid about him with such zest and power that he scattered the lines before him and escaped almost without a blow, greatly to the amusement of the older Indians who were spectators of the game. After six weeks more of captivity Stark was released on the payment of ransom by the General Court of Massachusetts.

While with the Indians, Stark gained an intimate knowledge of their nature and habits, which stood him in good stead later. In subsequent expeditions of the hunters Stark was generally selected as guide. When the French and Indian War broke out in 1755 Stark was commissioned Lieutenant in the Corps of Rangers enlisted under the leadership of the renowned Robert Rogers, whose fame as a partisan ranks with that of Marion, Sumter, and John S. Mosby. The scene of the exploits of these sturdy fighters was on Lake George, Lake Champlain, and the vicinity. Here they participated in several pitched battles; but their greatest service was rendered through scouting expeditions, gaining information of the plans of the enemy, cutting off their communications, and harassing them in every other way. During the campaign of 1758 against Fort Ticonderoga, Stark became an intimate friend of Lord Howe, the brother of Sir William Howe, of Revolutionary days. Lord Howe was killed in this battle, and the whole expedition failed through the incompetence of the British commander, Abercromby. The next year, in face of another attempt at its capture, Fort Ticonderoga was evacuated by the French without a contest, most of the troops having been withdrawn to Quebec to assist in the defense against General Wolfe. Stark bore a prominent part in this expedition.

Wolfe's great victory at Quebec brought the war virtually to a close, though military operations of a minor character continued for several years, the treaty of peace being signed in 1763. Stark resigned from the army in 1760, partly because he wished to be with his family and develop his property, and also because the overbearing insolence of young British officers toward the crude provincials was intolerable to men of the ability, experience, and independence of Stark. These young officers were appointed in England through their social and political connections. They knew nothing of actual warfare, but tried to show their authority and rank by their disdain of all persons and things colonial, especially venting their prerogatives on inferior officers. Stark left the service, however, with the expressed goodwill of the Commander-in-Chief, General Amherst, who promised he should resume his rank in the army should he ever return.

No unusual events happened to Stark during the interim between the ending of the French and Indian War and the commencement of the Revolution. With the approach of hostilities with England every man had to decide to which side he would adhere. Major Robert Rogers, who had passed the greater part of the preceding ten years in England, adopted the British side. John Stark's older brother William, who had fought under the British flag at Ticonderoga, Crown Point, and Louisburg, and had been with Wolfe at Quebec, found it hard to make up his mind. However, he applied for the command of one of the New Hampshire regiments; and when the Assembly gave preference to another, William Stark listened to the overtures made by the British, became a Colonel in the Royal Army, and was killed by a fall from his horse on Long Island.

John Stark, to whom the same overtures had been made by the British, steadfastly championed the cause of the Colonists. He served with great efficiency on the Committee of Safety for New Hampshire. Ten minutes after the news of the battle of Lexington reached him, Stark mounted his horse and rode as rapidly as possible to the scone of hostilities. Not less than 1200 men from New Hampshire followed his example. Stark was unanimously elected Colonel of the first New Hampshire regiment. At Bunker Hill Stark commanded on the left of the American line, and in that army of heroes was conspicuous for his gallantry and his skill as an officer. Some months after this battle the term of enlistment of Stark's regiment expired; but so great was his ascendancy over his men that in a few days his regiment was again full.

Later, when Washington's main army moved to New York to meet the attack of the British at that point, Stark was directed to participate in the campaign against the British in Canada. In this ill-fated expedition he bore a prominent part. Several small battles were fought in Canada, but with no success to the Americans, whose army under General Sullivan was withdrawn by way of Lake Champlain to the vicinity of Fort Ticonderoga. Here on July 8th, 1776, sixteen years after Stark had assisted in the capture of the fort by the British, Stark had the satisfaction of hearing read the Declaration of Independence.

Colonel Stark was now temporarily given the command of a brigade. In December he was ordered to join Washington on the right bank of the Delaware. He arrived on the 20th day of December, and participated with his usual vigor in the battle of Trenton "on Christmas night, in '76." Afterwards he fought in the battle of Princeton, and continued with Washington until winter quarters were established at Morristown, New Jersey. He was now ordered to New Hampshire to obtain recruits for the army, which duty he performed with much success.

Now for the first time Stark became the victim of the incompetence of the Continental Congress. In spite of his conspicuous services for his country, junior officers of far less experience and ability were, through political machinations, appointed over his head. Later Schuyler and Arnold were to meet similar treatment. Stark at once resigned from the army, though expressing entire fealty to the cause. He took with him the vote of thanks and confidence of the New Hampshire legislature.

As previously stated, the ensuing summer, 1777, found the American cause wrapped in gloom because of the slow but steady approach of the victorious army of Burgoyne. Washington was about the only public man who saw a gleam of hope; and his forecast of coming events is well worth quoting. In reply to a letter from General Schuyler expressing his apprehensions of the state of affairs, Washington, on July 17th, wrote as follows: "Though our affairs have for some days past worn a gloomy aspect, yet I look forward to a happy change. I trust General Burgoyne's army will sooner or later meet an effectual check; and, as I suggested before, that the success he has had will precipitate his ruin. From your accounts, he appears to be pursuing that line of conduct, which, of all others, is most favorable to us—I mean acting in detachments. This conduct will certainly give room for enterprise on our part, and expose his parties to great hazard. Could we be so happy as to cut off one of them, though it should not exceed four, five, or six hundred men, it would inspirit the people and do away with much of their present anxiety. In such an event they would lose sight of past misfortunes, and, urged at the same time by a regard for their own security, they would fly to arms and afford every aid in their power."

As previously stated, Stark had resigned from the army, deeply mortified at the treatment he had received at the hands of the Continental Congress; but now that an emergency arose in his own State he yielded to the urgency of his friends and accepted the command of the troops for its defense, stipulating only that he should not join the regular army, but should be allowed to move independently on the wings of the enemy in the New Hampshire Grants.

The general confidence in Stark caused the militia to assemble in large numbers. When Stark had gathered a respectable force General Schuyler sent orders for Stark's troops to join the main army in New York. Stark refused to obey, citing the orders of his State under which he was acting. This refusal was in due time reported to the Continental Congress, which urged the government of the State to require Stark to serve as directed by the National Military authorities. But even before the Continental Congress had adopted this resolution of disapprobation, Stark's wisdom was manifest in a great victory. Indeed, as soon as General Schuyler learned of the expedition of Colonel Baume, he highly approved Stark's plan of operations.

On the 13th of August Stark learned that the enemy in full force was approaching Bennington. He at once ordered a concentration of entire command in that vicinity. Colonel Baume had already informed Burgoyne that his plans had been based on erroneous information, and that reinforcements were necessary for the success of the raid; whereupon Burgoyne sent an additional force of Hessians under Colonel Breyman, numbering 642 men to the support of Baume. Before they arrived on the scene, battle had already been joined.

When Col. Baume approached to within a few miles of Bennington, resistance increased. Stark's main body was before him. Baume thereupon selected a good position and entrenched for a day. Stark determined to surround him, and for that purpose sent 200 men toward the right, and 200 toward the left, while Stark with the main body attached from the front.

The contrast in the equipment of the two armies was very marked. The Hessians wore immense boots, hats, swords, and muskets. The day was hot and rainy, and the Hessians were almost unable to maneuver. The Americans, on the other hand, were nearly all in shirtsleeves, and carried nothing but a gun and a cartridge box. When the Hessians saw these unequipped militia approach on their right and left flanks they did not recognize them as soldiers. The Indians in the British camp had had considerable experience with sharpshooters in shirtsleeves; and fearing they would all be killed or captured they fired one volley and took to the woods at top speed "while the going was good."

The three divisions of the embattled farmers now closed in, and the fight became furious. Every man in Stark's army was a Dick Deadeye. A Hessian head above the breastworks meant a dead Hessian. The irate farmers more than made up for their lack of military training by the fury of their attack. Stark was everywhere, animating his troops. His horse was shot under him, but he jumped on another. "We must beat the British today," he shouted "or tonight Molly Stark will be a widow." Urged on by his reckless exposure and his shouts of encouragement his men blazed away for two hours, when with a mighty rush they stormed the breastworks. Ammunition ran low but the farmers swung their guns as clubs and broke many a Hessian skull. The Hessians here, as elsewhere, showed themselves brave men on the defensive; but weighed down by their heavy equipment they were unable to run with any degree of speed. Besides, a retreating back formed an excellent target for the sharpshooters, who never missed the mark. Colonel Baume was mortally wounded, a large part of his force was placed *hors de combat*, hundreds held up their hands in token of surrender, while the residue escaped toward the west. These last soon met Colonel Breyman's reinforcements approaching the scene, and were saved for the time being.

Here it may be remarked that a benign Providence or an opportune rain had interposed to the great advantage of the Americans; for by it Colonel Breyman's forces had been delayed twenty-four hours. If not thus detained this force would have joined Colonel Baume in good time before the battle began, thus doubling his numbers, and making the issue exceedingly doubtful. Now, however, the Americans swept forward with almost undiminished numbers, raised to a high pitch of courage by their victory of the morning. They had tasted blood; and every man had the strength of ten, not so much because his heart was pure as because he smelled another triumph ahead.

Stark was also reinforced by 200 fresh troops. With these he hurled himself upon the enemy, and after an obstinate contest the British were compelled to flee. Stark pursued until darkness halted him. With one hour more of daylight it is probable that the entire British force would have been captured. The British lost 207 killed on the spot, 700 prisoners, as well as a quantity of arms. The Americans lost 30 killed and 40 wounded.

At Bunker Hill the American militia showed great steadiness when they were behind breastworks. In the battle of Bennington, conditions were reversed. Here the thoroughly drilled and equipped British regulars were behind fortifications, while the Americans were the attacking party. True, the Americans outnumbered the British two to one; but in an attack on defenses two to one was not at all out of proportion. Rarely in the battles of the American Revolution was there as great a display of courage and intrepidity as was exhibited by the militia in this affair.

The effect of this victory was exactly what Washington had anticipated in the letter previously quoted in this paper. As the discomfited Hessians straggled toward Burgoyne's camp on the Hudson the farmers everywhere within fifty miles of the scene came forward to join Schuyler. A month later Stark himself with his command joined the American army at Saratoga, now commanded by Gates. However the term of service of his men expired shortly thereafter; and just before the surrender of Burgoyne, Stark returned to New Hampshire to raise recruits and gathered supplies for the continuance of the contest.

In regard to Stark's disobedience in not joining Schuyler prior to the Battle of Bennington, it may be said that his act was not based merely on pique, but on a profound conviction that Schuyler's strategy was wrong in uniting all the American forces in front of Burgoyne. Stark claimed that Burgoyne's long line of communications was his weak point; that raids thereon in the neighborhood of Ticonderoga would strike Burgoyne a body blow; and that falling on detached troops would go far to discomfit the enemy. The letter of Washington shows that he too had some such scheme in mind. Stark's plan put 1500 troops at exactly the right place to overwhelm the British raid. Had he joined Schuyler as directed, Colonel Baume's expedition would most likely have resulted in great loss to the people of New Hampshire, relief for Burgoyne, the capture of Albany, and the success of the British cause.

Congress speedily recognized the services of General Stark by voting him the thanks of the country, and restoring him to the rank of which he had been unjustly deprived.

As for Burgoyne, the results at Bennington were fatal. He had relied on these raids into the countryside to keep the farmers from joining the American army by dispersing and otherwise terrorizing them. Exactly the opposite result ensued. He had hoped to secure much needed supplies for his army. Instead he lost everything in the way of food, guns, and ammunition that the party possessed. His force had been depleted by the loss of a thousand men, he was compelled to halt for a month where he was to obtain supplies from other quarters—a delay of inestimable value to the American army, which received daily large detachments of volunteers until Burgoyne was confronted and later surrounded by twice his numbers.

Napoleon once said, "In war, food, arms, ammunition, and discipline are one-fourth, morale the other three-fourths." Previous to Stark's victory the American army had known nothing but retreat—from Canada down to Saratoga; and retreat always tends toward loss of morale. The triumph at Bennington, farmers in the field against regulars behind breastworks, sent a thrill of confidence into every American heart. The British were not invulnerable. Saratoga might be a repetition of Bennington. Patriotic enthusiasm drove thousands to arms; and when Burgoyne twice attempted to break through, he found himself surrounded with a cordon of steel that compelled his surrender.

The subsequent career of General Stark was one of general service. He was sent to one point or another, in New York, New England, and in New Jersey, where the exigencies of the situation required his talents. Sometimes he was absent raising soldiers in Vermont and Massachusetts. His brigade was at West Point shortly after the discovery of Arnold's treason, and he was a member of the court-martial that condemned Major André as a spy. Later he was placed by Washington in command of the Northern Department with headquarters at Saratoga. His duties in this situation were mainly to run down marauders, and protect the inhabitants from raids. When Washington started on the campaign which ended at Yorktown, Stark predicted its success, and expressed great regret that he could not participate.

During the last year of the war Stark took an active part in allaying the spirit of discontent that had long existed in the army in reference to its treatment by the Continental Congress. The record of the armies of the Revolution had been so glorious that Stark used his best efforts to avoid any stain of revolt or other unhappy overt act on their history. In this he was markedly successful, his own sacrifices and prestige being a powerful reinforcement to his appeals.

After the army had been finally disbanded. Stark retired to his home, where he devoted the remainder of his days to his farm and his large family. He was visited by prominent people from this country and abroad, and received commendatory letters by the score, including a number from Jefferson and Madison. He took a keen interest in the war of 1812, but was too old to participate. Thus he glided gently down the stream of time, until, on May 8th, 1822, he reached the farther shore at the ripe age of 94. He was the last surviving general of the Revolution except General Sumter. He was buried with military honors near his home on the banks of the Merrimac. A granite obelisk now marks the spot, with an inscription that cannot be surpassed in eloquence—simply Major-General Stark.

MAJOR-GENERAL PHILIP SCHUYLER

Dr. L. S. Foster

As briefly as I can I wish to bring to your attention the career of a man, who was born a gentleman, reared a gentleman, who was imbued with the spirit of liberty and independence, who was a statesman, just to his fellow man, who carried the misfortune of disease through the greater part of his life, yet served his country with fidelity, a courageous soldier from his manhood to his death. He is no less a man than Major General Philip Schuyler, Born Nov. 22, 1733—died Nov. 18, 1804.

Of all the prominent men in public life in America during the last half of the 18th century, not one so distinguished for important services as General Schuyler has received so little attention from historian or biographer as he. His name is familiar to all who possess even a superficial knowledge of his country's history; and yet to all the details of his career in civil and military life are practically unknown. The really more important phases of his useful life are hidden or imperfectly made known. He did not leave any autobiography in the form of a diary or a narrative of his career, for this reason we have very little knowledge of his early life, except such as is preserved in family traditions and passages in the public records.

General Schuyler and his ancestors are so intimately connected with the life and traditions of New York or New Netherland, as it was called by the Dutch, it becomes necessary to review in brief the character of the people with whom he came in contact. When the Dutch began the settlement of New Netherland, all the Indians on Long Island and the Northern shore of the sound and on the banks of the Connecticut, Hudson, Delaware and Susquehanna rivers were in subjection to the Five Nations, as the different tribes were called. At that time they inhabited villages, cultivated extensive fields and orchards and traded far and near with the French and English. With these people the early settlers of New Netherland, and for an hundred years, the Schuyler family in particular, had much to do as traders in peace and as allies or enemies in war. The Iroquois possessed an exalted spirit of liberty and they spurned with disdain every foreign or domestic shackle of control. Almost an hundred years before Jefferson wrote the Declaration of Independence, Garangula, a venerable Onondaga Sachem, said to the Governor General of Canada, who had menaced the league with destruction, "We are born free, we neither depend on Yonondio, (meaning the Governor of Canada) nor Corlea, the Governor of New York; we may go where we please."

Such were the people with whom the Dutch settlers in the interim of New Netherland were brought into immediate contact; and from the hour they established a trading post at Albany to the close of the War for Independence, the Six Nations, (by this time the Tuscaroras, a community of Southern Iroquois, had joined them) occupy a large space in the history of the province. From the reign of William and Mary until far into that of George the Third, the name of Schuyler appears prominent among Indian Commissioners, for that family, because of their innate love of peace and justice to all men, were peerless in their influence over the dusky tribes of New York, except when Sir William Johnson ruled like a nabob in the Mohawk Valley.

The father of Philip Schuyler died in the autumn of 1741. Philip was then only eight years of age and was the oldest of five children, who were left to the care of their mother. The entire duties of guardian and guide for the children were therefore laid upon the mother, Cornelia Van Cortland Schuyler, a person of superior excellence and then in the prime of her early womanhood.

According to the English law of primogeniture, Philip inherited all of the large estate of his father and upon him the hopes of the family naturally depended. He entered upon his studies at New Rochelle with great zeal. Very soon however, the hand of disease was laid heavily upon him and for a whole year he was confined to his room with gout. It was the first experience of a malady that tormented him all his life, not withstanding he was always active and temperate in eating and drinking. The fortitude of the youthful martyr was sufficient to sustain him, and during the whole period of his sufferings he hardly relaxed his studies for an hour. When he reached the age of twenty-one the property which he received by entail was large, but his nature was too noble to be governed by the selfishness which the laws of primogeniture allowed and which universal practice sanctioned; so he generously shared his patrimony with his brothers and sisters. Philip Schuyler was innately just, noble and generous, and his act was nothing but a natural manifestation of these qualities.

During the French and Indian war he took an active part, being commissioned Captain and later, due to his courage and ability, he was advanced to Major. His activities and pronounced prominence in this conflict raised him in the estimation of the people of New York and the mother country. As we are dealing with him in connection with the War for Independence, suffice it to say that in all his engagements in the French and Indian War, he proved himself a gentleman, a patriot and a soldier. So without going into detail with regard to those engagements, we turn our attention to his activity during the War for American Independence.

Being imbued with the spirit of liberty and independence, he was always ready to do his part in whatever capacity he might be called. As a member of the New York Assembly before actual hostilities began, he stood by the Colonies in all their opposition to the wrongs promulgated by Parliament with regard to taxation. In the year 1775 he was elected by the New York Assembly without opposition to the Continental Congress in Philadelphia, where he took his seat May 15th and stood side by side with Washington, Jefferson, Lee and other leaders who stood solidly for Liberty and Independence. Very soon after taking his seat in the Congress, he won the admiration and confidence of those leaders in the making of American history.

To give you some idea of how he preferred peace to war, I quote part of a letter to his friend John Cruger, chairman of the Assembly's Committee of Correspondence, who was preparing for a voyage to England on account of ill health. "Of course long ere this you have received the news from Boston. My heart bleeds as I view the horrors of civil war, but we have only left to us the choice between such evils and slavery. For myself, I can say with Sempronius:

> "Heavens! Can a Roman Senate long debate which of the two to choose, slavery or death! No; let us arise at once," etc.

for we should be unworthy of our ancestors, if we should tamely submit to an insult and wicked ministry, and supinely await for a gracious answer to a petition to the King, of which, as a member of the Assembly who sent it, I am ashamed. I know there are difficulties in the way. The loyal and timid in this province are many, yet I believe that when the question is fairly put, as it is really so put by the massacre in Massachusetts Bay, whether we shall be ruled by a military despotism or fight for right and freedom, the great majority of the people will choose the latter. For my part, much as I love peace, much as I love domestic happiness and repose and see my countrymen enjoying the blessings flowing from undisturbed industry, I would rather see all those scattered to the winds for a time, and the sword of desolation go over the land, than to recede one line from the just and righteous position we have taken as free born subjects of Great Britain. I have watched the course of the political currents for many months with great anxiety, and have been for more than a year fully convinced that unless Great Britain should be more just and wise than in times past, war was inevitable. It is now actually begun; and in the spirit of Joshua, I say, I care not what others may do, as for me and my house, we will serve our country."

Two days before the conflict at Boston, the Continental Congress acting upon the sentiment in their petition to the King: "We have counted the cost of this contest, and find nothing so dreadful as voluntary slavery," had not only voted to raise an army of twenty thousand men, but had adopted the incongruous one before Boston, as a Continental Army, and appointed General Washington Commander-in-Chief of "all the forces raised or to be raised for the defense of the Colonies."

Artemus Ward, Charles Lee, Philip Schuyler, who had a few days before been placed on a committee with Washington to prepare rules and regulations for the government of the army, and Israel Putnam, were appointed Major Generals and composed the principals of Washington's Staff.

Washington left Philadelphia for Cambridge on the morning of the 21st of June 1775, accompanied by Generals Lee and Schuyler, and chosen members of his military family. Washington stopped by New York to spend the night and he and Schuyler spent the entire evening in earnest consultation concerning the present and prospective affairs of the Northern Department, to whose guardianship the latter was assigned. That Department included the whole of New York, a province then peculiarly situated both geographically and politically. It was an important link in the Confederacy uniting the New England provinces with those of the middle and southern. The Central and Western regions of New York were filled with the powerful tribes of the Six Confederated Nations of Indians, whose almost universal loyalty had already been secured by the agency of the Johnson family representing the King, while near the Seaboard and in the Metropolis family compacts and commercial interests were powerfully swayed by traditional and natural attachments to the Crown and, therefore, neutralized to a great extent the influence of the few sturdy patriots, who in the face of frowns and fears of the timid kept the fires of the Revolution burning with increasing brightness; thus you see the difficulties Gen. Schuyler had to confront. If these had been all, he most likely would have had success in every step taken, but alas Gen. Washington gave Gen. Schuyler the following instructions: "You are to take upon you the command of all the troops destined for the New York

Department, and see that the orders of the Continental Congress are carried into execution with as much precision and exactness as possible. Watch the movements of the Indian agent, Col. Guy Johnson, and prevent as far as you can the effect of his influence to our prejudice with the Indians. Obtain the best information you can of the temper and disposition of those people, and also of the Canadians, that a proper line may be marked out to conciliate their good opinion or facilitate any future operation. The posts on Lake Champlain you will please to have properly supplied with provisions and ammunition, and this I am persuaded you will aim at doing on the best terms, to prevent our good cause from sinking under a heavy load of expense. You will be pleased also to make regular returns to me and to the Continental Congress, once a month and oftener, as occurrences may require, of the forces under your command and of your provisions and stores, and give me the earliest advice of every piece of intelligence which you shall judge of importance to be speedily known. Your own good sense must govern you in all matters not particularly pointed out, as I do not wish to circumscribe you within narrow limits."

Those of you who have read the life of Napoleon, will be impressed with the similarity of the above commands to those he gave to a general he was sending to Egypt, then occupied by the British, when he was anticipating an invasion of that country; but the difference is, that he did not have the same confidence in his general that Washington had in General Schuyler. Washington closed his command with, "I do not wish to circumscribe you within narrow limits." Napoleon took care to remind his general, that when he replied, "I want no *ifs*, no *buts*, no *ands* and no *becauses*." Gen. Schuyler, after receiving his command, immediately began a vigorous execution of the same; he urged upon Congress the great necessity of supplying him with provisions, military supplies and men and other supplies necessary for the formation and movement of a large army, for he was contemplating an invasion into Canada by way of Lake George and Lake Champlain.

While Gen. Schuyler was making his plans for this invasion with as much speed as the circumstances would admit, Ethan Allen, with a commission from the Connecticut Assembly and with what force he could command, including the Green Mountain Boys, advanced as far as Bennington, where he was joined by Arnold with a small force collected in Massachusetts. After a spirited consultation as to who should command the combined forces, Allen decided to make a night attack upon the garrisons of Ticonderoga and Crown Point. In the early morning they crossed the Lake and entering the fort commanded by Captain De Laplace without much opposition, and rushing to the chamber of Captain De Laplace, beating on his door with a heavy sword and with a stentorian voice, said, "I demand a surrender!" De Laplace started from his bed, and opening the door recognized Allen. "Your errand?" he boldly asked the intruder. Pointing to his men, Allen answered, "I order you to surrender immediately!" "By what authority do you demand it?" asked the indignant De Laplace. "The Great Jehovah and the Continental Congress," said Allen with terrible emphasis and at the same time he flourished his sword over the head of the now terrified commander. De Laplace doubted Allen's divine authority. He knew that George was King "by the grace of God," but took council of necessity and surrendered the fortress. This success so impressed the impetuous Allen with his importance, that he decided to press on to the siege of the Fortress of St. John.

Gen. Schuyler sent Gen. Montgomery to aid in the siege of St. John and at the same time reminded Allen that a commission from the Connecticut Assembly was subordinate to that of the Continental Congress and therefore he must obey the officer in command; this Allen agreed to do, but chafing under restraint, he very soon broke this promise. Stimulated by his success at Ticonderoga, eager for greater honors, and connected enough to believe that if he made an effort to capture Montreal, the Canadians would flock to his aid, he started without orders to gain his objective. He succeeded in crossing the St. Lawrence, but alas, his fate was near the end, for an escaped captive had alarmed the garrison and the city, and all must become prisoners if an attempt should be made to recross the river. Allen would not leave his men. "This," he said, "I could not reconcile to my feelings as a man much less us an officer, and I therefore conclude to maintain the ground if possible, and all should fare alike." Major Campbell with a mixed multitude composed of regular troops, Canadians and Indians, then in Montreal came down upon the invaders and a sharp conflict ensued. Allen commanded skillfully and fought bravely until only about thirty or forty of his men remained. He was taken prisoner and sent to England.

The irrepressible courageous Arnold, without orders, eager for all the glory, rushed with all the men he could command through almost a wilderness from Massachusetts to the St. Lawrence, for fear that Gen. Montgomery, Sullivan or Allen, would reach Quebec in advance of his small army and gain a victory.

He reached the Plains of Abraham with nearly half of his force down with sickness, and yet under these conditions, conceived the idea that he could storm and take the strong Fortress of Quebec. To save him from utter destruction the immortal Montgomery had to hasten to his relief, poorly equipped as he was with men and supplies. He lost his life in the attempt. Thus hasty, impetuous soldiers without orders caused the Americans to make a hasty retreat from Canada with Gen. Burgoyne at their heels. Such soldiers were also responsible for the last chance of the Continental Army to take Canada.

In the meantime Gen. Schuyler was taken ill and had to return to Ticonderoga, there he found some troops and others soon arrived. He, therefore, at once issued orders for the most of them to embark to reinforce Sullivan, then in Canada. Fever and rheumatism had almost reduced him to a skeleton and he found no relief at Ticonderoga. He was also constantly annoyed by the bad conduct of some of the troops, and in his vexation of mind and body, he wrote as follows to the Continental Congress: "The vexation of spirit under which I labor, that a barbarous complication of disorders should prevent me from reaping those laurels for which I have so unweariedly wrought since I was honored with this command; the anxiety of mind I have suffered since my arrival here lest the army should starve, occasioned by a scandalous want of subordination and attention to my orders in some of the officers that I left to command the different posts; the vast variety of disagreeable and vexatious incidents that almost every hour arise in some department or other not only retard my cure but have put me back for some days past. If Job had been a general in my situation, his memory had not been so good for patience. But the glorious end we have in view and which I have a confident hope will be attained will atone for all."

In reply to this letter the President of Congress wrote: "I am directed by the Congress to express the approbation of your conduct as stated in your letter," and he concluded by saying, "It is with great concern that the Congress hears of your indisposition. They desire me to assure you of their warmest wishes for your recovery and to request that in discharging the duties of your station, you will not omit the attention due to the reestablishment of your health." Fortunately, very soon thereafter, Schuyler's health improved and upon the urgent solicitation of his officers, he consented to leave Ticonderoga and go to his headquarters at Albany. Following the disasters of the forces in Canada which gave him much concern, Schuyler was satisfied that Burgoyne would make Albany his objective and would advance by way of Lake Champlain and Oswego, and he therefore implored Congress to send forces and supplies as rapidly as possible to reinforce Ticonderoga and Crown Point; but Congress was slow and apparently indifferent, not realizing the urgency of Schuyler's request. In the meantime Burgoyne was advancing south by way of Lake Champlain and Oswego as Schuyler had anticipated, with a large force of British regulars, Canadians, Hessians and Indians.

At this critical period Congress appointed Gates Commander-in-Chief of the army in Canada, with instructions to proceed to Albany and advise with Gen. Schuyler. When he reached Albany he was cordially received by Gen. Schuyler and from him first learned officially, that the army he was sent to command was out of Canada and his occupation gone. Gates was disappointed but not disheartened. He had strong friends in Congress and he knew how earnestly they desired to have him in command of the Northern Department. He gave the broadest construction to his commission and claimed that he had supreme control under Congress of the army lately in Canada wherever it might be and consequently was the military head of the Northern Department. Without consulting Gen. Schuyler he proceeded to act upon this assumption by appointing subordinate officers. This matter of difference between Schuyler and Gates was soon brought to a conclusion by a letter from Gen. Schuyler to Gen. Washington in which he said: "If Congress intended that Gen. Gates should command the Northern army wherever it may be, as he assures me they did, it ought to have been signified to me, and I should then have immediately resigned the command to him; but until such contention is properly conveyed to me, I never can. I must therefore entreat your Excellency to lay this letter before Congress, that they may clearly and explicitly signify their intentions, to avert the dangers and evils that may arise from a disputed command; for after what Gen. Gates has said, the line must be clearly drawn, as I shall until then stand upon punctilios with Gen. Gates that I would otherwise with pleasure waive; but that the service may not be retarded, nor suffer the least from a difference of opinion between Gen. Gates and me, I have determined to remain here."

This letter was sent to Congress by Gen. Washington, when on the 8th of July that body, "Resolved: That Major-Gen. Gates be informed that it was the intention of Congress to give him command of the troops while in Canada, but that they had no design to invest him with a superior command to Gen. Schuyler, while the troops should be on this side of Canada; etc." So was quieted for a while the movement on the part of the New England delegates for depriving General Schuyler of the command of the Northern Department and giving it to Gates. It only slumbered, however, as we shall see later, for Schuyler's public and private enemies were industriously circulating the most absurd and scandalous falsehoods concerning him, while Congress refused to comply with his repeated requests for a court of inquiry.

After the controversy as to who was to command the Northern Department, Gen. Schuyler sent Gates to Ticonderoga, while he had a conference with the Six Nations to endeavor to persuade them to assume a neutral position during the war. On his return, hearing of the continued schemes and false accusations against him, he wrote to Gates as follows: "I find the jealousies and false accusations with respect to me have not yet subsided in the country. I am advised that some committees at the Eastward in this and adjacent States are trying me. I wish Congress might at last comply with my entreaties and order an inquiry on the many charges made against me, that I may no longer be insulted. I assure you that I am sincerely tired of abuse, that I will let my enemies arrive at the completion of their wishes by retiring as soon as I have been tried, and I will attempt to serve my injured country in some other way, where envy and detraction have no temptation to follow me."

On the 16th day of August 1776, Gen. Schuyler wrote to Congress: "If my character has been so barbarously traduced, and the miscarriages in Canada so generally attributed to malconduct in me, it somewhat alleviates the chagrin I feel that Congress has appointed a committee to inquire into the causes of the miscarriages in Canada. But as I am confident the misfortunes in Canada are to be imputed to more causes than those mentioned in the Resolutions of the 30th ult. (the Committee reported it as their opinion, that the short enlistment of the Continental troops, the want of hard money and the prevalence of smallpox had been the chief causes of the miscarriages in Canada) and as I rush that my conduct should undergo the strictest scrutiny, Congress will therefore permit me to entreat them to charge the committee above mentioned or to appoint another to minutely inquire how far, if at all, any of the miscarriages in Canada are to be imputed to me. If I am the cause of them, let me meet with the detestation of my fellow citizens; if not, and others are, let the public resentment be transferred to the proper object."

In the meantime Schuyler tendered his resignation and on October 2nd, Congress resolved: "That the President write to Gen. Schuyler and inform him that Congress cannot consent, during the present situation of their affairs, to accept his resignation, but requests that he continue the command which he now holds; that he be assured that the aspersions which his enemies have thrown out against his character have had no influence upon the minds of the members of this house, who are fully satisfied of his attachments to the cause of freedom, and are willing to bear testimony of the many services which he has rendered to his country; and that in order to put calumny to silence they will at an early date appoint a committee of their own body to inquire fully into his conduct, which they trust will establish his reputation in the opinion of all good men." In spite of the resolutions Congress unjustly appointed a committee to confer, not with Gen. Schuyler, but with Gen. Gates upon what is proper to be done in the Northern Department. Such treatment would naturally anger a sensitive gentleman.

He wrote to his friend Gen. Scott on the 13th of October, "I have suffered such brutal outrage from Congress, that every gentleman who has ever honored me with his friendship, ought to blush for me, if I did not resent it. The treatment I have experienced puts it out of my power to hold any office, the appointment to which must be made by Congress. A late instance of their conduct towards me is equally replete with brutality and folly; they have sent a committee to confer with my inferior officer upon what is proper to be done in this Department, and resolve that they will not consent to my resignation." To his friend Robert R. Livingston, he wrote: "A more brutal insult could not be offered, an insult which I will not bear with impunity from any body of men on earth. Although I am fired with the highest resentment at the ill usage, I must entreat you to not be alarmed, as I shall steadily make the good of my country my first object, and thus heap more coals on the heads of my enemies."

The commissioners who went to Canada to investigate the causes of the disaster to the American forces in that Province, saw with their own eyes and heard with their own ears, what noble and notable services Schuyler had performed and was continuing to perform. The commissioners were disturbed by the evident intrigues of Gates and rebuked him for his expressed suspicion of Schuyler and his evident unkind feelings toward him. Samuel Chase, one of the commissioners, in a letter to Gates, recommended him to place the most unreserved and unlimited confidence in Gen. Schuyler. "Be assured, Sir, of his integrity, diligence, ability and address." But all these things passed for naught in the mind of the schemer Gates and his friends, who were bent on having Gates appointed to the Northern Department.

Upon the earnest solicitation of Gen. Washington and many other Generals, Schuyler decided to remain at the head of the Department, and the committee that expected to confer with Gates as to the needs of the Northern Department, realized that it was just to confer with Gen. Schuyler. Gen. Washington never failed in his confidence in Gen. Schuyler as a gentleman and soldier and rendered him all the support in his power in his effort to collect troops and supplies to combat the invading army of Burgoyne. Schuyler was vigorous and persistent in calling upon Congress and States for troops; his energy apparently had no limit. In the meantime Ticonderoga was evacuated. By no means was Schuyler responsible for this, as was stated by Gen. St. Clair, who was in command of the fort at the time. This event, however, gave Gen. Schuyler great concern and if possible hastened his efforts to meet the invading army. He sent Arnold to Fort Stanwix to aid Gen. Herkimer in forcing the enemy from that post, as has been so ably described by Compatriot Stauffer, and Stark and Warren to Bennington, which has been given you in detail by Compatriot Krebs. The success of the American armies at both forts gave Schuyler much encouragement and he was determined that Burgoyne should not realize his ambition of eating his Christmas dinner in Albany as he had boasted.

While Schuyler was devoting his entire time to the needs of the army, collecting a force of twenty thousand troops and sufficient supplies, and was preparing to crush Burgoyne, the schemer Gates had with the aid of his cohorts in the Congress from the New England States poisoned the minds of members of Congress with falsehoods. He had used every conceivable design to accomplish his purpose of supplanting Gen. Schuyler. The Congress, deceived by those misrepresentations, finally acted against their best judgment and appointed Gates to the command of the Northern Department. Congress within the whole period of its existence never committed a more grievous crime; but not many months passed before they realized the great injustice they had done to one of their most capable generals. Schuyler, stung to the quick by this unprecedented action of Congress of not giving him an opportunity to combat the false charges made by his enemies, vehemently urged Congress to appoint a court of inquiry. Gates was kindly received by Gen. Schuyler who offered his assistance, but when Gates had a conference with his officers he never invited Gen. Schuyler to meet with them. This prompted Gouverneur Morris to remark: "The new commander-in-chief of the Northern Department may if he pleases neglect to ask or disdain to receive advice, but those who know him will, I am sure, be convinced that he needs it."

Immediately after the action of Congress placing Gates in the command of the Northern Department, the citizens of Albany and Albany county held a mass meeting deploring the action of Congress and condemning its unjust treatment of so worthy a citizen and soldier as Major General Schuyler. A copy of the resolutions adopted were sent to Gen. Schuyler. He replied at once, in part, as follows: "However chagrining the Resolutions of Congress of the 29th and 30th of July, taking the command of the Northern Department from me were, I have a consolation which none can deprive me of in the conscious reflection that I have done my duty both before and since the evacuation of Ticonderoga and I trust the strictest inquiry into my conduct will evince it; perhaps the Hon. Congress was under the disagreeable necessity of sacrificing the feelings of an innocent individual to the general weal of the whole. If so, time will make it appear and I will not repine at having once more unjustly suffered in the cause of my country."

Strange to relate the court-martial Gen. Schuyler had so earnestly sought was not appointed until the 20th of January 1776, and the decision of the court-martial was not made to Congress until the 3rd of December 1778. The report was as follows: "The court having considered the charges against Major General Schuyler, the evidence, and his defense, are unanimously of opinion that he is not guilty of any neglect of duty in not being at Ticonderoga as charged, and the court does therefore quit him with the highest honor." The result of the court-martial was no surprise to his friends, nor to the public at large. Because the record of Gen. Schuyler's civil and military character while in the Northern Department was found to be perfectly clean, the tongue of slander ceased. Congress before it realized that Gates was such an egotistic schemer made another grievous error in November 1777 when it appointed Gates President of the Court of War and Ordnance, a position which he used to further an intrigue with the clique known as the "Conway Cabal," consisting of Thomas Conway and his New England friends. The plan was for Gates to supplant Gen. Washington in the chief command of the army. Congress, having now begun to realize that Gates was an egotistic schemer, thwarted his plans. He was a traitor to his superior officers, Washington and Schuyler, and should be placed in the same class with Gen. Charles Lee, who suffered the British to make a prisoner of him.

It would be too tedious and would consume too much of your time to go into detail concerning the battle and surrender of Gen. Burgoyne; suffice it to say, that Gen. Schuyler had prepared the way for that event which so cheered the hearts of the American people. While Gen. Schuyler's enemies were making false charges and abusing him, he like a true patriot and soldier was preparing for Burgoyne's defeat. He had ordered all provisions and army supplies of every kind to be found in the country through which Burgoyne's army had to pass, taken away or destroyed. By the execution of this order, Burgoyne's army by the 1st of October was in a pitiable plight, for his base of supplies was in Boston, too far away for him to obtain his needs. That was a large factor in the surrender which Gates was in no way responsible for. Gen Schuyler, at the time that Gates had been given the command, had by his energy and persistent demand for troops and supplies accumulated an army of twenty thousand troops, while Burgoyne had not more than nine thousand.

For all the final preparations for the battle Gates deserves no credit. For the movements of the troops he deserves no credit. The officers in the field did their outmaneuvering with the aid of that accomplished gentleman and Soldier Gen. Morgan, and when Arnold rushed in against the protest of Gates, all the hopes of

Burgoyne were crushed. There was no chance of his escape; he had to surrender, although Gates was not aware of the fact until Burgoyne asked for terms. Those historians who have studied all the facts connected with the battle and surrender of Burgoyne do not hesitate to say that Gates spent his time in his tent and the glory of its success belongs to Major General Schuyler, Gen. Morgan, Arnold and the other generals who were on the field of battle and not to the scheming egotistic and unscrupulous Gates, who in his report to Congress did not mention the names of any of the generals who had brought about the surrender.

Col. Trumbull in his painting of Burgoyne's surrender of his sword to Gates, for the rotunda of the Capitol at Washington, represented one person in citizen's dress, a dark brown suit. It was intended to be Major Gen. Schuyler. This was supposed to be a representation of a military scene; why should a man in citizen's dress be in it? Because Trumbull knew that Gen. Schuyler deserved the honor.

The intriguer Gates was sent by Congress to the Southern Department, where he met with an ignominious and shameful defeat at Camden, South Carolina—not because of lack of men, for he had one thousand more men that Cornwallis; it was a lack of generalship. Washington, to show his confidence in Gen. Schuyler's ability as a soldier, urged him to take the command of the Northern Department, but he declined the honor, preferring to remain a member of Congress, where the New York Assembly had unanimously elected him.

A brave, manly man, just to his fellow men, charitable to the conquered foe was Major Gen. Philip Schuyler. No braver soldier over drew sword on the plain of Waterloo or on the field at Yorktown than he. He was a true Knight from "gilded spur to quivering plume." There never was a time from the beginning to the end of the Revolution that he was not ready to exclaim, as did the immortal Henry, "Give me Liberty or give me Death."

BARON VON STEUBEN

J. Luther Kibler

Baron von Steuben was one of the outstanding characters in the Revolutionary War. His entry into that conflict marked an epoch in the progress of the War for American Independence. His services as the great drillmaster of Washington's Continentals, is a matter of general knowledge. But the story of this great general as a man as well as a warrior cover a larger canvas. His soldierly qualities are best understood by one knowing his personal traits of character also. Baron Steuben was a wonderful man. His personality combined deep human sympathy with the strict disciplinary spirit of the professional soldier—his life combining the extremes of two opposite poles of thought and action in a glorified antithesis. Much of interest and of profit may be learned from the story of Baron Steuben; yet it is safe to say that the youth of America are barely familiar with some of the most significant chapters in his life history.

Frederick William Augustus Henry Ferdinand, Baron von Steuben was, literally, a citizen of two worlds, Old and the New. A look into his life in the Old World is essential in fully appreciating his services rendered to the New World, the New World politically as well as geographically. For the map of the United States—if there had been independence for the Thirteen Colonies—is as it is today because von Steuben arrived at a most opportune time. His life, therefore, resolves itself into two great epochs, and he lived in two great historic periods—under the rule of Frederick the Great and in the time of George Washington's supremacy as the greatest

American. Frederick Wilhelm Augustus Steuben, who was one of the first great German-Americans, was the son of William Augustine Steuben. He was born at Magdeburg, Germany, on November 15th, 1730. Already in his childhood his military life began while he was with his father during the War in the Crimea. At the age of 14 he was with his father at the Siege of Prague (1744) as a volunteer in the War of the Austrian Succession. In 1762 he became aide-de-camp to Frederick the Great. Thus from infancy to his retirement, Steuben's life, except one brief period, was spent in fortress or in camp. However, his education had not been neglected. As a youth he studied mathematics, history and literature—three fascinating subjects. When he left the army after the Seven Years' War, Frederick the Great, King of Prussia, gave him a benefit—a benefit that yielded him 1200 florins, 400 thalers, extra income yearly in addition to his army pay. This benefit was the canonry of the Cathedral of Havelberg—a martial life giving place, in part, to that of a canon in the church. How many people know about the religious side of Steuben's life? He did have religious convictions, it is certain. His grandfather was the author of *An Able Commentary on the New Testament and the Apocalypse*. Evidently, some type of religious training was a heritage he "held in fee."

Returning to his estate at Wilhelm, he was made grand marshal to the Prince of Hohenzollern–Hechingen, with another 1200 florins added to his income. But his services in war were in demand outside of Germany. The King of Sardinia and the Emperor of Austria each asked him to join his army. Soon after Prince Margrave of Baden made him a Knight of the Order of Fidelity and chief in command of the Margrave's troops; this increased his emoluments by 2000 florins more. With such a salary, estimated at about $3,000 in American money, Steuben did not need to emigrate to America as a soldier of fortune. Hence, one would ask, what circumstances led him to the aid of the Continental Army? He came—he saw (with astonishment)—he helped Washington to conquer. But why did he join the American Revolution? What induced him to leave Europe behind him forever and venture his military knowledge and valor in the doubtful fortunes of America?

Did he volunteer in the cause of American liberty for the sake of Freedom alone? Was he moved by nothing but mercenary motives? How his coming to America came to pass forms a chapter of incidents of most intriguing interest. The account of his contact with the American situation and of his decision to come to America—all induced by the French—helps us to understand the character of this distinguished man of Mars.

While he was a Grand Marshal in the service of the King of Prussia, Frederick the Great, he met Count St. Germain, the French Minister of War. They became friends. But he had also met some English noblemen while they were traveling in Germany, and who urged him to visit them in England. In 1777 he set out on this mission of friendship going by way of Paris. Here he again (in May 1777) met Count St. Germain, with the sequel that he never saw England, but our own America instead. Then it was that St. Germain surprised Steuben by suggesting to him that he go to America where he would have an opportunity for military glory. The French Minister of War was well aware of the needs of the Continental Army, and that Baron Steuben's knowledge of military tactics would be of incalculable benefit to Washington's undrilled aggregation of raw recruits. The following exchange of views passed between these two men on whom hung, in a greater or lesser degree, the destiny of Washington's army in the struggle to hold the soil of the Colonies against the invading British forces.

Steuben to Germain: "What would you advise me, not as a minister, but as a friend?"

Germain to Steuben: "Sir, as a Minister, I have no advice to give you on these subjects; but as your friend I would never advise you to do anything which I would not do myself, were I not employed in the King's service."

Germain was also instrumental in furthering Steuben's acquaintance with the secret agency for America in the French Capital; he gave him a letter to Beaumarchis. The Baron afterwards met Franklin and Silas Deane. Here now were courtier, philosopher, diplomat and soldier in close association. But Steuben left Franklin in anger, we are told. He then returned to consult Beaumarchis, and called again to see St. Germain at Versailles where the minister invited him to his own home.

The American envoys were anxious to secure Von Steuben's services for the undisciplined troops of the Continental Army, just as Count St. Germain also was interested in such an arrangement. The French minister was "fully resolved on depriving England of her colonies," for he knew that our great weakness lay in our "want of discipline and ignorance of military tactics," as Headley presents the situation. As offsetting Germain's flattering promises, Steuben spoke of his age, his then lucrative position, and the uncertainty of the outcome in America, and also of his ignorance of the English language. All these circumstances might have been discounted had Franklin and Deane been able to offer the Baron some definite form of remuneration. The outlook was so discouraging that von Steuben returned to Germany. But a letter from St. Germain followed him stating that a vessel would soon sail for America, and he urged him to return and embark, adding that a satisfactory arrangement should be made. After arranging all matters pertaining to his estate and his finances, Baron von Steuben returned to France, embarked for the War in America, and on December 1st, 1777, arrived at Portsmouth, New Hampshire.

The former Field Marshal of Frederick the Great carried with him letters of introduction from Franklin and Deane to Congress and to Washington. Congress received him with every mark of respect. He proposed to serve in the American Army as a volunteer; if his services were not satisfactory or if the American cause did not succeed, he was to receive nothing; but on the contrary, should the American cause succeed, he was to be reimbursed for the financial losses he suffered in order to cast his fortunes with the colonies fighting for independence. Congress accepted those general, generous terms. Forthwith Steuben set out for Valley Forge. Here he inaugurated a new era in the history of American Arms.

Now picture this scene as described by Headley in his *Washington and His Generals*. "Steuben was astonished and declared that no European army could be kept together under such suffering. All discipline was gone and the troops were no better than a ragged horde, with scarcely the energy to struggle for self-preservation. There was hardly any cavalry, but slender artillery, while the guns and accoutrements—a large portion of them—were unfit for use. Our army had never before been in such a state, and a more unpropitious time for Steuben to enter on his work could not have been selected. Nothing daunted however, and with all the sympathies of his noble nature aroused in our behalf, he began as soon as Spring opened to instruct both officers and men. His ignorance of our language crippled him at first very much; while the awkwardness of our militia, who gathered as they were from every quarter, scarcely knew the manual exercises, irritated him beyond measured, They could not execute the simplest maneuvers correctly, and Steuben, who was a choleric man, though possessed of a soul full of generosity and the kindliest feelings of human nature, would swear and curse terribly at their mistakes, and when he had exhausted all the epithets of which he was master, would call on his aide and ask him to curse in his stead. Still the soldiers loved him, for he was mindful of their sufferings, and often his manly form was seen stooping through the doors of their hovels to minister to their wants and relieve their distresses."

The results of Steuben's work was apparent in the actions of the American Army in the battles that followed in 1778—at Monmouth and at Stony Point and Paulus Hook. After the taking of the two last-named places at the point of the bayonet, von Steuben was so well pleased that he remarked: "We are beginning to walk." Later he wrote in French a manual of discipline and inspection for the army at the request of Washington and Board of War and had it translated into English. The title was *Regulations for the Order and Discipline of the Troops of the United States*. It was published in 1779.

In 1780 Baron von Steuben was able to present an army that could maneuver to the surprise of those who doubted the ability of the Continentals to approach Europeans in military evolutions. He was proud of his men, and was accustomed to bestow rewards upon those especially efficient. Steuben was a member of the board which condemned Major André for his part in Arnold's treason. Himself the soul of honor, Steuben could not hesitate in pronouncing the death sentence of that excellent but unfortunate British officer.

When the northern laurels of Horatio Gates had turned to weeping willows at the battle of Camden, Baron Steuben was sent south with General Nathaniel Greene, who placed him in command in Virginia. As Inspector-General he had the rank of a Major-General. But with all his recruiting in this State, his command was generally but a small body of troops, for Virginia soldiers were needed in the Carolinas in opposing Cornwallis and his generals. Thus Virginia was drained of her manpower.

When Benedict Arnold made his raid into Virginia, Steuben had but 150 men to oppose him. With this small force he defied the traitor by refusing to let him secure the tobacco in Richmond without molestation, at the price of sparing the city from the torch. So when Arnold had fired the public buildings and plundered private property, Steuben boldly followed him down the James; and by the time several thousand militiamen were collected, Arnold was in camp at Portsmouth. Washington sent a division of troops under Lafayette from the north to aid in the plan of Governor Jefferson and Baron Steuben to capture Arnold, but the failure of French vessels to arrive in time to hold Arnold in the Chesapeake allowed the marauder to escape. Lafayette returned to the north and Steuben was again in command under General Greene in Virginia, except that the State militia were under General Thomas Nelson.

But in April 1781, the State suffered another invasion when General Phillips came with 2500 men. Reaching the vicinity of Petersburg, he found Steuben opposing him with 1000 militia and greatly retarding his progress. Lafayette, meantime, was hastening from the north again, this time to save Richmond. Steuben, in ill health, was superseded by Lafayette, and for a while retired above Richmond to recuperate. However, this change in command, by order of General Greene, was effected in such a manner as to avoid offending the Baron, who followed the campaign in Virginia, as Cornwallis withdrew towards Portsmouth. Finally, in the Siege of Yorktown, Steuben had charge of one of the three Divisions of Infantry, Lincoln and Lafayette being in command of the other two.

He was in actual command at Yorktown when Cornwallis beat a parley for a truce to offer terms for capitulating. When Lafayette came to relieve him at the usual hour, he stubbornly refused to leave, saying that European etiquette required that the officer who receives overtures should keep his post till the capitulation is either signed or broken. It would appear that Steuben was reasonably right. That he should participate in the ultimate defeat of the British army after his drill tactics had contributed so much to bring about that result, was indeed a fitting end of Steuben's active military career.

It has been said that next to his services a Inspector-General, the field of Steuben's most important activities was Virginia in the winter of 1780–81 and during the Siege of Yorktown. General Steuben was the only American officer at Yorktown who had ever been present at a siege; he had been at Prague (as already noted) and at Schweidnitz; and at the end of what we call the French and Indian War, but in Europe called the Seven Year's War. But the effects of Steuben's inspectorship of Washington's army was felt in the battles that finally compelled Earl Cornwallis to leave the Carolinas and move up into Virginia to meet his Waterloo at Yorktown. The Continentals—the regulars—proved the value of Steuben's drill methods at Guilford Court House and at Eutaw Springs, and even at disastrous Camden. When all is said, the verdict of history marks Steuben as the organizer of the American Army in the Revolution. To illustrate: Lafayette's "dear light infantry" history places to the credit of Steuben who originated this type of military organization.

After the advent of this great German soldier at Valley Forge, it is recorded that "The War Office, instead of having to count an annual loss of from 5,000 to 8,000 muskets, could enter upon its records that in one year of Steuben's inspectorship only three muskets were missing, and they were accounted for."

The influence of Steuben's work in America on military organization in Europe should not go unnoticed here. A quotation from *The German Element in the War of Independence* is significant indeed. "In the formation of the light infantry he became an inventor, sending back a lesson from the New World to the Old, from

Frederick's pupil to Frederick himself." We are told that Frederick accepted the improvement and Europe followed his example. This improvement refers to fighting according to American conditions, which included Indian methods of warfare. So European military science became indebted to Steuben for his adaptation of Prussian tactics to New World circumstances

We shall now leave the Baron as a warrior and consider his post-military days as a private citizen. The first incident that invites one's attention plainly marks Steuben as an extraordinary person from the standpoint of generosity, especially. Just before he left Yorktown, he sold his horse to provide means for publicly entertaining Lord Cornwallis. When the army disbanded at Newburgh, he observed the dejected look of Colonel Cochrane and inquired the cause. Learning that the Colonel had a family in a nearby tavern, but with neither money nor a home, Steuben offered to pay his respects to Mrs. Cochran and her daughters. He immediately visited the family and emptied the entire contents of his purse on the table of their home in a garret. He had scarcely returned when a wounded soldier lamented the lack of a fare to cross the ferry to New York. The Baron's pocket was empty; so he at once borrowed a dollar and gave it to the distressed negro.

Steuben made his home in New York after the war, living in winter at 216 Broadway. Here he spent his time as a reader and a thinker, and attended religious services at the German Reformed Church. For eight long years he waited for Congress to remunerate him for his military services to the rise of American liberty, freedom and independence. At last Congress ended its dishonorable halting and partially settled with him. Lack of a definite contract was the lame excuse of such ungrateful non-activity. And the settlement finally made was at the instance of the persevering efforts of Washington and Hamilton. The annuity granted our German benefactor was $2500, about half the amount he sacrificed in Germany in order to cast his fortunes with those of the Continental Army.

Still, we are told, this disappointment and consequent privations did not embitter him. Friendship was the source of his happiness, and he was ever the old soldiers' friend. "He was eccentric in his habits, frank, blunt, and irritable, and always expressed his sentiments without regard to friend or foe. But whenever he happened to be blameworthy in giving offense, he never hesitated to humbly apologize," as anecdotes on record strikingly prove.

His latter days were spent in New York State. Virginia and New Jersey had donated small tracts of land to General Steuben, but New York gave him a whole township of land (16,000) in Oneida County, about twelve miles from Fort Schuyler, now Utica. Here, from a high ridge extending through the tract, he could see land in seven different counties. He lived in a log house with a frame addition of two rooms. He never married, and servants attended to his household wants. Most of this rough pioneer region he gave away or sold to veterans of the Revolution on terms almost equal to giving it away.

Here Steuben farmed methodically like George Washington did at Mt. Vernon, and like him also kept a diary of his agricultural expenses. "Molly" was the name of his horse he kept for riding over his estate. His leisure was spent in playing chess or in reading Voltaire and Gibbon. Near the end of his life he was made a regent of the University of New York.

The following quotation from Headley's *Washington and His Generals* is such a. fine tribute to Baron Steuben that I give it in full: After referring to his township of land near Utica, Headley continues— "Here the old aide-de-camp of Frederick having built himself a log-house, and cleared off sixty acres of land, sat down for the remainder of his life. With his trusty servants and some few friends who still clung to him with romantic attachment around him, he watched the current of his years drift peacefully away without a sigh for the courtly splendors he had left behind him in the old world.

"Notwithstanding the injustice with which he had been treated, he never seemed inclined to leave his adopted country. Its free institutions suited well his bold and independent spirit, and he loved it like a father to the last. His life passed in acts of generosity and beloved by all, he was enjoying a vigorous old age, when, on November 25th, 1797, he was suddenly struck with paralysis, and lived but three days after. He directed just before his death, that he should be buried in a forest near his house in his military cloak, with the star of honor, which he always wore, placed on his breast. His weeping servants and a few rustic neighbors formed the procession that bore him to his solitary place of burial; and there in the still woods with his martial cloak around him, and the star flashing on his breasts they laid the old warrior down. His stormy career was over, and he who had passed his life on the battlefield had not a flag to droop over his hearse, or a soldier to discharge his farewell shot above his grave. He was left alone in the forest with the tall stems of the trees standing like sentinels about him, and the wind sighing through their tops his only dirge."

Summing up what I have gathered together in this brief review of a notable career, and expressing an individual opinion concerning Steuben's biography, I am firm in my belief that American youth needs to know what were the distinguishing characteristics of this great man in a greater measure than they have ever been able to learn from scrappy accounts of his services to the army under Washington, most of which somehow, omit to tell what kind of man he was, an essential omission; for his example must inspire all who know how he actually felt and acted towards his fellowman as both soldier and man. His human side has been too much overlooked by sketch writers. Only in a different way was his place in the American Revolution as unique as was that of Lafayette.

In retrospect I give the following quotation from Headley's *Washington and His Generals* as a suitable close to this sketch of the man about whom Americans of today know too little. The trite tribute reads: "Steuben was a firm believer in the Christian religion, and a constant attendant on divine worship when in the city (New York). He sleeps well beneath the soil of the land he helped to free; and though the nation refuses to erect a monument to his worth, when we cease to remember his deeds we shall be unworthy of the heritage he left us."

It is gratifying to know, however, that since *Washington and his Generals* was written, indeed, a long time afterwards, a beautiful statue-monument was erected to his memory where his remains now rest in a second tomb; near the place of their first interment, in Oneida county, New York, not far from Utica.

In 1930 a gentleman from Utica, New York, stopping in Williamsburg en route to Florida, gave the writer the story of the removal of Steuben's body from his first grave to its present location. His grave, apparently, had been almost entirely neglected until a highway engineer in excavating for an improved public road in the vicinity of the famous Baron's old home, partially uncovered his remains (either necessarily or accidentally) and they were removed to a nearby spot and reburied. Here a memorial was at last raised to honor the subject of this sketch. The monument is a beautiful work representing the Warrior of Freedom on a high pedestal, similar to the two chief statues at Jamestown Island.

The writer is fortunate in having a photograph of this monument, through the kindness of a business friend in New York City. A large picture of this monument would be worthy of a prominent place in one of the Yorktown shrines because of the conspicuous services Baron von Steuben rendered to the American cause at the Siege of Yorktown.

THE REVOLUTIONARY BATTLE OR ENGAGEMENT AT HAMPTON

EDWIN K. PHILLIPS

You will note that the term Revolutionary is used, since the gamecock town has figured actively in every war of any consequence that has been fought in this country. Because of the larger or more important events of the Revolution which occurred in our section, we have overlooked almost entirely this engagement, which was the first battle in Virginia.

The number of troops engaged was by no means imposing, and while no exact figures are available, it appears that the Americans in the first day's fighting numbered about 200 and in the second 300 men. The British were somewhere between the two figures with the chances favoring the former. The fighting occurred on October 24th and 25th, 1775, and you see, was about six months after Lexington and Concord and four months later than Bunker Hill.

Several Continental Congresses had already met in Philadelphia and steps were being formulated for united defense action. Companies of troops were organized in every county in Virginia, but to quote from an historian of the times: "It was not war, nor was it peace. The very ordinance by which these troops were raised was filled with professions of allegiance and fidelity to King George III; professions whose sincerity there is the less reason to doubt because they are confined to the exercise of his constitutional powers and stand connected with an expression of their firm determination to resist any attempt on the liberties of the country. The only intelligible purpose therefore, for which the troops were raised was a preparation for defense and against an attempt to enforce the parliamentary taxes upon the colony."

By direction of the Committee of Safety in Virginia, the colors of these very troops bore the name of the district on one side and on the other, "Virginia for Constitutional Liberty." Virginians were still Englishmen, but Englishmen who were taking a most decided stand for their rights.

In order to appreciate and comprehend the incidents and facts leading up to the engagement at Hampton, it might be best to make a brief résumé of the political conditions in Virginia in the year 1775.

Lord Dunmore, the last of the Royal Governors, through arrogance and lack of understanding, was making converts to the American Cause even faster than Patrick Henry's fiery eloquence. On April 19th, 1775 (the day after the battle of Lexington and Concord) he ordered the gunpowder from the Powder Horn in Williamsburg secretly removed to a British Man-of-War in the James River. Like many other foolish maneuvers this hurt the Crown far more than the powder in the hands of the Patriots could have done. In the excitement following the news of the movement of this powder, armed men from all over the colony moved on Williamsburg with the Hanover men under Patrick Henry in the lead. Immediate hostilities were averted, however, by Dunmore's forwarding the cost of the gunpowder to the Hanover men before their arrival in town. The payment of this money amounting to 330 pounds, was acknowledged by a receipt from Patrick Henry dated May 4th, 1775, at Dencastle's Ordinary, New Kent County. Exactly a month and a day later occurred an incident which caused the Governor to flee from Williamsburg to the safety of the British warship *Fowey* at Yorktown.

The following is an account of the incident published in the Williamsburg newspaper: "Last Monday night," says Purdie, "an unfortunate accident happened to two persons of this city, who, with a number of others, had assembled at the Magazine to furnish themselves with arms. Upon their entering the door one of the guns which had a spring on it, and was charged with eight fingers deep with swan-shot, went off and lodged two balls in one of their shoulders; another entered at his wrist and is not yet extracted. The other person had one of his fingers shot off, and the next to it so much shattered as to render it useless, by which sad misfortune he is deprived of the means of procuring a livelihood by his business. Spring guns it seems, were placed at other parts of the magazine, of which the public were totally ignorant, and certainly had any person lost his life, the perpetrator or perpetrators of this diabolical invention might have been justly branded with the title of murderers."

A writer says further, "Early on the next morning, Lord Dunmore with his family fled from the palace to return to it no more, and took shelter on board the *Foway* from the vengeance which he knew he so justly deserved—no commotion, however, had ensued to justify his retreat. The people, indeed, were highly indignant, but they were silent and quiet. The suggestions of his lordship's conscience had alone produced his flight."

After moving to Yorktown the Governor carried on considerable correspondence with the Assembly in which he made certain demands and conditions in answer to their request that he return and resume his duties. He finally demanded that they meet aboard the warship. The Assembly, however, adjourned with the following resolutions: "That his Lordship's message requiring the house to attend him on board one of his Majesty's ships of war, is a high breach of the rights and privileges of this house."— "That the unreasonable delays thrown into the proceedings of this house by the Governor and his evasive answers to the sincere and decent addresses of the representatives of the peoples, give us great reason to fear that a dangerous attack may be meditated against the unhappy people of this colony."— "It is, therefore, our opinion, they say, that they prepare for the preservation of their property and their inestimable rights and liberties with the greatest care and attention."— "That we do and will bear faith and true allegiance to our most gracious sovereign, George III, our only lawful and rightful King; that we will, at all times, to the utmost of our power, and at the risk of our lives and properties, maintain and defend his government in this colony, as founded on the established laws and principles of the constitution; that it is our most earnest desire to preserve and strengthen those bonds of amity with all our fellow subjects in Great Britain, which are so very essential to the prosperity and happiness of both countries."

Lord Dunmore then moved himself and his forces to Norfolk, while the patriots mobilized in Williamsburg, and encamped in the rear of the college. Dunmore's forces being mostly naval, the ranking officer, Mathew Squires by name, began their campaign of pillaging, marauding, and negro stealing along the shores of the York and James River and Hampton Roads. The evident intention was to change the defensive attitude of the colony by annoying and irritating the population, and at the same time draw to his forces those characters to whom a campaign of this kind would appeal. How well he succeeded we shall see!

On the night of September 2nd, 1775, while sailing a tender on one of his marauding expeditions from the James to the York River, a violent storm drove the vessel ashore in the mouth of Back River. Evidently fearing the wrath of the people of that section whom he had so frequently robbed, the worthy officer and his men made their way secretly through the woods to the shores of Hampton Roads and contrived to return to Norfolk.

The next morning the vessel was burned and we find on September 10th the Captain addressing the following letter to the Committee of Hampton:—

"*Otter* Sloop, Norfolk River
September 10th, 1775

Gentlemen:

Whereas, a sloop tender, manned and armed in His Majesty's service, was on Saturday the 2d instant, in a violent gale of wind, cast on shore in Back River, Elizabeth County, having on board the undermentioned king's stores which the inhabitants of Hampton thought proper to seize; I am therefore to desire that the King's sloop, with all the stores belonging to her be immediately returned or the people of Hampton, who committed the outrage, must be answerable for the consequences. I am, gentleman, you humble servant,

Matthew Squire."

On receipt of this letter it was at once forwarded to Williamsburg. The commanding officer there dispatched a hundred men under Major James Innes to the town's assistance. Squire must have had news of this movement, however, since he seems to have been content to cruise about Hampton Roads, seizing the passage of boats with their slave crews as a means of reprisal for the loss of his stores and vessel. The Williamsburg newspaper makes the following comment: "These boats and negroes it is likely he intends taking into the King's service to send out pirating for hogs, fowls, etc., a very pretty occupation for the captain of one of his Majesty's ships of War." We see further how popular this officer was from the following issue of this same paper: "We hear that the renowned Captain Squire of his Majesty's slooper *Otter* is gone up the bay to Baltimore in Maryland on his old trade it is to be presumed, of negro-catching, pillaging the farms and plantations of their stock and poultry, and other illustrious actions, highly becoming a squire in King's Navy. Some say his errand was to watch for a quantity of gunpowder intended for this colony, but that valuable is now safely landed where he dare not come to smell it."

Meanwhile the Committee of Hampton forwarded the following answer to the Captain:

"To Matthew Squire, Esq., Commander of His Majesty's Sloop *Otter* in Hampton Roads

Hampton, Sept. 16, 1775

Sir:

Yours of the 10th instant directed to the Committee of the town of Hampton reciting that a sloop tender of His Majesty's service was, on the 2nd instant, cast on shore near this place, having on board some of the King's stores, which you say were seized by the inhabitants, and demanding an immediate return of the same, or that the people of Hampton must answer the consequences of such outrage, was today laid before them, who, knowing the above recital to be injurious and untrue, think proper here to mention the facts relative to this matter. The sloop, we apprehend, was not in His Majesty's service, as we are well assured that you were on a pillaging or pleasuring party; and although it gives us pain to use indelicate expressions yet the treatment received from you calls for a state of the facts in the simple language of truth, however harsh it may sound. . . .

"Although we know that we cannot legally be called to account for that which you are pleased to style an outrage and notwithstanding we have hitherto, by you, been treated with iniquity, we will, as far as in our power lies, do you right upon just and equitable terms: *First*, we, on behalf of the community, require from you the restitution of a certain Joseph Harris, the property of a gentleman of our town, which said Harris, as well as other slaves, have been long labored and often employed, with your knowledge in pillaging us under cover of night of our sheep and other live stock. *Secondly*, we require that you will send on shore all boats with their hands, and every other thing you have detained on this occasion, and *lastly*, that you shall not, by your own arbitrary authority, undertake to insult, molest or detain the persons or property of anyone passing to and from this town, as you have frequently done for some time past.

"Upon complying with those requisitions we will endeavor to procure every article left on our shore, and shall be ready to deliver them to your pilot and gunner, of whose good behaviour we had had some proofs.

We are, etc.
The Committee of Eliz. City County and
Town of Hampton."

You can see from the firm tone of this letter that the men of Hampton had nearly reached the breaking point. It was evidently the climax; for Squire under the Governor's orders moved against the town. An account of the Engagement in the papers reads as follows:

"On Wednesday night last a party from an armed tender landed near Hampton, and took away a valuable negro slave and a sail from the owner. Next morning there appeared off the mouth of Hampton River a large armed schooner, a sloop, and three tenders with soldiers on board, and a message was received at Hampton from Capt. Squire, on board the Schooner, that he would that day land and burn the town on which a company of regulars and a company of minute men, who had been placed there in consequence of former threats denounced against that place, made the best disposition to prevent their landing; aided by a body of militia who were suddenly called together on the occasion. The enemy, accordingly, attempted to land, but were retarded by some boats sunk across the channel for that purpose. Upon this they fired several small cannons at the provincials without any effect, who in return discharged their small arms so effectually as to make the enemy move off with the loss of several men as it is believed. But they had, in the meantime, burnt down a house belonging to Mr. Cooper on the river. On intelligence of this reaching Williamsburg about nine o'clock at night, a company of riflemen was dispatched to the aid of Hampton, and the Colonel of the 2d regiment sent to take the command of the whole, who, with the company, arrived about eight o'clock next evening. The enemy had in the night cut through the boats sunk, and made passage for their vessels, which were drawn close up to the town, and began to fire upon it soon after the arrival of the party from Williamsburg; but as soon as our men were so disposed as to give them a few shots, they went off so hastily that our people took a small tender with five white men, a woman and two slaves, six swivels, seven muskets, some small arms, a sword, pistols, and other things and several papers belong to Lt. Wright who made his escape by jumping overboard and swimming away with Mr. King's man, who are on shore, and a pursuit it is hoped may overtake them. There were two of the men in the vessel mortally wounded; one is since dead, and the other near his end. Besides which we are informed nine were seen to be thrown over board from one of the vessels. We have not a man wounded. The vessels went over to Norfolk, and we are informed the whole force from thence is intended to visit Hampton this day. If they should, we hope our brave troops are prepared for them, as we can with pleasure assure the public, that every part of them behaved with spirit and bravery and are wishing for another skirmish.

"At sunrise the enemy's fleet was seen standing in for the shore, and having at length reached a convenient position, they lay with springs on their cables and commenced a furious cannonade. Double-headed and chain shot, and grape, flew in showers through all parts of the town; and as the position of the ships enabled them to enfilade, it was thought impossible to defend it even for a few minutes. Nothing could exceed the cool and steady valor of the Virginians; and although, with few exceptions, wholly unacquainted with military service, they displayed the countenance and collection of veterans. Woodford's commands to his riflemen, previous to the cannonade, were simply to fire with coolness and decision, and observe the profoundest silence. The effects of this advice were soon visible; the riflemen answered the cannonade by a well-directed fire against every part of the line, and it soon appeared that no part of the ship was secure against their astonishing precision. In a short time the enemy appeared to be in some confusion; their cannonade gradually slackened, and a signal was given by the commander to slip their cables and retire. But even this was attended with the most imminent danger. No man could stand at the helm in safety; if the men went aloft to hand the sails, they were immediately singled out. In this condition two of the schooners drifted to the shore. The commander of one of these in vain called on his men to assist in keeping her off; they had all retired to the hold, and declared their utter refusal to expose themselves to inevitable destruction. In this exigency, deserted by his men, he jumped into the water and escaped to the opposite shore. The rest of the fleet had been fortunate enough to escape, although with some difficulty, and returned to Norfolk."

Another contemporary advises that the American commander, Col. Woodford, on the retreat of the British ordered the troops around to the mouth of Hampton Creek to out them off and insure their capture. This troop movement was delayed, however, by the report that a body of British had been landed and were moving on the town from the land side. This report was unfounded, and the town was not molested again.

If you will pardon another newspaper reference I would like to quote the following, showing that Capt. Squire himself did not escape unscathed.

"Williamsburg, Nov. 3rd,—The Riflemen and soldiers of Hampton desire their compliments to Capt. Squire and his squadron, and wish to know how they approve the reception they met last Friday. Should he incline to renew his visit, they will be glad to see him, otherwise, in point of complaisance, they will be under the necessity of returning the visit. If he cannot find the ear that was cut off, they hope he will wear a wig to hide the work; for perhaps it may not be necessary that all should know chance had effected that which the laws ought to have done."

The effects of the Battle of Hampton were far reaching. Virginia, the oldest, richest and most influential of the colonies was at last in open warfare with the representatives of the King. The confidence gained by their victory have showed the way to victory at Great Bridge and the final expulsion of Lord Dunmore.

Coachwhip Publications

CoachwhipBooks.com

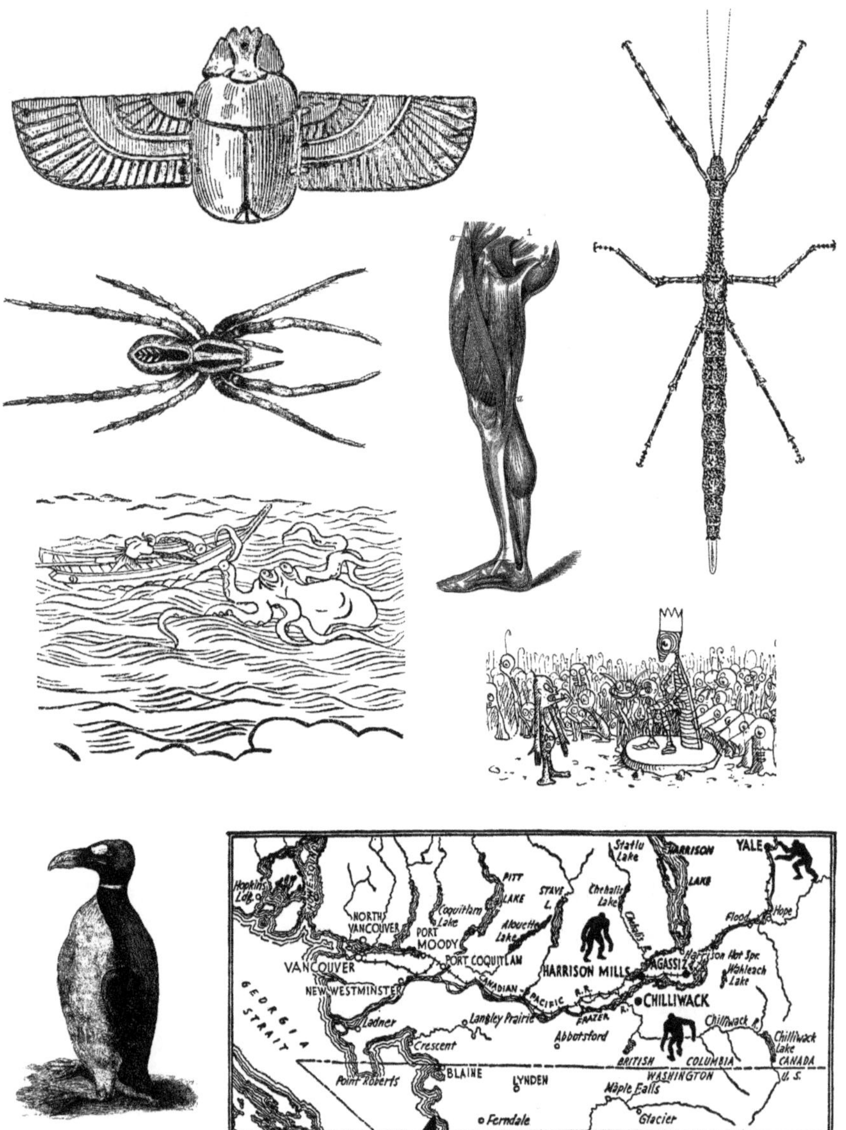

Also Available

CoachwhipBooks.com

The War of 1812

ISBN 1-61646-065-2

Also Available

CoachwhipBooks.com

Strategy in the Civil War

ISBN 1-61646-064-4

Also Available

CoachwhipBooks.com

Handbook for Spies

ISBN 1-61646-067-9

Also Available

CoachwhipBooks.com

Psychological Warfare

ISBN 1-61646-055-5

www.ingramcontent.com/pod-product-compliance
Lightning Source LLC
Chambersburg PA
CBHW030715110426
42739CB00030B/418

* 9 7 8 1 6 1 6 4 6 1 0 1 0 *